D0875774

Spenser's Allegory
of Love

२

Spenser's Allegory of Love

Social Vision
in Books III, IV, and V
of *The Faerie Queene*

James W. Broaddus

Madison • Teaneck
Fairleigh Dickinson University Press
London: Associated University Presses

Associated University Presses
440 Forsgate Drive
Cranbury, N.J. 08512

Associated University Presses
25 Sicilian Avenue
London WC1A 2QH, England

Associated University Presses
P.O. Box 338, Port Credit
Mississauga, Ontario
Canada L5G 4L8

The paper used in this publication meets the requirements
of the American National Standard for Permanence of Paper
for Printed Library Materials Z39.48–1984.

Library of Congress Cataloging-in-Publication Data

Broaddus, James W., 1928–
    Spenser's allegory of love : social vision in Books III, IV, and V
of The faerie queene / James W. Broaddus.
        p.   cm.
    Includes bibliographical references and index.
    ISBN 0-8386-3632-2 (alk. paper)
    1. Spenser, Edmund, 1552?–1599. Faerie queene. 2. Spenser,
Edmund, 1552?–1599—Political and social views. 3. Literature and
society—England—History—16th century. 4. Epic poetry, English-
-History and criticism. 5. Social ethics in literature. 6. Body,
Human, in literature. 7. Love in literature. 8. Sex in literature.
9. Galen—Influence. 10. Allegory.   I. Title.
PR2358.B73   1995
821'.3—dc20   95-1119
                                                                    CIP

PRINTED IN THE UNITED STATES OF AMERICA

To the memory of my son
James Colson Broaddus (1958–95),
who was allotted only half a lifetime

Contents

Acknowledgments

My first personal expression of thanks goes to Richard Frushell, who did a careful and helpful reading of my first attempt at Spenser scholarship and who later suggested that my Renaissance psychophysiological approach to the characters and their adventures in the middle books of *The Faerie Queene* should be worked out in a book-length study.

Thomas Derrick, Russell Meyer, Sarah Feeny Welch, Benjamin Lockerd, Renée Ramsey, and Judith Anderson read early versions of the introduction and did their duty by refusing to tell me that my efforts were adequate.

My primary debts are to those I refer to in the text. I am indebted to those whose insights I have appropriated and to those whose insights resulted in interpretations against which I have attempted to sharpen my own.

I thank the editor of *English Literary Renaissance* for permission to use my essay, "Renaissance Psychology and Britomart's Adventures in *Faerie Queene* III," *ELR* 17, no. 2 (1987): 186–206. Revisions of parts of that essay appear in chapters 1 and 3. I also thank the Johns Hopkins University Press for permission to quote from *The Works of Edmund Spenser: A Variorum Edition*, edited by Edwin Greenlaw et al. (Baltimore, 1932–57). All citations to Spenser's works are from this edition.

Spenser's Allegory
of Love

Introduction

THE most apparent indications that Books III, IV, and V of *The Faerie Queene* can be read as a unit are that the Britomart quest provides a narrative thread for all three books and, taken together, the titles of the books—*Chastitie*, *Friendship*, and *Iustice*—constitute a broad reference to the Renaissance concept of earthly love. I propose to pursue these and other indications that III, IV, and V can be read to constitute an integrated vision.[1] Using words from Spenser's Letter to Raleigh, my thesis is that these books constitute a "continued Allegory, or darke conceit" whose "generall end . . . is to fashion a gentleman or noble person" in a social and specifically Elizabethan "vertuous and gentle discipline."[2] The discipline was to be effected by engaging the psyche of the reader with a group of quests so interwoven and interrelated as to prompt an allegorical reading of all three books as a vision of the commonwealth bound by the sublunary, social manifestations of the love that binds the cosmos. And that vision of chaste, sexual love, of friendship, and of justice as elements of a comprehensive social love was to be a "speaking picture" worn, Sidney-fashion, in the tablets of its readers' memories, moving its readers, including Elizabeth, toward a better understanding and acceptance of their proper roles in the social hierarchy.

Although the titles of the three books reflect the basic hierarchical structure of Spenser's allegory of love, a grasp of the vision requires a shift in focus from book to quest. The distinction between book and quest is not important for studies of I, II, and V (when considered by itself, i.e., when Britomart's appearance in Book V is, by means of a kind of double-think, both related to and detached from her earlier adventures), and VI because one can, without destructively oversimplifying, equate book and quest in those books, each book consisting essentially of a series of episodes that are part of or related to the quests of Redcrosse, Guyon, Artegall, and Calidore. But the interwoven quests in Books III and IV have always been perceived to disrupt this scheme and thus prevent those books from being "legends" of chastity and of friendship in the same way as Book I is a "legend" of holiness and Book II a "legend" of temperance. No one has satisfactorily related quest and book in what are usually considered to be the middle books, III and IV.

The key to the project is the ability to read the Britomart quest for Artegall in its entirety and as it relates to the lesser quests of Scudamour for Amoret, Florimell for Marinell, and Timias for Belphoebe. And to follow these heroes and heroines on their quests requires an understanding of them more as romance characters, more as fictional personages or selves, than as types or personifications or, in Paul Alpers's phrase, as "congeries of characteristics." Characterization, like other aspects of *The Faerie Queene*, is "both/and" rather than "either/or."[3] But an adequate approach to Spenser's characters as selves requires an understanding of self in terms of its Renaissance analogue, self-love. My investigation into the interiors of the characters will be guided by the science Spenser and his contemporaries used to understand the self as a subject of conscious discourse. Like David Lee Miller, I pursue Elizabethan psychodynamics; but Miller pursues, at least in part, unconscious directionality as understood in Lacanian psychology, while I pursue conscious intentionality as understood in Elizabethan psychology.[4] Self-love was, according to the Renaissance psychologist Thomas Wright, the God-given "inclination, faculty, or power" of every thing, animate and inanimate, to conserve itself. Wright cites fire, which "continually ascendeth vpward, because the coldnesse of the water, earth, and ayre much impeacheth the vertue of his heate"; heavy substances, which "descend to their centre for their preseruation"; and animals, which flee their enemies. Reducing all activity to primal love and hate, as does Spenser in his depiction of Concord outside the Temple of Venus (4.10.31–36), Wright concludes: "God hath enabled euery thing to eschew his enemie, and enioy his friend."[5] As with the larger cosmos, the ordered energies in Spenser's social vision are as vital as the ordering principles.

The characters in Spenser's allegory of love are moved by self-love so understood. Most of the characters in the middle books, the virtuous as well as the vicious, are selves primarily as they give expression to the urgings of sexual desire. Next to preserving our very selves, we express our self-love, our instinct for self-preservation, in that complex of desires that moves us to perpetuate ourselves through offspring. In addition, love, i.e., sexual desire expressed through a properly ordered psyche such as Britomart's, also "breeds" in each "gentle hart" a "desire of honour" (3.1.49). Lust, i.e., sexual desire expressed through an improperly ordered psyche such as Malecasta's, breeds the opposite: "Such loue is hate, and such desire is shame" (3.1.50).

At the heart of Spenser's vision are the inevitable components of social visions: energy and order. The source of the energy is fictionalized as the love that moves the characters on their quests, and the sublunary source of that love is to be found in Spenser's use of Galenic sexual physiology. Galen generally followed Aristotle, who has been the source for previous examinations of the generative processes in *The Faerie Queene*, but not Aristotle on generation. Aristotle did not believe that male seed was produced by the testicles or that females produced seed at all. In Galen's system, however, while the heart is the source of life, the testicles, male and female—in Galenic physiology ovaries were understood to be internal testicles that also produced seed in the form of semen—are the source of the dynamic life, augmenting the heart in supplying the body with vital heat. Consequently, in Spenser's allegory they are, ultimately, the source of the energy necessary for a healthy commonwealth. Galen's belief that the accumulation of seed in the testicles is the physiological cause of sexual desire provides the entrée to *the* crucial episode in which Britomart falls in love, the chronological beginning of Spenser's allegory of love. That sexuality is a dominant concern throughout *The Faerie Queene* is evident. What has not been evident is that statements—such as that love "breeds" in each "gentle hart" a "desire of honour" and that love is the "roote" of "honor and all vertue" (4.prol.2)—express what were perceived to be actual physiological as well as psychological processes, no matter what etherealizing notions may also be evoked by them. An understanding of the major characters as fictional personages who function psychically and physically according to Renaissance psychophysiology is essential to an understanding of Spenser's representation of sexuality, male and female.[6] And an understanding of Spenser's representation of sexuality is essential to a perception of his social vision.

The Neoplatonic bias of the scholarship on Books III and IV, the predilection to move out and up from the fictional situation to the uppermost levels of being at every opportunity, has precluded sustained interest in the physiology of love.[7] But the mythology of sexual desire, which has its basis in the equation of Venus with seed, enables physiological interpretations of the birth of Amoret and Belphoebe, the Garden of Adonis, the Temple of Venus, and the Marriage of the Medway and the Thames. And these interpretations are directly related to the psychic and physiological forces that move both the questing characters and those who are the objects of the quests. What I understand as the middle books of the poem could be called "Spenser's allegory of seed" almost as accurately as "Spenser's allegory of love." It is the focus on energy and life that has made Books III and IV so attractive to the modern reader, and it is the focus on what Spenser understood as the necessary subordination of energy and life that has made Book V so unappealing. However, if we are to understand Spenser's social vision, all three books must be read together. Spenser's is in part a conventional Renaissance vision of society as a sublunary hierarchy analogous to the cosmic hierarchy. Both the cosmos and the vision are systems of dynamic tensions. The energies of the cosmos originate in the self-love of the elements; in Spenser's vision the energies necessary for the commonwealth originate in the self-love of the characters. The potentially subversive impulses in both the elements and those characters in the poem who are representations of proper members of the commonwealth are subordinated rather than suppressed—the difference is crucial—because the energies expressed in the impulses of both are necessary to their overall systems.

When Spenser's characters are understood as fictional personages created within the framework of Renaissance science, the quests that are woven together to form these middle books can be separated out and explicated. Explicating a Spenserian quest, whether Redcrosse's or Britomart's, is like explicating one of those neo-Gothic, allegorical Elizabethan portraits—the Unton Memorial Portrait is the best example—in which the convention of space is presented as "a constant alternation or movement in the subjective experience of the observer as he views the elements of the work successively in time" rather than one defined space that is presented to the focused eye of the viewer.[8] The Spenserian narrative equivalent is to be found in the absence of causality, in the disappearance of characters, in the different versions of events—in all that prevents us from reading the quests as representations of actions like those told by a narrator with a fixed and consistent point of view. However, like the Unton picture, whose various scenes are to be read separately and as a comprehensive depiction of Unton's journey through life into death, Spenser's peculiarly isolable but related episodes, sometimes stories in themselves, are not quite paratactically assembled into quests. And these quests are, in their own peculiar way, somewhat like Aristotelian plots, imitations of actions.[9] For each of the questers, union with a lover is the goal; and that goal is achieved, *however problematically*, in each of the quests. When Spenser's quests are so read, the "allegorical cores" in the middle books—the Garden of Adonis, the Temple of Venus, Isis Church, and so forth—can be read not merely as thematically related to the virtue expressed by a book but as components in a quest. And when the quests that are woven together to form Books III, IV, and V are read together as a "continued Allegory, or darke conceit," they can be read as constituting a comprehensive social vision.

The structural principle that organizes the sexually driven quests—Florimell for Marinell, Scudamour for Amoret, and Britomart for Artegall—into an allegory of love is, as one might expect, hierarchical; the relationships among the quests parallel the sublunary hierarchy implied by the titles of the books, *Chastitie*, *Friendship*, and *Iustice*. Spenser expresses the familiar Renaissance drive toward symmetry and correspondence by creating homologous structures of quests and books. To begin at the lowest level, the emphasis in Florimell's quest for Marinell is on the individual in that the fundamental problems of the story are to awaken one individual's (Marinell's) capacity for virtuous love and to preserve another's (Florimell's). It is the level of significance that accounts for the story's being played out apart from society and against a natural background of land and sea and of the movement of the rivers to the sea, the source of all physical life. Proteus, a creature of nature, is an appropriate enemy of love on this level. Amoret and Scudamour are also individuals finally able to love properly. (Convinced that Spenser proceeded through quest, I am also convinced that the discarded 1590 ending of Book III was scheduled for reintroduction somewhere in the unfinished portion of the poem.) But the House of Busyrane, the primary obstacle in Scudamour's quest for Amoret, creates a larger, societal context for this quest because Busyrane is a threat not just to Amoret but to social order.

Britomart is typically perceived to be the organizing *figure* of Books III and IV, a "human embodiment" of both the Heavenly and Earthly Venuses (for Thomas Roche) or a *Venus armata* (for Kathleen Williams).[10] In this reading of III, IV, and V, Britomart's is the organizing *quest*, the apex that subsumes the quests of Florimell for the love of Marinell and Scudamour for the love of Amoret into a hierarchical structure and thus structures the bulk of Spenser's allegory of love. When we understand how the continuation of Britomart's quest into Book V relates those lesser quests, as well as her own adventures in III and IV, to the exploits of Artegall and Arthur in Book V, we perceive the basic structure of Spenser's allegory of love. The quests are narrative structures, but Spenser's social vision is an allegorical structure that also includes the quest of Timias for the love of Belphoebe as well as the friendship *stories* (as opposed to quests) and the false friends *episodes* (as opposed to stories) of Book IV.

Britomart's quest through Books III and IV and into Book V to find and ultimately to rescue Artegall, together with the earlier Book V adventures of Artegall and Arthur, prepares us for what in this study is the climactic episode of the middle books at Mercilla's castle. The ultimate expression of love-as-justice, the relationship of Mercilla-Elizabeth to her kingdom, is given its final, overt expression there; and the episode is the controlling center for Arthur's rescue of Belge and Artegall's rescue of Irena, quests that express the proper place of Elizabethan England in human affairs. That episode is the ultimate expression of love-as-justice, but the full expression of the discipline is to be found by following the adventures of Britomart and the rest from the chronological beginning in the episode in which Britomart falls in love up to and including those adventures of Artegall and Arthur. An understanding of justice gotten from Book V only, despite strenuous efforts of scholars to apply classic definitions of justice, to emphasize the brief comments about equity and clemency in the episode at Isis Church, and to downplay the presence in the poem of Spenser's contemporary England, must necessarily focus on the suppression of disorder. When Spenser's whole allegory of love is the referent, justice becomes a broader concept of social harmony, but the forms of and degree of subordination that Spenser advocates in his social vision will remain foreign and distasteful to modern sensibilities. We live in a different hierarchy and subordinate ourselves to different gods.

The organizing concept for Spenser's vision is hierarchy; one of the two major organizing metaphors, or "darke" conceits, is the monarch as head and the subjects as members of the body politic. Whatever final plans Spenser may have had for Gloriana when he wrote the Letter, in the poem as we have it Elizabeth's "two persons" are expressed not nearly so much in the Faery Queen and Belphoebe as in Mercilla and Belphoebe. These two characters are crucial to Spenser's metaphorical restructuring of that (in Kantorowicz's phrase) "organological whole," the Elizabethan state. We can associate Mercilla with Elizabeth's Body politic and Belphoebe with Elizabeth's Body natural as long as we keep in mind that the two "bodies" were not separate—to quote Plowden, the king's "natural Body is conjoined [to] his Body politic . . . and the Body politic includes the Body natural." Belphoebe and Mercilla represent Elizabeth in both capacities. The Body natural is emphasized in Belphoebe and the Body politic in Mercilla. Belphoebe is, in addition to being a "vertuous" lady, also a "beautifull" lady, and consequently her story fictionalizes the romantic affection that apparently governed the expression of the relationships between Elizabeth and her courtiers. The fictional Belphoebe shadows the real-life fiction of the beautiful Elizabeth; the idea of Elizabeth as sexually desirable provided a socially acceptable fiction by which males in that patriarchal society could enthusiastically subordinate themselves to her as a female as well as a monarch. Timias's final submission, however, is almost exclusively to Belphoebe as a reflection of Elizabeth's majesty. And although Mercilla's role is almost entirely reflective of Elizabeth's "politic capacity" (as in Blackstone's comment on the legal ubiquity of the king: "His Majesty in the eye of the law is always present in all his courts, though he cannot personally distribute justice"), she is also a character who expresses emotion. The concept of the monarch's two bodies *is expressed in* these two characters; the concept does not define the characters.[11]

The other controlling metaphor for the middle books is the dance, the dance of love, the underlying concept for which, as with the metaphor of the "bodified" state (another of Kantorowicz's terms), is hierarchy. I am pursuing, within the middle books of *The Faerie Queene*, the dynamics of the interaction of the monarch and her subjects, both of whom are sources of power and authority—a proper complementarity is the goal. And Tillyard's image of the cosmic dance, "degree in motion," "divine hierarchies . . . sped on a varied but controlled peregrination," *when applied to patterns of human behavior within the social hierarchy*, is appropriate to the task.[12] It is as a dance, a dance of male and female and of masculine and feminine, that we can best comprehend the quest of a virtuous character for the love that will properly unite him or her with one virtuous member of the other sex: "Kind Nature first doth cause all things to love, / Love makes them daunce and in just order move."[13] And it is as a dance that we can perceive the whole hierarchy of quests as an allegorization of the proper relations of subjects to monarch and monarch to subjects. Until the schematized movements of the dance are perceived, the surface movements in the stories, just like surface movements in the real world, appear to be chaotic. Spenser's readers are to perceive the dance in the middle books of *The Faerie Queene* just as they are to perceive the dance of the cosmos, through imagination and understanding. And when Spenser's "gentleman or noble person" has internalized the dance, Spenser's allegory of love has done its work.

As I read it, Spenser's social vision is a conservative but not merely orthodox vision that explores and qualifies—rather than merely accepts or, on the other hand, questions the validity of—the dominant social discourse of his day. Spenser harps on degree as unceasingly as did some of his less-inspired contemporaries; but for him true social harmony is not merely the ordering of energies that would, if not ordered, bring chaos. Spenser celebrates those energies. Spenser's vision is grounded on the physical, physiological, psychological, and social science of his day, but it is not merely an orthodox rendering of that science. That Spenser had a refined understanding of the interworkings of cultural, economic, and political entities is clear from *A vewe of the present state of Irelande*. The political purpose of the middle books of *The Faerie Queene,* however, was not, as it was with the *Vewe*, to reconstitute a society but to institute moral reform within individuals in a society. And so the focus is on individuals, not as members of social and economic organizations but as divided more fundamentally into monarch and subject, noble and commoner, young and old, and, most importantly, into male and female. Especially important are Spenser's unorthodox emphasis on the role of sexual passion in a healthy commonwealth and his variation on the means by which sexual energy is to be channeled into socially productive activities. Despite the qualifications, however, the middle books of *The Faerie Queene* are the expression of a true conservative who sought to solve social problems through the reformation of individuals, i.e., through moving individuals to accept the official view as their own.[14]

I will proceed by separating out and explicating the quests that are woven together to form these middle books—a procedure significantly different from the usual separating out and discussing of the major characters and/or the major episodes. The Britomart quest will be examined in two parts. Chapter 1 will treat the initial Book III stages of the quest, which provide, among other things, an understanding of chaste, sexual love and its relationship to fortune and Providence, forces that intertwine both in the Faeryland adventures and in Spenser's history from Troy to Elizabeth. An understanding of this relationship is necessary for examination of the lesser quests—those of Florimell for Marinell in chapter 2 and Scudamour for Amoret in chapter 3. Chapter 4 will treat Timias's quest for the love of Belphoebe, a love allegorical of the love between Elizabeth and her courtiers, as opposed to the larger love that unites her with all members of the commonwealth. Chapter 5 will examine the friendship stories and false friends episodes, which will have been effectively separated out by the assembling the other Book IV episodes into their appropriate quests. The friendship stories and false friends episodes broaden the social implications of the poem by incorporating into Spenser's allegory of love the more social virtue of friendship and its opposite: the social chaos that results when unsubordinated self-love, or pride, governs relationships within groups of people. Chapter 6 will begin with an examination of Artegall's initial Book V exempla of justice. This will be followed by an examination of the Book V Britomart episodes in which the love that unites the pairs of lovers is related to the love that unites the commonwealth. And all of the foregoing explications of quests and stories and episodes are preparation for the examination of the culminating adventures of Artegall and Arthur, which have their symbolic center at Mercilla's castle, the symbolic center for Spenser's allegory of love. I do not ignore the arrangement of episodes into books, but in my reading the primary structural components of Spenser's allegory of love are the quests, not the books.

My topic is what I consider to be the middle books of the poem, but that III, IV, and V can be read as the expression of a single, if complex, virtue, and more to the point, a single discipline enables a bare construal of the entire poem from a single point of view: its intended effect upon its readers. The virtues change from book to book, but the "vertuous and gentle discipline" of subordination by which Spenser's readers were to be moved toward those virtues remains the same. Understood in its simplest terms, Book I would move its readers toward that subordination of self to the Christian faith that would preserve their immortal souls. Similarly understood, Book II would move them to subordinate within themselves their sensitive or animal faculties, or souls, to their higher rational, judgmental faculties, or souls. Completing the private virtues, chastity, expressed both as virginity and as chaste sexual love, I shall argue, is the product of the proper subordination of the sexual appetite, a product of the vegetal soul. And, finally, the more obviously social virtues of friendship, justice, and courtesy are virtues to be achieved by the subordination of self to external social bonds. What I suggest is a refinement of the traditional division of the poem into the private and public virtues, a refinement in which the poem is to effect a continuing discipline of the expression of the human soul in both the private and the public virtues.

To the extent that critical approach governs objectives, my project results from a mix. Like a New Critic, I attempt to read these middle books as a unified vision, but like an Old Historicist, I pursue a Renaissance allegorical rather than an organic unity. Although I do not share the Old Historicists' apparently unqualified assumption of a transhistorical human nature, I do share their operating assumption that we can cultivate a historical imagination that can provide an access, however impure, to Renaissance artifacts and, at the same time, can enable a divestiture, however partial, of our own acculturation. After all, only through imagination (or its less cognitive counterpart, empathy) do we have access of any kind even to contemporary cultural artifacts, human and otherwise; and such access requires a divestiture, however partial, of our own proclivities.

Like a New Historicist, I pursue a Renaissance social rather than a timeless, autonomous, aesthetic, New Critical vision; but like a New Critic I remain in what Stephen Greenblatt identified as the "presumed center of the literary domain," arrived at "through sustained, scrupulous attention to formal and linguistic design." I do not follow him out to the "margins" of the text.[15] I suggest that staking out both a center and borders for Spenser's essentially conservative social vision must precede truly successful New Historical readings of the middle books of Spenser's poem. I have been influenced by the anthropological bent of the New Historicists, but their critical practices enable neither the discovery of organizing principles *within* literary works nor sustained explication consequent to the discovery. The New Historicist mind-set, a qualification of and development from, as well as corrective to, the Old Historical and the New Critical, is satisfied only when a reality contrary to, or apart from, the official version of things is found. However, if we are to inquire intelligently into whether or how or to what extent the middle books of *The Faerie Queene* question or depart from the official ideology, we must also understand at the same time the extent to which they express the official ideology, a goal best pursued within what are now referred to as traditional critical methodologies. Although my reading will not satisfy those for whom postmodernism represents a major paradigm shift, it will provide them with an interpretation to deconstruct.

In a perspective on Derrida and deconstruction most helpful to one doing a modern rather than postmodern reading of a text, M. H. Abrams points out that for Derrida the deconstructive enterprise is a "deliberate and sustained duplexity," that in "reading texts there is a double procedure, [in Derrida's words] 'two interpretations of interpretation.'" What Abrams calls a "reading$_1$," finds "a passage 'lisible' and understandable, and makes out, according to a procedure that Derrida shares with common readers, the determinate meanings of the sentences he cites . . . he *construes* the passage." What Abrams calls a "reading$_2$" and Derrida calls "a 'critical reading' or an 'active interpretation' goes on to disseminate the meanings it has already construed."[16] My point is that we have not had a "reading$_1$" of the middle books of *The Faerie Queene* and so have not been prepared for a "reading$_2$."

To use Harry Berger Jr.'s word, we have as yet not had an "innocent" reading of the middle books, a reading that makes coherent the "allegorical and narrative schemes directly conveyed by the storyteller's discursive practices," the "story" that Berger, following recent trends in Spenser scholarship, understands to be significant primarily as it is contested within the poem. Specifically, Berger argues that "the culture's dominant discourses on attitudes toward gender, desire, marriage, morality, justice, and religion" are parodied within the poem. My purposes lead me to look for something beyond, something suggested by, an "innocent" reading of "story" rather than to query how an "innocent" reading of "story" may be subverted.[17]

1

Britomart's Initiation

As Spenser's social vision reveals itself in the quests that are woven together to form the middle books, it is an essentially conservative vision that accepts the status quo insofar as the status quo has maintained traditional values; and consequently the purposes of his vision are to be achieved by reinvigorating traditional social values within individuals. The most commonplace of social commonplaces, as in William Starkey's "Dialogue between Cardinal Pole and Thomas Lupset," provides the entrée. Cardinal Pole describes the ideal: "[I]n a cuntrey, cyty, or towne, ther ys perfayt cyuylyte, ther ys the true commyn wele, where as al the partys, as membrys of one body, be knyt togyddur in perfayt loue and vnyte." And Lupset describes the impediment that unsubordinated self-love poses to the achievement of the ideal: "For me semyth playnly wyth vs euery man, vnder the pretens[e and] colour of the commyn wele, regardyth the syngular, by the reson whereof our cuntrey lyth rude, no thyng brough[t] to such cyuylyte as hyt myght be by gud pollycy." The essentially orthodox, specifically Elizabethan "vertuous and gentle discipline" *toward which* Spenser would have the middle books of his poem "fashion a gentleman or noble person" would enable the expression of the self-love described by Lupset as the true love described by Cardinal Pole.[1]

In the Renaissance, the fundamental source of energy in all things was understood to be a form of self-love or self-preservation. Every "creature," animate and inanimate, the psychologist Thomas Wright tells us, has "an inclination, faculty, or power to conserue it self."[2] Self-love was at the same time the source of a destructive eccentricity, a hatred of order, which, as in *An Hymne in Honovr of Love* (78–84), is found most clearly in the elements prior to their being shaped into the cosmos by God's love. Wright says God imparted self-love to human beings "that we might thereby be stirred vp to attempt those actions which were necessary for vs, or flie those inconueniences or harmes which might annoy vs." However, the grant of self-love was made to prelapsarian, rationally controlled human beings; in our fallen state, despite its necessity, self-love is the nurse of the passions and thus functions as "an inordinate inclination of the soule, affecting too much the pleasures of the body against the prescript of right reason" (*Passions of the Minde*, 13, 14). It was a true dilemma for an orthodox thinker; and Wright responded to it with what Kenneth Burke would call a secular prayer that rational control be the efficient cause of virtuous behavior.

Self-love is also the fundamental source of energy in the middle books of *The Faerie Queene*, but Spenser departs from Wright's typical psychological moralizing by not accepting the energies deriving from self-love, from our instinct for self-preservation, as a given. Spenser accounts for, promotes, and celebrates the energies of life; and he is unique in his view that they are more vigorous and vital when properly disciplined than when given free rein. Lewis noted the obverse in his view that evil does not appear in Spenser as it does in Marlowe, Shakespeare, and Milton, as "abounding and upsurging" energy. In Spenser, Lewis says, even when initial appearances are to the contrary, as with Pyrochles, evil is not expressed as real energy but as "agonized frenzy."[3] For Spenser, the solution to the problems of love is not the suppression of real energy deriving from inordinate passion but the creation of the real energy necessary for heroic deeds by properly subordinating passion. Also, although Spenser believed the lower faculties of the soul should be subordinated to the higher faculties, he does not, at least for those in love, depend upon the direct rational control of the emotions.

In Spenser's love psychology, or rather love psychophysiology, the imagination, when properly fashioned, directs the emotions and appetites toward good and away from evil by submitting sensory data to the reason "under the forme of Good or Evill."[4] As explained by Milton's prelapsarian Adam, reason will function correctly unless "by some fair appearing good surpris'd / She dictate false, and misinform the Will" (PL 9.354–55), i.e., unless the reason, looking to the imagination for images of the external world on which to make judgments, finds distorted, false images that have the appearance of the true and thus necessarily comes to a false conclusion. The problem with fallen human beings is that our corrupted imaginations present false images to the higher faculties. Spenser would have his poem shape the psyches of its readers so that actual good is perceived as "fair appearing good" and consequently proper choices become possible in matters in which the passions would seem to govern. And, crucial to the explication of the interwoven quests, this same psychophysiology operates within the more fully realized characters. The imaginations of these characters control their higher faculties and thus direct their adventures according to the same principles by which Spenser would have the shaped imaginations of his readers control their higher faculties and thus direct their lives.

Britomart, Spenser's most clearly realized character in the middle books, not only figures forth the ordered energy necessary for contributing members of a healthy commonwealth, but the reader is privileged to observe the fashioning of her imagination of love into that which makes her Spenser's preeminent "ensample." We have often been told that Britomart's psychology, except as it has been perceived to reflect a balance or a completeness of some kind, is peripheral to Spenser's purposes.[5] My contention is that when her psychology *and* her physiology are understood, in the way of Renaissance science, as parts of her larger psyche, she provides the entrée to Spenser's allegory of love. The major virtuous characters in the middle books, Britomart included, are selves primarily as they give expression to the urgings of sexual desire and secondarily as they give expression to the desire for honor, which derives from the urgings of sexual desire within a properly ordered psyche: *the* refrain in the love stories is that from true love, love that "choseth vertue for his dearest Dame," spring "all noble deeds and neuer dying fame" (3.3.1). And these noble deeds are finally expressive of the efforts necessary to maintain the commonwealth.

I

I begin my examination of Spenser's social vision at its chronological beginning. After Britomart is smitten with Artegall's image in the magic mirror, she becomes pale, melancholy, and "full of fancies fraile." She wakes up oppressed with dreams and "fantasticke" sights and then again begins to "thinke of that faire visage, written in her hart" (3.2.27–29). She goes to church for relief, but she cannot keep her mind on the "holy herse" because her "loue-sicke hart to other thoughts did steale." Returning home, she falls into her fit again because "no powre / Nor guidance of her selfe in her did dwell" (48–49). A Renaissance psychologist such as Thomas Wright, always fearful of the role of the imagination in the passions' subversion of the rational faculties, would diagnose her emotional condition as follows:

> [W]hatsoeuer we vnderstand, passeth by the gates of our imagination, the cosin germane to our sensitiue appetite, the gates of our imagination being preuented, yea, and welnie shut vp with the consideration of that obiect which feedeth the passion, and pleaseth the appetite; the vnderstanding looking into the imagination, findeth nothing almost but the mother and nurse of his passion for consideration. (*Passions of the Minde*, 51–52)

And falling in love, whatever the psychological system, is not merely a psychic experience. Britomart is specified as one of those who "buxome are and prone" to "Imperious Loue" (3.2.23); and now that love has awakened in her, she begins to produce the seed necessary for procreation. Or, perhaps, we are to understand that since Britomart has begun to produce the seed necessary for procreation, the vision of Artegall causes her to fall in love. Robert Burton quotes Guastavinius who, following every authority from Hippocrates onward, declares *ob seminis abundantiam crebrae cogitationes, veneris frequens recordatio et pruriens voluptas* [from an abundance of seed (come) frequent thoughts, constant memories of venery, and itching pleasure]; and then Burton adds "an earnest longing comes hence, itching body, itching mind."[6] One of Burton's recommended authorities, the physician Helkiah Crooke, gives a traditional explanation of the physiological basis of sexual frustration, saying it stems from the retention of seed in the testicles, female as well as male—in the Galenic tradition ovaries were understood as internal testicles. Following Galen, Crooke said that if you dissect the organs of women that have "long refrayned the vse of men, you shall finde their vesselles and Testicles full of seede." He also said that "sometimes when their genitalles are full of seede they grow into woodnesse and rage of lust, and euen to bee starke mad indeede; but after that seede is auoyded they come againe vnto themselues."[7]

The chaste Britomart does not go mad, but her desperation is reflected in her open envy of the viciously unchaste Myrrhe, Biblis, and Pasiphae, who, in Britomart's words, "how euer shamefull and vnkind, / Yet did possesse their horrible intent" and die. Britomart laments, "[I] Can haue no end, nor hope of my desire, / But feed on shadowes, whiles I die for food" (3.2.43–44). Glauce recognizes that the physiological cause of Britomart's passion and pain is an excess of seed and attempts to effect a cure. The herbs: rue, savine, camphor, calamint, and dill, which she puts in what is apparently a poultice (49), are, according to Upton, said "to abate the desires of venery" (*Variorum*, 3:221). Camphor, says Burton, is "in the highest degree inimical to lust" and is one of the herbs he recommends for drying up the seed (*Anatomy of Melancholy*, 3:194). Although Glauce is not shown to administer the herbs to Britomart—because Spenser imagined it as a poultice to be applied to the groin?—the comment that neither Glauce's herbs nor charms nor counsel brought Britomart relief (3.3.5) indicates that the herbs are to be perceived as medicine.

The episode cannot be adequately understood apart from the inescapable physiology of the time: the Galenic theory of bodily humors, in which both male and female seed were humors or fluids concocted by the testicles from blood, one of the four humors. Nor can it be adequately understood apart from the dominant psychological imperative of the time, the moral control by the higher faculties of the lower, here the moral control of vegetal soul, that part of or aspect of the soul responsible for generation. But that moral control is not to be achieved by rational suppression. As Glauce opines, "reason" may "represse" passion "ere it strength haue got" (3.2.46), but Britomart's passion is clearly beyond the stage that can be controlled by rational suppression. Britomart's actions, which in one way or another relate to her love for Artegall, are never choices determined by a victory of reason over passion.

The Neoplatonic bias of modern Spenser scholarship on Book III has precluded serious interest in the physiology of love; but that physiology, expressed allegorically and mythologically in the equation of Venus with seed, underlies the middle books. The Marriage of the Medway and the Thames, generally perceived to reflect the natural cycle of life, more specifically allegorizes the cause of generation, the confluence in the womb of male and female seed. In Galenic physiology, conception results when female seed is loosed from the testicles through the Fallopian tubes into the womb, the womb draws the male seed from the vagina into itself, and the two seeds are mixed and then actuated by the womb. And so the confluences of the rivers, the Isis with the Thame and the Medway with the Thames, are ready-made metaphors for marriage and also for sexual intercourse and conception (as are the confluences of the Molanna and the Fanchin (7.6.53) and the Bregog and Mulla in *Colin Clovts Come Home Againe*, 141–45). The physical allegory of the Venus myth in the marriage pageant, initiated by the reference to the birth of Venus brought about by Saturn's castrated testicles falling into the sea (4.12.2), is especially applicable to a physiological interpretation of the confluence of the Medway and the Thames because that confluence takes place in a part of the sea, the estuary of the Thames. As Leone Ebreo explains, "Hence they say that she [Venus] sprang from the blood of the testicles and from the foam of the sea; and this means that animals are born of the seed of the male, which is the blood of the testicles, and of the subtle seed of the female, which is like to foam."[8] That same Venus is allegorized, through a different metaphor and with emphasis on the operation of form on matter, in the Garden of Adonis. The seeds of the parents, Crooke informs us, contain in them "the Idea or forme of the singular parts of the body [but] are neuer actuated, neuer exhibite their power and efficacy, vnlesse they be sown and as it were buried in the fruitfull Field or Garden of Nature, the wombe of the woman" (*Microcosmographia*, 270–71). It is surely just as significant that the organs of generation are symbolized in two major episodes of Books III and IV as that those organs are not included in Alma's castle; Alma has not yet felt "*Cupides* wanton rage" (2.9.18). My contention is that when Spenser celebrates the physiological Venus in the seas—"O

What an endlesse worke haue I in hand, / To count the seas abundant progeny"
(4.12.1)—and the physiological Venus in the Garden of Adonis, taking her "fill"
of Adonis's "sweetnesse" (3.6.46), he is at the same time celebrating the physiology of love in the pairs of virtuous lovers.

Nevertheless, so determining have been Neoplatonic assumptions, Britomart's response to love is typically either etherealized or perceived as inadequate,
even defective. Love begins in Britomart, according to William Nelson, "with an
envisagement of what the beloved should be. . . . [and] The ideal having been
imagined, the lover must then find its fleshly counterpart." On the other hand,
Kathleen Williams says Britomart "gives way to the exaggerated feminine terrors
of an Ovidian heroine." And Maureen Quilligan makes light of Britomart's passion by arguing that her complaints about an "vlcer" or "running sore" and en-
trails that "flow with poysnous gore" (3.2.39) are exaggerated, sounding "more
like a clinical account of stomach cancer than a conventional complaint of love."[9]
Exactly. Britomart thinks she is suffering from something like a stomach cancer
but actually describes symptoms, both psychological and physiological, of her
newly awakened and powerfully aroused sexuality. Initially the innocent Britomart
had imagined that blood was flowing from the wound made by her swallowing a
"hidden hooke" along with the bait (the attractive image of Artegall), a reference
perhaps to the onset of menstruation, to the onset of female sexual maturity.
Now, however, her condition has intensified; the still innocent Britomart now
imagines that the wound "ranckleth" (festers) so that all her

> entrailes flow with poysnous gore,
> And th'vlcer groweth daily more and more;
> Ne can my running sore find remedie,
>
> (3.2.39)

This is no merely periodic flow that she experiences; she is describing a malaise
from which she gets no relief and she does not exaggerate. Her words express
her not to be discounted sense of her new psychophysiological state.

The passage is a significant part of the whole charming image of an innocent
and powerfully sexed pubescent female in the throes of an overpowering passion; the image is an integral part of Spenser's allegory. James Nohrnberg's impression that "One feels in Britomart a surplus of energy" touches upon part of
what I am attempting to explicate systematically.[10] At the heart of Spenser's allegory of love is Galenic physiology; and for a Renaissance understanding of the
sexual basis of the energy of life, we return once more to Helkiah Crooke, re-
membering that in Renaissance physiology females also had testicles:

Surely the power and vertue of the Testicles is very great and incredible, not onely to make the body fruitefull; but also in the alteration of the temperament, the habit, the proper substance of the body, yea and of the manners themselues. In these [the testicles] doth *Galen* place, beside that in the heart, another hearth as it were of the inbred heate, and these are the houshould Goddes which doe blesse and warme the whole bodye. (*Microcosmographia*, 24l)

The problem of the middle books is how to harness the energies of self-love, expressed allegorically as the love that moves the lovers on their quests. The operative force in the direction of Britomart's natural affection is her imagination of love, i.e., the way her imagination gives ethical coloration to those images that have a sexual content. Britomart's imagination is controlled by the single image of a virtuous knight. Before she looked into the mirror, she had lusted after no one (3.2.23); she had *no* imagination of love. After she looks into the mirror, her natural affection is inextricably bound to the image of Artegall. Because the mirror has the power to "shew in perfect sight, / What euer . . . in the world . . . [that] to the looker appertayn[s]" (19), she sees Artegall as he truly is. The stanzas that describe the image are not merely an attempt to recreate in words the visual image that Britomart sees; the intent is to communicate in words the manly virtue inherent in the visual image that she sees. His comeliness, his "manly face, that did his foes agrize, / And friends to termes of gentle truce entize," the Phoebus simile, the soundness of his armor, etc., all combine to create an image of manly virtue (24–25). The poem operates in two directions here. The stanzas are, as Paul Alpers maintains the poem in general is, a rhetorical appeal to the reader,[11] informing and shaping the reader's imagination of manly virtue with an image of a true knight; they are an example of Sidney's "speaking pictures." However, contrary to Alpers, the stanzas are at the same time part of a story in which that image of a true knight informs and shapes the imagination of a character within the story and consequently directs her sexual appetite. Our final goal is to understand how Spenser exercised his own imagination in the creation of his vision of Elizabethan England and how he expected his vision to impact on the imaginations of his readers; and the starting place in this study is with the imaginations of the characters.

When Artegall and Britomart meet, her image, with its "modest countenance" so "goodly graue, and full of princely aw," has an effect on his imagination comparable to that of the image in the mirror on Britomart's imagination. Artegall's imagination, however, is that of a mature knight, not an innocent girl: "it [the image of Britomart] his ranging fancie did refraine, / And looser thoughts to lawfull bounds withdraw" (4.6.33). The lines record a fairly complex experience.

But it is an experience, like Britomart's falling in love, that is separated from any notions about the rational control of the emotions. The attractive sexuality of Britomart's image first caused Artegall's fancy to conjure up images that pleased his appetite and led him into loose thoughts. But then the virtue of the image that captured his imagination corrects his imagination of love and draws those loose thoughts to "lawfull bounds." And, most important to Spenser's allegory of love, "Whereby the passion grew more fierce and faine, / Like to a stubborne steede whom strong hand would restraine" (33). For Spenser, virtuous love is not merely good or pure or proper; it provides the energy and direction for a purposeful life. Britomart is Spenser's preeminent "ensample" of natural, healthy sexuality—if we understand "natural" to be the nature, say, of the elements bound into an orderly cosmos. Britomart's intrinsically ordered sexuality, i.e., chastity, energizes and at the same time gives direction to her quest to find Artegall. But intrinsically ordered means bound and bound means subordinated. Britomart's sexual appetite is bound to the image of Artegall in her imagination; and when they meet she becomes bound to him as a woman to a man: she "yeelded her consent / To be his loue, and take him for her Lord" (41). There is no understanding of true love in any of its senses in the middle books apart from subordination. Lust is "free," i.e., inconstant, chaotic, weak and fitful; love is ordered, bound, constant, and powerful. Lust would destroy social concord; love orders male and female into a complementarity essential to social concord.

The contrast between chaste love and lust first appears in the Castle Ioyous. Beginning with her initial appearance, Malecasta's story is a case history of the corruption of the psyche. That her "wanton eyes, ill signes of womanhed, / Did roll too lightly, and too often glaunce" (3.1.41) is a reflection of her radical inconstancy. Wright observed that as harlots may be marked by "the light and wanton motions of their eyes," so can "honest matrons" by "their graue and chast lookes" (*Passions of the Minde*, 29). Malecasta is to be contrasted to *Womanhood* in the Temple of Venus, who

> stedfast still her eyes did fixed rest,
> Ne rov'd at randon after gazers guyse,
> Whose luring baytes oftimes doe heedlesse harts entyse
>
> (4.10.49)

and with Triamond's Canacee, who "vnto her lookes a law she made, / That none of them once out of order went" (4.2.36). The extent of Malecasta's corruption is revealed when she sees Britomart, who has remained armed and has only "vented vp her vmbriere" (3.1.42). Malecasta thinks Britomart is a "fresh and lusty knight" and begins to whet her physical appetites by exercising her higher faculties, by vexing "with vaine thoughts her falsed fancy" (47). Wright warns that when the rational faculties become confirmed in vice there is no help: "for when the witte is once perswaded . . . then the soule is confirmed almost in malice" (*Passions of the Minde*, 54). Even more, Malecasta has given her will the "bridle" and her "wanton will" is used as a "coale to kindle fleshly flame" (50). Wright seems almost despondent about people whose "wicked" wills command the wit "to finde out reasons to pleade for Passions : for this corrupteth, yea wholy destroyeth the remorce of conscience, the carefull guardian of the soule" (*Passions of the Minde*, 54). And, almost as if to confirm Wright's general prognosis, Malecasta, "giuen all to fleshly lust," "poured forth in sensuall delight, / That all regard of shame she had discust, / And meet respect of honour put to flight" (3.1.48). Malecasta is only the first of the characters in Spenser's allegory of love who function like Sidney's examples of Tantalus and Atreus. Neoplatonic assumptions have resulted in too much attention on shortcomings, real and imagined, in the virtuous characters and not enough on the contrast between the virtuous and the vicious.

The observation that love stirs up "sensuall desire" in the "baser wit," whose "idle thoughts . . . Are wont to cleaue vnto the lowly clay . . . And in lewd slouth to wast his carelesse day" (3.5.1) contains the complex of lewdness, idleness, and weakness that is consistently associated with inconstancy; and we have only to remember the Seven Deadly Sins to understand how, for Spenser, sexuality expressed in a life of idleness and sloth brings sickness of the body as well of the soul. Spenser's inclusive term for the corruption of sexual desire caused by the complex of idleness, lewdness, inconstancy, etc., is "lust," as in one of his comprehensive statements on the difference between chaste love and lust, just after the episode in which Britomart falls in love:[12]

> Most sacred fire, that burnest mightily
>   In liuing brests, ykindled first aboue,
>   Emongst th'eternall spheres and lamping sky,
>   And thence pourd into men, which men call Loue;
>   Not that same, which doth base affections moue
>   In brutish minds, and filthy lust inflame,
>   But that sweet fit, that doth true beautie loue,
>   And choseth vertue for his dearest Dame,
> Whence spring all noble deeds and neuer dying fame:
>   (3.3.1)

Passages such as these have suggested to Neoplatonists that for Spenser even the truest love between mortal males and females is, in Nelson's words, only a "pale and distorted" reflection of the "generative power of the divine."[13] I read such passages as having a more positive, explicitly Christian tonality. I believe Spenser is saying that the true love that unites the unlikes, males and females, is an expression of the same love by which God formed the cosmos from the unlike elements. Friendship, on the other hand, is an expression of the love or attraction that, moved by God's word, caused the like atoms of earth, water, air, and fire in the confusion of Chaos to assemble into the separate strata of the cosmos. This difference will, I trust, become clearer and more significant in chapter 5, "Social Concord in Miniature."

The whole of the Castle Ioyous, usually approached through the tapestry of Venus and Adonis,[14] is better understood as the outward manifestation of Malecasta's inner state. The merely sensual relationship of the mythological pair in the tapestry is a reflection of the merely sensual lives of the damsels and squires "Dauncing and reueling both day and night, / And swimming deepe in sensuall desires" (3.1.39)—there are corrupting as well as ordering dances in *The Faerie Queene*—but the corruption inherent in such a life is seen most clearly in Malecasta herself. Malecasta's "sighes, and sobs, and plaints, and piteous griefe," like Britomart's, are the "outward sparkes of her in burning fire" (53). But Malecasta's emotions are weak and transitory: "Her fickle hart conceiued hasty fire, / Like sparkes of fire, which fall in sclender flex" (47). And they are finally poisonous: "the false instilled fire / Did spred it selfe, and venime close inspire" (56). Real energy came only after the elements were properly bound into the cosmos, and real energy and strength are generated in human beings only when they are properly subordinated. Within *The Faerie Queene*, the solution to the problems of love is not, as it is with the Renaissance psychologists, to suppress real energy deriving from an inordinate passion but to create the real energy necessary for heroic deeds by properly subordinating the passion. As with Britomart.

There is a simple but fundamental difference between the ways sexual desire functions within the virtuous and the vicious. In Britomart, the operation is from the vegetal soul up, from the concoction and storage of the seed in the testicles to the expression of the resulting sexual desire through the higher faculties, which are governed by an imagination possessed by the image of a virtuous loved one. In Malecasta, the process is initiated by what we must call the "higher" faculties, although they have been corrupted by inconstancy, and those faculties then goad the appetites into action. Britomart is captured by love and her sexual appetites are thereafter governed by that love. Malecasta is, so to speak, in charge of her sexual appetites and, being "free," i.e., unsubordinated to a good external to

herself, exercises them at will. Sexual desire in Britomart provides the psychic
and physical energy necessary for noble deeds. Malecasta's desires lead only to a
self-gratification in which self-love is allowed to manifest itself as it chooses:
"Such loue is hate" (3.1.50). Lewis is right to say that in Books III and IV we get
the conflict between the "romance of marriage" and the "romance of adultery,"
in that marriage is the goal of the virtuous loves.[15] But marriage certainly does
not appear in the fiction as a nurturing institution; it protects neither Scudamour
nor Amoret. When Britomart is treated as a fictional personage, she is illustrative
of "married love" only if the phrase is taken to mean a permanent commitment
of the sexual appetite to one other. The focus of the chaste love stories is not on
marriage but on the psychophysiological state necessary for a chaste marriage:
psychologically constant and physiologically healthy, i.e., with testicles full of
seed.

Britomart's response to the Castle Ioyous and to Malecasta reflects her virtuous imagination of love. She defends constancy in love in her jousts with
Malecasta's knights outside the castle. She is genteel but condemnatory toward
Malecasta's initial advances and is outraged when she finds what she thinks is a
"loathed leachour" in her bed (3.1.62). That she, with Redcrosse, beheld "with
scornefull eye . . . [the] lasciuious disport . . . [and] loath'd the loose demeanure
of that wanton sort" in the castle clearly reflects her chaste imagination of love,
as does her (and Redcrosse's) view of the Castle as "The image of superfluous
riotize" (40, 33). Also, that Gardante, Parlante, et al. are "all but shadowes" to
her indicates that the false social amenities attendant upon the sensual life make
no impression upon an imagination possessed by the single image of a virtuous
knight (45). These first two episodes in Book III provide the understanding of
chaste love and its opposite, lust, necessary for a reading of the rest of Britomart's
adventures in Book III as expressions of the energies created by chaste love and
the threat to those energies posed by those who do not properly subordinate
natural affection.

But what about the wound? When Britomart discovers Malecasta in her
bed, she goes for her sword, thinking to "gride" a "loathed leachour" (62). And
while she stands before the bed in her "snow-white smocke, with locks vnbownd,"
i.e., feminine and vulnerable, but "Threatning the point of her auenging blade"
(63), i.e., masculine and aggressive, she is wounded by an arrow shot by Gardante,
a figure straight out of *The Romance of the Rose*. Then with the wound comes the
"staines of vermeil" on her "lilly smock" (65). The evocativeness of the image is
reflected in the critical attention that it has received, but the notions evoked have
been diffuse and speculative. Roche says the wound "represents the ever present
dangers of maintaining chastity unimpaired in the active life" and that with the

wound comes a realization "that love is something other than an interior passion. Her encounter at Castle Joyous forces her into an awareness of love in
others and of herself as a love object." Roche also says "perhaps Spenser is telling
us that Britomart has partially succumbed to the beauty of Castle Joyous and
thus deserves this slight wound."[16] But where are the words that reflect such
"realization" or "awareness" on Britomart's part or even that she has "succumbed"? James Nohrnberg's ambivalent response to the wound is instructive.
He seems to accept the traditional interpretation that the wound "expresses the
extent of Britomart's vulnerability," but he also says it is "less obvious what particular erotic susceptibility is symbolized."[17] Perhaps because I attempt to approach Spenser's characters through Renaissance psychology, which is short on
insights into such nuances of intellectuality as "awareness" and "realization," I
do not see within Spenser's characters the complexities that Roche sees in
Britomart. And since I find no evidence of susceptibility in Britomart, I would
say that if any deficiency is expressed by the wound, it would be the "deficiency"
of innocence, that attendant upon her characterization generally as a virtuous
but unsophisticated, even awkward, young woman experiencing the difficulties
of a newly awakened appetite and attendant passions. Finally, however, I depart
from previous readings of the Castle Ioyous episode not because they find vulnerability or even susceptibility in Britomart but because they focus on Britomart's
imperfections rather than on the contrast between the virtuous Britomart and
the vicious Malecasta. My objectives in these middle books are to be reached by
seeing the adventures of the characters in Faeryland as prefiguring the actualities
and potentialities in the Elizabethan commonwealth rather than by holding the
virtuous characters up to modes of existence found in higher levels of being.

II

The full range of social and political implications that Britomart's chaste
love has for Elizabeth's England becomes clear only in the continuation of
Britomart's quest in Book V. Spenser's allegory of love must be read cumulatively and retrospectively. We are, however, introduced to one of the means by
which those implications are made clear at the beginning of her quest. Britomart's
fictional role to find and bring Artegall back to Britain not only makes her an
"ensample" of chastity, it also creates her historical role to initiate the line of
descendants that culminates in Elizabeth and consequently in the Elizabethan
state, which was conceived to inhere in the body of the monarch.

Merlin begins his recitation of the history from Britomart and Artegall to

Elizabeth with a direct evocation of the tree of succession, a popular symbol for the immortality of the realm:[18] "For so must all things excellent begin, / And eke enrooted deepe must be that Tree, / Whose big embodied braunches shall not lin, / Till they to heauens hight forth stretched bee" (3.3.22). This prophetic image had been carefully prepared for in the previous episode. Glauce remarks there that Britomart's love pangs had caused her to lose both "leafe and fruit, both too vntimely shed" (3.2.31), and Britomart says that her plight causes her to languish "as the leafe falne from the tree" (3.2.39). Her suffering is described as the "root and stalke" that "so bitter yet did tast, / That but the fruit more sweetnesse did containe" (3.2.17). And while such an image may evoke notions of evolution in the modern mind, Merlin makes clear that the historical forces inherent in the tree of succession are Providence, fortune, and human endeavor:

> It was not, *Britomart*, thy wandring eye,
>   Glauncing vnwares in charmed looking glas,
>   But the streight course of heauenly destiny,
>   Led with eternall prouidence, that has
> Guided thy glaunce, to bring his will to pas:
>
>   (3.3.24)

And his answer to Glauce's obvious question, "what needs her to toyle, sith fates can make / Way for themselues, their purpose to partake" (25), describes the ambiguous part that human endeavor has in the unfolding of Providence:

>   Indeed the fates are firme,
>   And may not shrinck, though all the world do shake:
>   Yet ought mens good endeuours them confirme,
> And guide the heauenly causes to their constant terme.
>
>   (25)

Merlin's two statements accurately describe the part that "mens good endeuours" play in Spenser's chronicle history, where Providence works only in very large ways, where, for the most part, good and evil fare much the same, and where fortune often controls not only the entire lives of human beings, good and evil, but also large stretches of history. However, Providence intervenes intermittently through the course of history, and the final purposes of Providence are served by the accession of Elizabeth and the creation of the Elizabethan commonwealth. In the broad sweep of history, Providential love finally controls fortune.

That Spenser's chronicle history is traditional and "medieval" suggests that he would understand the society produced by such historical forces also to be traditional and "medieval." Arthur Ferguson describes the enervating effect that the "bastard cyclicism" inherent in the concepts of fortune and mutability had on the development in Elizabethan England of a modern historical consciousness of history. Perceptions of history as a record of social change rather than as a storehouse of timeless examples for the use of the moral philosophy were in their infancy.[19] Consequently, that Spenser included a complete, traditional, *labored-over* history from Troy to Elizabeth (3.9.40–51; 2.10; and 3.26–50) in his masterpiece argues that Spenser either had a conservative, even medieval, conception of his own society or that he thought such a conception appropriate to his purposes. And that Spenser, as "Poet historical," set in the past stories whose characters were also to be such timeless examples supports that argument.

That as an antiquarian Spenser was able to divorce himself from the mythology and theology of *Irish* history does not, at least for me, argue the contrary. Spenser recognized the danger of relying on the Irish chronicles and the oral tradition on which they were based—"remembraunces of bardes which vse to forge and falsefye euerie thinge as they liste"—and supplemented those sources with a general reading among authors ancient and modern. Out of these, together with "comparison of times likenes of manners and Customes Affinytie of wordes and names properties of natures and vses resemblaunces of rightes and Ceremonies monimentes of Churches and Tombs and manie other like circumstances," Spenser says, "I doe gather a likelyhode of truethe, not certainlye affirminge anye thinge but by Conferringe of times nacions languages monimentes and such like I doe hunte out a probabilitye of thinges. . . ." (*A Present vewe of the state of Irelande* [*Variorum,* 10:84-85]). As Ferguson observes, "No self-styled antiquary of that day ever put the methods of the new antiquarianism more succinctly than the author of *The Faerie Queene.*"[20] But should we be tempted to conclude from the *Vewe* that the historical forces that inform *The Faerie Queene* are mere propaganda, we should also consider that it is just as likely that Spenser could divorce himself from the theology of history when considering the barbaric Irish society but not when considering the English. Although one can find in Tudor England generally, and in the *Vewe* specifically, evidence of a groping toward an understanding of history as a record of social change, the notion that *The Faerie Queene* reflects both an awareness of and sympathy for the evolutionary forces that we see at work in Elizabethan England is, I believe, a fanciful projection of our notions back onto a Renaissance artifact.[21]

Just as in the chronicle history, although fortune seems at first to dominate in the individual Faeryland quests, the quests end, however problematically, with virtuous love controlling fortune. The middle books can be read as a variation on Boethius's view that humankind should control fortune through understanding, that we should "rise above" that which is under the control of fortune by under-standing how fortune is finally subordinated to Providence and so focus our lives on that which is above the realm that fortune controls. Stated baldly, Spenser's theme is that the characters' exercise of virtuous endeavor, the product of virtu-ous love, enables the control of fortune in the very fabric of their lives because virtuous endeavor leads them away from the pitfalls and vagaries of a corrupt life and it also aligns them with the aims of Providence in this world. And that such a theme informs both the fictions that are woven together to form these middle books and the historical framework for the fictions reinforces the overall conser-vative, medieval outlook in these books. But the bald statement does not reflect either the complexities or the ambiguities. What we get in the characterization of the virtuous, for example, is not so much an actual control of self-love as a struggle toward that control. And although the quests do end with love control-ling fortune, those endings are ambiguous if not perplexing. That love controls fortune in Spenser's allegory of love is, finally, a statement of faith similar to the statement of faith that Mutability, i.e., fortune writ large, will come under the control of God's love.

Britomart's encounter with Marinell after she leaves the Castle Ioyous and takes leave of Redcrosse illustrates the struggle of the virtuous to control fortune through love. The flashback to Britomart's falling in love and her meeting with Merlin had been occasioned by her conversation with Redcrosse about Artegall after they left Malecasta's castle. Britomart, having been pleased by Redcrosse's noble characterization of Artegall and thinking "to beguile her grieuous smart" (3.4.6), portrays Artegall in her "feigning fancie . . . as fittest . . . for loue" (5). But she succeeds only in causing the "deepe wound" in her heart to deepen (6). This emotional state produces her complaint to the sea, in which she perceives her life to be at the mercy of love and fortune: "Loue my lewd Pilot hath a restlesse mind / And fortune Boteswaine no assurance knowes" (9). In Britomart's impassioned imagination, it is not just that fortune controls love but that both love and fortune are chaos principles.

Of the several methods that Wright uses to analyze the passions, the most applicable here is the division into those that dilate the heart and thereby pro-mote action and those that contract the heart and thereby inhibit action: "al passions may be distinguished by the dilation, enlargement, or diffusion of the heart; and the contraction, collection, or compression of the same: for (as after-wards shall be declared in all Passions) the hart is dilated or coarcted more or less" (*Passions of the Minde*, 24). We must remember the circular logic that consti-tuted demonstration for Renaissance psychologists. Since the heart was under-stood for good reasons to be the seat of appetite and motion, and since one can

observe paralysis in the demeanor and actions of those who are grieving, it stood
to reason that grief is a passion that contracts the heart and thereby inhibits the
flow of vital spirits. In this particular case, Britomart brings a temporary emotional paralysis on herself by augmenting the conflict between the dilating passion of desire and the contracting passion of sorrow. In order to relieve Britomart's
pain, Glauce reminds her of Merlin's prophecy and the providential aspect of her
quest—the reader had been reminded of it by the reference to Elizabeth immediately before the episode (3.4.3)—but the "cure" is psychological. When chal-
lenged by Marinell, Britomart, "Conuerting" the contracting passion of sorrow
into the dilating, "coosen" passion of wrath, is now moved by two dilating passions, "Loue and despight," which "attonce" kindle her courage (12). (Shakespeare
describes the same process and uses much the same terminology in Malcolm's
urging of Macduff to "Let grief convert to anger; blunt not the heart, enrage it"
[*Macbeth* 4.3.229]).

The point of the episode is the contrast between Britomart, whose
lovesickness causes her to engage herself with what she perceives to be the accidents of fortune, and Marinell, whose unhealthy abstinence from love results in
a life in which he attempts to avoid them. The usual practice in *Faerie Queene*
scholarship would be to examine the interlacing of the Britomart with the Florimell
quest at this time, but my plan is to separate out the different quests. Briefly,
however, fortune, Providence, and human character are integral to the Florimell
quest from the beginning when Cymoent, through her misguided effort to control fortune, follows what she thinks is Proteus's advice to keep her son, Marinell,
from love. She succeeds only in putting him on Fortune's Wheel. On the other
hand, Florimell, whose sexual desires, like Britomart's, are inextricably bound to
the image of a virtuous knight, goes on a quest to find her love and thereby
submits herself to the accidents of fortune. Britomart's quest is the catalyst in
Florimell's minor quest, because Britomart's defeat of Marinell sets into motion
the providential forces that undo Cymoent's attempt to control fortune and finally bring Marinell and Florimell together.

The continued contrast between the sexuality that moves Britomart on her
quest and the sexuality that moves the defective characters to an unsubordinated
self-love provides the coherence necessary for a sustained reading of Britomart's
adventures in Book III. In the next episode, at Malbecco's castle, Paridell, like
the earlier Malecasta, sees himself as a free agent; and the love play with Hellenore
could have taken place in the Castle Ioyous. When Hellenore understands
Paridell's intentions and sends at him a "firie dart, whose hed / Empoisned was
with priuy lust, and gealous dred" (3.9.28),

He from that deadly throw made no defence,
> But to the wound his weake hart opened wyde;
> The wicked engine through false influence,
> Past through his eyes, and secretly did glyde
> Into his hart, which it did sorely gryde.
> But nothing new to him was that same paine,
> Ne paine at all; for he so oft had tryde
> The powre thereof, and lou'd so oft in vaine,
That thing of course he counted, loue to entertaine.

(29)

A practiced amorist like Malecasta, Paridell is looking for "loue to entertaine" with anyone he finds attractive; and, consequently, like Malecasta, when he sees an opportunity, whets his physical appetites by exercising his higher faculties. He wills his heart to open to the dart thrown by Hellenore, and it is the "false influence" of his will that serves to draw the dart to his heart. And, just as with Malecasta, the pain that results from this dissipated passion is false and weak, "Ne paine at all." Inconstancy in Paridell is, as it is with Malecasta, coincident with psychic dislocation; but with Paridell inconstancy also takes on an intellectual dimension. Paridell's imagination of history is of a piece with his imagination of love and both reflect the emptiness, the sterility, of a life devoted only to self. He tells his version of the Troy story only because he thinks his attractiveness as a speaker will help him seduce Hellenore; and his account is full of weakness, distortion, and emptiness of purpose. He sees history as the working out of "direfull destinie" and Troy as "nought, but an idle name." For him, Paris is the "Most famous worthy of the world" (3.9.33–34); and he simply forgets, to some extent because his attention is on Hellenore, all about Aeneas and Rome and Brute and Troynouant. As Paridell says, "my wits bene light" (47). Paridell perceives himself to be a free agent—he later dumps Hellenore after he uses her, declaring that he will not be clogged—but actually he is a captive of a narrow and self-defeating hedonism that puts him at the mercy of whatever fortune brings.

Britomart is on an arduous quest to find her one true love; and consequently the energy that moves her is different from and stronger than that deriving from the psychic explosion that moves Paridell to fight her outside the castle, just as her love for Artegall is different from and stronger than the lust that moves Paridell. Marinell and Paridell, each in his own way, demonstrate the sterility of a life in which sexual desire is expressed merely as an unsubordinated self-love; and, because such a life is without direction, each has become captive (Marinell only temporarily) to fortune. Britomart has an imagination of life and history that is equivalent to her imagination of love. History for her is not Paridell's "direfull destiny," but is, as it was explained to her by Merlin, the positive unfolding of Providence through the heroic endeavors of the virtuous. And life is not, as it is for Cymoent and consequently for Marinell, to be lived in fear of one's destiny. For Britomart life is an opportunity for "faire endeuour"—Britomart's phrase for her offer of help to Scudamour outside the House of Busyrane (3.11.15). Britomart not only has a proper imagination of history, but also plays a part in a history that contrasts with Paridell's. Paridell is the end product of a history, beginning with Paris, in which the moving forces are lust and fortune; Britomart is in the middle of a history sometimes temporarily moved by lust and fortune but finally moved by love and Providence.

In this episode, Britomart's encounter with a contrasting character is part of a larger story, the story of an old miser, Malbecco, who, when deprived of both his treasures, his young wife and his money, seeks a "life" that will continue to express his miserliness without those treasures. The story of Malbecco's physical transmogrification—he had chosen from the beginning to live in fear and to feed on his suspicions and so remains psychologically constant throughout the story— provides the context for the smaller fictions: the contrasting histories of the descendants of Paris and Aeneas and the reenactment of the fall of Troy by Paridell and Hellenore, as well as the encounters of Britomart with Paridell. And, besides providing its own version of lust, the Malbecco story serves as a comic foreshadowing of the grand climax to Britomart's adventures in Book III at the House of Busyrane. Like Busyrane, Malbecco attempts to master by nonsexual means a young woman suited to a sexual life; like Busyrane, Malbecco creates a little world in which his desires are temporarily fulfilled; and, like Busyrane, he lives to see his world destroyed. Both Malbecco and Busyrane attempt to control fortune through false love, through an unsubordinated self-love. The Malbecco episode is an important episode in Britomart's quest; but its peculiarities remind us that as artistic wholes Spenser's quests are like those neo-Gothic Elizabethan portraits, the Unton "story picture" in particular, in which "Inscriptions, emblems, symbolic objects and whole inset scenes," as Roy Strong says, "are meant to be read separately as well as together."[22]

Malbecco provides a new and different contrast to Britomart. Malecasta and Paridell corrupt by inconstancy what otherwise could be healthy sexual desire, but Malbecco's problem is not inconstancy. The point of his vacillations between his desire for Hellenore and his desire for his money is not that he is inconstant to Hellenore but that his affections for both are the product of mere acquisitiveness, that his affection for Hellenore has no physical basis. His testicles are empty of seed. He is "old, and withered like hay, / Vnfit faire Ladies seruice to supply"

(3.9.5) and consequently lacks "courage," both in the purely sexual sense and also in the related sense of purpose and spirit, the "courage" that moves Britomart, Florimell, and Scudamour on their quests. Malbecco is male but not masculine. Malbecco's attempt to possess Hellenore in the way he possesses his money is one of the attempts—like that of Proteus and Cymoent (and possibly Busyrane)— of the aged to appropriate for their own purposes the energies of youth, the energies necessary not just to the individual but to the commonwealth. And that those attempts invariably fail, that the energies of youth prevail over the fears and desires of age, makes Spenser's an appealing allegory of love. That those energies are ultimately validated by their subordination to the good of the state makes Spenser's allegory, at least to the modern mind, much less appealing.

Britomart's taking off her armor reveals the spectacular contrast between the forces that energize virtue and the forces that govern the dark interior of Malbecco's world. When she doffs her helmet, her braided locks, like sunbeams that had been hidden as behind a cloud, now "shew their golden gleames" and "through the persant aire shoote forth their azure streames" (3.9.20). And when she takes off her body armor, which "the faire feature of her limbs did hyde," and lets down "her well plighted frock . . . with careless modestee," she is revealed to be the "fairest woman wight, that euer eye did see" (21). But she is a "woman wight," like Minerva who, having conquered the giants, took off her helmet and untied her shield "to rest in glorious victorye" (22). Both Britomart and Minerva are chaste, modest, and, we must not forget or minimize, powerful. And now it is fair rest after "faire endeuour" for Britomart, just as it was for Minerva.

The Malbecco story is instructive about Spenser's storytelling in that the canto 9 and canto 10 portions of the story cannot be intelligently read apart from each other. But for some reason—to more effectively parody the Troy story through Malbecco's forced choice between his money and his wife?—Spenser has Paridell's seduction of Hellenore, although already accomplished in canto 9 except for the physical act, begin again in canto 10. Spenser sacrifices verisimilitude and point of view, but he does not sacrifice theme. The point of the second episode of seduction is that which is implied in the marriage from the beginning: Malbecco's hesitation between attempting to save his wife or his money clearly indicates that she can be nothing more than one of his possessions, an external object for his internal miserliness. Hellenore sets fire to Malbecco's treasury and then cries rape:

> Ay when to him she cryde, to her he turnd,
> And left the fire; loue money ouercame:

But when he marked, how his money burnd,
He left his wife; money did loue disclame:
Both was he loth to loose his loued Dame,
And loth to leaue his liefest pelfe behind,
Yet sith he n'ote saue both, he sau'd that same,
Which was the dearest to his donghill mind,
The God of his desire, the ioy of misers blind.

(3.10.15)

For the most part, Malbecco illustrates the paralysis of mind that results from conflicting, simultaneous passions. From the beginning Malbecco's psyche had been an arena for the conflicting passions of fear and desire: desire for Hellenore and his money and, lacking the courage necessary for a healthy possessiveness, fear of losing them. Malbecco's present dilemma is caused by the *same* passion, desire, for two different objects, Hellenore and his money, which cannot be simultaneously possessed. After he loses Hellenore, the emotional torment caused by simultaneous, *conflicting* passions begins again to dominate him. Renaissance psychologists believed that unrelieved passions in conflict cause serious internal damage, both psychic and physical.[23] Malbecco is "Full deepe emplonged . . . and drowned nye" in "huge waues of griefe and gealosye . . . Twixt inward doole and felonous despight . . . And all the passions, that in man may light, / Did him attonce oppresse, and vex his caytiue spright" (3.10.17). Grief contracts Malbecco's heart, and jealousy, a mixture of fear and desire, both contracts and dilates it. Malbecco's "inward doole" is also in conflict with another dilating passion, "felonous despight."

In her encounter with Marinell, Britomart cured her temporary emotional paralysis by converting the contracting passion of sorrow into the dilating passion of wrath (3.4.12). This is not possible for Malbecco. When he spies Hellenore dancing with the satyrs and proud of being their "May-lady," the "bitter thoughts [that] engore" his heart conflict with the fear that prevents him from taking action; and yet, despite the nine demonstrations that night that her affections lie elsewhere, his desire for Hellenore, such as it is, remains constant. Spenser's depiction of an obsession that obliterates rationality and self-respect is exquisite. Malbecco wakes Hellenore from her postcoital slumber, upbraids her for her looseness, attempts to persuade her through moral argument to leave "that lewd / And loathsome life," and finally completely abases himself by forgiving her in advance, promising to take her back "With perfect peace, and bandes of fresh accord . . . As if no trespasse euer had bene donne" (3.10.44–51).

The loss of his last and truest love, his gold, is what finally destroys the remnants of Malbecco's humanity. Now deprived of the last of external objects for his miserliness, he is left only with the internal state that caused his life to be what it was in the first place and flees, a battleground of powerful conflicting passions:

> Griefe, and despight, and gealosie, and scorne
> Did all the way him follow hard behind,
> And he himselfe himselfe loath'd so forlorne,
> So shamefully forlorne of womankind;
> That as a Snake, still lurked in his wounded mind.
>
> (3.10.55)

Through the corrosive effect of the emotional state that had governed his life from the first, he has destroyed all of the ties to the external world. He voluntarily builds his "balefull mansion . . . In drery darknesse, and continuall feare" of a huge rock that threatens to fall on him at any time, and so he dares not sleep. He cannot even rest in tranquility because of the external manifestations of his inward emotional turmoil, the "roring billowes" that "beat his bowre so boystrously" (58). But Malbecco from the start had lived in "continuall feare" of losing Hellenore. He had always fed on "toades and frogs," which had bred a "filthy bloud, or humour rancorous, / Matter of doubt and dread suspitious" in his "cold complexion." He had always lived with the "curelesse care" that doth

> consume the hart,
> Corrupts the stomacke with gall vitious,
> Croscuts the liuer with internall smart,
> And doth transfixe the soule with deathes eternall dart.
>
> (59)

Malbecco's psychophysiological state had from the beginning precluded him from devoting himself in any real way to anyone other than himself. At the end of the story, his essentially superfluous physical being has disappeared and his whole existence is reduced to that miserable self now totally separated from the larger world and now living totally within itself.

Perhaps we should see Malbecco and his inability to love as an allegorization of the "rugged forhead" who "with graue foresight / Welds kingdomes causes, and affaires of state." Burleigh had apparently complained of the poem's "magnifying" of "louers deare debate; / By which fraile youth is oft to follie led" (4.proem.1). Spenser's response is that "Such ones ill iudge of loue, that cannot loue" (2) and Malbecco is, so far, the clearest illustration of a character who cannot love. Greenlaw made a good case for believing that Spenser was consistent over the years in his support to those who, in opposition to the penuriousness, vacillation, and greed that moved the policies of the lords Burleigh advocated a more vigorous foreign policy for England.[24] And Malbecco's pitiful inability to make use of the energies natural to Hellenore introduces a theme to be developed more fully in Florimell's quest: the appropriation by the old of the energies of youth is an abomination. Again, *perhaps*, we are to see in Malbecco that the appropriation of the energies of England by the Cecils is also an abomination. Paridell's recitation reminds Britomart of her "countries cause" (3.9.40); it may well have been meant to remind the Elizabethan reader of the same.

Another contrast between Britomart and a lesser character is developed when she, having left Malbecco's Castle, comes upon Scudamour. He is alone and "all wallowed / Vpon the grassy ground," "groueling" with his armour scattered about (3.11.7–8), a different Scudamour from that self-confident male who won Amoret in the Temple of Venus. Like Malbecco, Scudamour is torn by conflicting passions. He has despaired of rescuing Amoret from Busyrane and has retreated within himself, full of grief for Amoret and hatred for himself. Perhaps his sighs and sobs, thought by the psychologists to cool a heart undergoing the severe stress of a strong passion,[25] enable Scudamour to speak and thereby give vent to those passions. This relief lasts only for a moment, however, before the warring passions again choke off the "remnant of his plaintife speach," creating a severely passionate, unvented, and thereby life-threatening, internal state (8–12). Britomart is not being an alarmist when she fears for Scudamour's life.

Scudamour has fallen into an emotional state like that of Boethius at the beginning of the *Consolation*, although Scudamour has not lost his belief in God. But he has despaired of justice in this world because he can not understand why the wicked Busyrane has been permitted to prevail:

> Or hast thou, Lord, of good mens cause no heed?
> Or doth thy iustice sleepe, and silent ly?
> What booteth then the good and righteous deed,
> If goodnesse find no grace, nor righteousnesse no meed?

(3.11.9)

Britomart, like Lady Philosophy, recommends stoicism as a general antidote to the ways of the world, but, unlike Lady Philosophy, Britomart's solution to Scudamour's plight is action, a pledge to rescue Amoret or die in the attempt. Lady Philosophy would have us rise above fortune by understanding how fortune is subordinated to the larger scheme of Providence. Spenser's more optimistic view is that through virtuous endeavor we ally ourselves with Providence and thereby eventually control the operation of fortune in our own lives. Accordingly, Britomart offers virtue and "faire endeuour": "Perhaps this hand may helpe to ease your woe, / And wreake your sorrow on your cruell foe, / At least it faire endeuour will apply" (3.11.15).

The virtue that enables Britomart to enter the House of Busyrane—it is Britomart, not Scudamour, who has the proper attitude toward life and endeavor and can consequently pierce the flames—is the virtue that she manifests throughout her adventures. And the contrast between the singleness of purpose in Britomart and the internal conflict caused by warring passions in Scudamour provides an introduction to the House of Busyrane, Spenser's most important image of the destructive turmoil caused by improperly managed self-love or self-preservation. In Spenser's vision, only when self-love is expressed as true, chaste, constant love, love as it is embodied both physiologically and psychologically in Britomart, can it energize the noble deeds necessary to the health of the nation. Britomart's adventures in Book III provide the understanding of chaste love and the relationship of chaste love to the intertwining forces of human character, fortune, and Providence necessary for an examination of the lesser quests as components of Spenser's social vision. Britomart's rescue of Amoret from the House of Busyrane is, however, better examined as the climax of Amoret's progression from her birth to the Garden of Adonis to the Temple of Venus to the House of Busyrane. And so, following the example of my favorite author, I now feel free to leave Britomart and move to the quest, Florimell's, that best suits my present purposes.

2

Florimell's Quest for the Love of Marinell

WHEN Florimell is understood as a fictional personage, the basis for her characterization is the same as that for Britomart (or Amoret, for that matter): she loves virtuously.[1] When the image of Artegall in the magic mirror takes possession of Britomart's imagination, her appetites and passions, now permanently attached to that image, move her to undertake an arduous, dangerous quest to find Artegall. We do not get an episode in which Florimell falls in love, but her love for Marinell causes her also to attempt an arduous, dangerous quest. And that Marinell's image has permanently occupied her imagination is clear from her continuing love for the uninterested Marinell and, more explicitly psychological, her resistance to Proteus's attempts to displace Marinell's image (3.8.38–42). Florimell's characterization differs from Britomart's in that Florimell is all feminine while Britomart contains both masculine and feminine.

Florimell's femininity, however, is not to be understood simply as weakness.[2] Virtue in the middle books of *The Faerie Queene* is more than the product of victory in combat; it is right behavior in a world in which both internal and external forces militate against right behavior. Florimell is a heroine and her quest is heroic, because with the aid of Providence she, in her own feminine way, defeats those forces that would prevent the rightful and healthy expression of her sexual being in a proper marriage. This is not to say, however, that Spenser was a harbinger of equality between the sexes. Spenser's allegory of love envisions a proper complementarity, not a proto-equality, of male and female, of masculine and feminine.

The science of the day provides a useful if tangential look at sexual differentiation in *The Faerie Queene*. In the Galenic system both sexual and gender differences—I use "gender" throughout to denote masculine and feminine, not male and female—were physiological and were caused by the difference in the temperament of male and female seed. Renaissance physiologists rejected Aristotle's view of conception as the action of the male seed on concocted menses in favor of the two-seeds theory, and in doing so they also rejected Aristotle's theory of the female as an error or aberration of nature. As agents in reproduction, the sexes were viewed as complementary and almost as equal, because generation required not only a mixture of seeds but a place for the mixture to take place and the means of nurturing the fetus after conception. In the following quotation from Crooke, woman appears as equal, but he usually acknowledges that the male seed provides "the greatest part of the Formative power" (*Microcosmographia*, 271).

But because man was too hotte to performe this office for his heate consumeth all [the excess blood] in him and leaueth no remainder to serue for the nourishment of the infant it was necessary that a woman should be created . . . which might affoord not onely a place wherein to cherish and conceiue the seede, but also matter for the nourishment and augmentation of the same. Both these sexes of male and female doe not differ in the *kinde* as we call it or *species*, that is, in the essentiall forme and perfection; but onely in some accidents, to wit, in temper and in the structure and scituation of the parts of Generation. For the female sex as well as the male is a perfection of mankinde: some there bee that call a woman *Animal occasionatum*, or *Accessorium*, barbarous words to expresse a barbarous conceit; as if they should say, A Creature by the way, or made by mischance; yea some haue growne to that impudencie, that they haue denied a woman to haue a soule as man hath. The truth is, that as the soule of a woman is the same diuine nature with a mans, so is her body a necessary being, a first and not a second *intention of Nature*, her proper and absolute worke not her error or preuarication. (258)

That the threefold generative role of the female was not viewed as more than equal to the single role of the male reveals the underlying, unscientific, patriarchal predisposition at work even in the scientific perspective. And when the perspective is more social than scientific, Aristotle's (and others') understanding of the sexes as polarities—male as active, formative, and perfected, and female as passive, material, and deprived—was too congenial to Renaissance patriarchal needs to be abandoned. The difference in vital heat that resulted in almost equal and complementary reproductive roles for males and females also accounts for polarizing differences between male and female, because that which is "hotter" is more vigorous, more noble, and more refined than that which is "colder." When the hotter male seed and the colder female seed combine in the womb, the sex of the child is determined by which seed dominates:

[T]he fruite prooueth male or female, because of the temper of the seede and the parts of generation, either by heat thrust out, or for want or weakenes of the heate reteined within : wherefore a woman is so much lesse perfect then a man by how much her heate is lesse and weaker then his; yet as I saide is this imperfection turned vnto perfection, because without the woman, mankinde could not haue beene perfected by the perfecter sexe. The great Maister workman therfore of set purpose, made the one halfe of mankinde imperfect for the instauration of the whole kind. . . . (216–17)

This quotation is most interesting because elsewhere Crooke, benefiting from the advances in anatomy made in the Renaissance, denies Galen's theory that the female generative organs are merely an inverted version of the male. But as Thomas Laqueur makes clear, scientific advances in the Renaissance provided no escape from the Galenic model. Crooke's views of males and females as social creatures clearly supports Laqueur's thesis that in pre-Enlightenment texts, "*sex,* or the body, must be understood as the epiphenomenon, while *gender,* what we would take to be a cultural category was primary or 'real.' . . . it was precisely when talk seemed to be most directly about the biology of the two sexes that it was most embedded in the politics of gender, in culture."[3]

Crooke's lengthy treatment of the question, "Of the Temperament of women, whether they are colder or hotter then men," begins with biology but ends with culture. At first Crooke treats gender differences such as patterns of skill, gestures, demeanor, etc., as primarily biological, sexual, differences, because the concept of vital heat included qualities we also associate with "temperament": mental balance, inclination, and character (272–73). He presents arguments that women are hotter—it was a matter of some controversy—and then overturns all of those arguments. But all of that is merely preliminary to the argument of social necessity:

It behoued therefore that man should be hotter, because his body was made to endure labour and trauell [travail], as also that his minde should bee stout and invincible to vndergoe dangers, the onely hearing whereof will driue a woman as wee say out of her little wits. The woman was ordayned to receiue and conceiue the seede of the man, to beare and nourish the Infant, gouerne and moderate the house at home, to delight and refresh her husband foreswunke with labour and well-nigh exhausted and spent with care and trauell; and therefore her body is soft, smoothe and delicate, made especially for pleasure, so that whosoeuer vseth them for other doth almost abuse them. (274)

One can find sentiments comparable to those in the latter statement here and there in *The Faerie Queene,* as when the Leveler Giant in Book V is "admired much of fooles, women, and boys" (5.2.30), in the comment about "wauering wemens wit" (3.12.26), in the cynical observations of Satyrane and the Squire of Dames (3.7.57–61), and, most importantly, in the condemnation of Radigund and her Amazons for having "shaken off the shamefast band, / With which wise Nature did them strongly bynd" (5.5.25). But the mere presence of openly patriarchal or even explicitly antifeminist sentiments is not what is important. The essence is that there is a continuum of attitudes in *The Faerie Queene* comparable to that in Crooke and that the perspective determines the attitude. Male and female and masculine and feminine are complementary and the female and femininity are at the very least of equal value to the male and masculinity in the Garden of Adonis. Indeed, as Maureen Quilligan observes, "In a sense, Adonis' position is merely Verdant's passivity seen from a different perspective—one that insists on the cosmic legitimacy of the female Eros' triumph over a male Thanatos."[4]

The Garden of Adonis, however, is about principles, and in that sense it is a scientific treatise. The irreconcilable problem that the representation of female and femininity in *The Faerie Queene* poses to present-day sensibilities is that, for Spenser, the means by which all things play their proper parts in actual life is subordination; and true love between the male and female characters in the stories requires the subordination of the female to the male. After Britomart has been both wooed and won, she takes Artegall as her lord (4.6.41); and from that time on, however masculine she is in her relationship with others, she is feminine, i.e., dependent and yielding, in her relationship with Artegall. Britomart's characterization contains both masculine and feminine, but those qualities remain separate rather than amalgamated into androgyny. Spenser is, however, consistent about subordination. Free, unbound, unsubordinated males like Paridell are defective; and virtuous but unsubordinated males like Marinell and Artegall are incomplete prior to their falling in love. Males were to subordinate themselves not to females but to the love that unites the two—as in Paul's counsel for wives to submit themselves to their husbands and husbands to love their wives (Eph. 5:22–25). The problem in the story of Florimell and Marinell is solved when Marinell is finally able to love, to subordinate himself to love. It is the attitude toward, not the place of, male and female and masculine and feminine, that makes *The Faerie Queene* an interesting Renaissance text on sexuality.

Florimell's quest differs from Britomart's in that Florimell's takes place exclusively in the natural world of forest, shore, and sea. All three heroines of the chaste love quests are, of course, creatures of nature in that they are "buxome . . . and prone" to the god of love. The first three episodes in Amoret's story—her birth, her adoption by Venus, and her rearing in the Garden of Adonis—take place on the same "level of nature" as does the Florimell story. But the Temple of Venus, in addition to presenting courtship as an expression of natural forces, also puts it in a social context; and Busyrane's attempt to subvert Amoret's love for Scudamour is an attack on one who represents the expression of love within the social institution of marriage. Florimell's quest, however, takes place exclusively in the natural world; and Proteus, the prime enemy of constancy in this quest, is a creature of the natural world living apart from others in his bower at the bottom of the sea. Proteus is the antithesis of the natural forces that move the virtuous heroes and heroines to fall in love as well as the antithesis of that which enables the virtuous to remain constant in their loves. And the forces that move the central allegorical episode, the Marriage of the Medway and the Thames—those absolutely fundamental and natural forces that move the rivers to their confluence in the sea—are allegorical of the natural, physiological forces that move individual males and females to union.

Although the marriage pageant has always been examined apart from the adventures of Florimell and Marinell, it becomes central to an understanding of those adventures when it is understood as a metaphor not only for the overall generative cycle but also for the generative processes within the individual human being.[5] There are three groups in the pageant that have a familial relationship, and all three proceed properly with parents first and children following. First are Neptune and Amphitrite, followed by their issue, the sea gods and founders of great nations. Then come Ocean and Tethys, followed by their offspring, Nereus. And then comes the wedding party of the groom, the Isis and the Thame, followed by their son, the Thames. Because Spenser is topographically correct, we never lose sight of the rivers as rivers. The Isis and the Thame are the parents of the Thames in that they as rivers become the Thames at their confluence. The Thames and the Medway marry in that their waters flow together in the estuary of the Thames. At the same time, the descriptions of the Isis as weak, crooked and blind, sustained by her tributary grooms, the Churne and the Charwell, and the Thame, bowed down by Oxford, are descriptions of aged parents who take part in and support the quest of their son to achieve fruition in marriage. The natural movement of the river from source to mouth reflects an idealized cycle of life in which there are proper and healthy relationships between parents and offspring, proper and healthy relationships between old and young, and proper relationships between male and female. In the natural world, ideally conceived, such is the generative cycle. The old give way to the young, become the young, in endless succession, and the cycle proceeds with the inexorability of the moving waters of a river. The aged parents march before their son "full fresh and iolly" (4.11.27) to his union with the lovely Medway:

Her goodly lockes adowne her backe did flow
        Vnto her waste, with flowres bescattered,
        The which ambrosiall odours forth did throw
        To all about, and all her shoulders spred
        As a new spring; and likewise on her hed
        A Chapelet of sundry flowers she wore,
        From vnder which the deawy humour shed,
        Did tricle downe her haire, like to the hore
Congealed litle drops, which doe the morne adore.

(4.11.46)

Here in the figures of the Medway and the Thames are the images of youth and spring and morning and growth, the images of life—the description of the Thames is brief, but "fresh" in "full fresh and iolly" refers to the fullness of a stream in the spring and also means "blooming." This complex of youth and life is what the aged parents and the other figures in the pageant support by their presence in their proper places. Cymoent, Marinell's mother, is a part of the pageant in her appointed place as a daughter of Nereus. She and her sister sea nymphs follow the Medway and thereby remind us that the marriage takes place in the sea, the source of all life.

The confluences of the rivers are, however, more than an allegorical representation of the generative cycle. In Renaissance physiology, conception takes place through the confluence of the male and the female seed in the womb. When the two "Potentially Animated" moistures, male and female, combine in the womb, conception follows (Crooke, *Microcosmographia,* 285); and consequently the confluences of the rivers are metaphors for sexual intercourse and conception. The myth of Venus's birth, caused by Saturn's castrated testicles falling into the sea, reinforces the physiological significance. To account for the sea's incredible fertility, we are told, the "antique wisards well inuented, / That *Venus* of the fomy sea was bred" (4.12.2). Leone Ebreo explains the physical allegory: "Hence they say that she sprang from the blood of the testicles and from the foam of the sea: and this means that animals are born of the seed of the male, which is the blood of the testicles, and of the subtle seed of the female, which is like to foam."[6] The relating of Venus to seed and to the sea is especially appropriate to the episode, because the confluence of the Medway and the Thames actually takes place in the estuary of the Thames, a part of the sea. The Marriage of the Medway and the Thames is an allegory of the natural generative cycle unchecked, uninhibited, and uncorrupted by all that which works against the expression of love and generation among human beings in the postlapsarian world. The only "problem" in the "lives" of the Medway and the Thames is her delay (4.11.8), which, as with Milton's Eve in the Garden, is natural even to the prelapsarian female. The pageant is a dance of love in which the partners are idealized forces of nature, in which a complementarity of youth and age, of male and female, is achieved effortlessly.

Since the confluences of the rivers are the product of nature pure and simple, since they are inevitable, they do not fall under the sway of fortune and so do not need an exercise of character or the operation of Providence. But Florimell and Marinell must live in a world where fortune seems to hold sway and where forces opposing the chaste expression of healthy physical desire seem to prevail. The theme of the narrative is that the exercise of the virtue of chaste love makes possible in the real world the kind of life that comes so inevitably to the Medway and the Thames. The forces in the story proper that would deny the expression of natural affection are reflected primarily in two characters, Cymoent and Proteus. There is a direct contrast between the role Cymoent plays in the marriage pageant and the role she plays in the rest of the story. As a part of the pageant she is a part of life as life is symbolically presented there. As a character in the story, as a parent herself, she manifests some of the worst aspects of age; she is cautious and afraid of life, and she seeks to guide her son's life by guiding him away from life. Although very unlike Malbecco and Busyrane and Proteus, Cymoent would, like those villains, appropriate to her own purposes the energies of youth; and so her affection for her son is, as long as she attempts to circumscribe his life, properly understood as another form of the mismanagement of self-love.

The mainspring of the story, the effort of Marinell's mother to control Marinell's life, is a misguided effort to control fortune. In effect, she puts him on Fortune's Wheel. In order to "aduance his name and glorie" beyond what Marinell had already achieved in his many battles, Cymoent prevailed upon Nereus to endow her son with treasure "Boue all the sonnes, that were of earthly wombes ybore"; and so he came to possess the treasures resulting from the "ouerthrow / And wreckes of many wretches, which did weepe, / And often waile their wealth, which he [Nereus] from them did keepe." Marinell acquired "Exceeding riches and all pretious things, / The spoyle of all the world, that it did pas / The wealth of th'East, and pompe of *Persian* Kings" (3.4.21–23). All of the elements of Marinell's life before his encounter with Britomart—doing battle, cultivating the pride ensuing from his victories, and protecting the treasures amassed from the misfortunes of others—reflect the quality of life of one on the revolving Wheel.

Marinell's characterization is appropriate to his place on the Wheel. There is a fragility to Marinell's masculine pride that is most clearly reflected in his defeat by Britomart but apparent before. The reason Cymoent went to Proteus for the prophecy was that she feared Marinell's "too haughtie hardines" (3.4.24). Marinell is possessed by an unsubordinated self-love. He will not, or cannot, subordinate himself to love, and so his masculinity is self-enclosed and expressed as emptiness and slothfulness. In contrast to the Medway and the Thames, who move to the sea in order to partake of life, Marinell guards his sterile treasures, which have been taken from the sea. James Nohrnberg rightly reads the treasures on the strand as suggesting "an avarice of seed" and also a kind of onanism.[7] In order to join the minuet of love, the dance of life, the female must subordinate herself to the male, and the male must subordinate himself to love, to the dance itself. Marinell's life, though not immoral, is sterile; and his inner weakness is clearly revealed by his empty boasting before his fight with Britomart and when he falls defeated, "groueling" like a passive sacrificial ox on the "pretious shore" (3.4.17). The encounter illustrates how healthy sexual desire provides the basis for heroic endeavor and how unhealthy sexual desire underlies the opposite. In Book III, as elsewhere in *The Faerie Queene*, the problems attendant upon the expression of human sexuality are consistently the product of idleness and in-constancy; the solution to those problems is consistently the product of heroic endeavor and constancy. Britomart's defeat of Marinell is, of course, finally provi-dential in that it sets in motion the forces, only apparently under the sway of fortune, that will finally bring Florimell and Marinell together.

Florimell, like Britomart, is one of those who "buxome are and prone" to "Imperious Loue" (3.2.23) and, like Britomart, she is one of those governed by and sustained by her need to consummate her love in marriage. When she hears of Marinell's defeat and possible death, she goes on her quest to find him dead or alive. When they finally come together at the marriage feast, the force of her love pierces his heart, enabling him to fall in love and thereby to leave his immature, static stage in life. The story, in essence, is the victory of the forces of life over the forces that would deny life, and Florimell is a true heroine, a truly feminine hero. She has no masculine qualities, she wins no jousts with strange knights, and she destroys no magic houses. She does, however, venture out on a dangerous and difficult quest; and her steadfastness in love, the essence of the virtue of chastity, while not expressed in Britomart's "stout hardiment," is equal to that of Britomart. As her dwarf says, "Liues none this day, that may with her compare / In stedfast chastitie and vertue rare" (3.5.8); and when we come back to the story in Book IV, we are told that it was her "constant mind" (4.11.2) that enabled her to resist Proteus. When Proteus captured Florimell, his efforts were directed toward sup-planting the image of Marinell in her psyche. Proteus boasted he was a god, "But she a mortall creature loued best"; he made himself into a "mortall wight," but she said she "lou'd none, but a Faerie knight"; then "like a Faerie knight himselfe he drest," and so forth. However, nothing could affect her, "so firmly she had sealed vp her brest" (3.8.39–40). Her steadfastness is an expression of heroic virtue (3.8.42); Florimell's constancy, like Britomart's, is expressed as "faire endeuour."

Florimell's quest to find Marinell, unlike Cymoent's quest to make life safe for him, causes her to contend with the accidents of fortune rather than attempt to avoid them. When Florimell ventures out from the protection of the court, armed only with her love for Marinell, she submits herself to fortune. She is forced to travel afoot after her palfrey gives out: "Need teacheth her this lesson hard and rare, / That fortune all in equall launce doth sway" (3.7.4). From the time she leaves the court until she is thrown into Proteus' dungeon, Florimell's movements are governed by those who, happening to cross her path, are moved by her beauty to attempt violation. Her ultimate fate, however, is not a matter of fortune any more than is Britomart's or, for that matter, Elizabeth's and England's. When she flees the old witch's monster and comes to the shore, thinking to leap into the sea, "It fortuned (high God did so ordaine)" (3.7.27) that the old fisherman's boat was there to provide her with a temporary safe haven. Her plight on the boat seems to be directed by the goddess Fortune herself as the "cruell Queene auengeresse" (3.8.20), but Providence again arranges her rescue, this time by Proteus. Explicitly, the heavens "of voluntary grace" and "soueraine fauour towards chastity" effect her rescue, "So much high God doth innocence embrace" (3.8.29). Merlin and the narrator know that fortune is under the ultimate control of Providence. Florimell does not; she knows only that she loves Marinell, that her love for him is constant, and that she must find him dead or alive. Nevertheless, despite her ignorance, she accomplishes in her realm what Merlin says "mens good endeuours" (3.3.25) will accomplish in Britomart's.

The attempts to destroy Florimell's capacity for virtuous love reinforce the conflict between the old and the young that is manifested in Cymoent's attempts to govern Marinell's life. The attempts also provide another contrast between the ideal world of the marriage pageant, where the old support the quests of the young, and the chancy world in which the pair of lovers must learn to live. All the enemies of love who attempt to despoil Florimell, with the possible exception of the forester, whose age is indeterminate, are old: the old witch, whose son is smitten with Florimell, the old fisherman who attempts to rape her, and especially old Proteus. The desires of the forester and the fisherman, although debased, are natural; Proteus's desires are a perversion of natural affection.

As a fictional personage, Proteus obviously embodies mutability, and he is consequently the enemy of order, of constancy in love. But it is less obvious that his inconstancy, much more than Malecasta's, entails lifelessness, a lack of vital energy. Proteus does not mismanage and so corrupt what otherwise would have been a healthy "naturall affection"; in Proteus, as in Malbecco, the source of "naturall affection" is defective, and so self-love in Proteus is corrupted from the start. Spenser's use of Ariosto helps to make the point. Ariosto's Proteus is a passionate lover; and when we remember the role of vital heat in Renaissance psychophysiology, we can see that Spenser's Proteus owes more to Ariosto's old impotent hermit who captures Angelica than he does to Ariosto's Proteus. When Ariosto's Proteus sees the beautiful maiden on the beach, his sexual desire is expressed through a play on hot and cold: in Harington's translation, "That though he dwelt in waters salt and cold, / Yet fresh hote love on him had taken hold. / Which heate when all the sea could not asswage, / He thought her milkwarm flesh could only quench" (8.46–47).

Spenser's Proteus is quite different; all of his characteristics militate against real physical desire, against "fresh hote love." He is old and he is cold, "An aged sire with head all frory hore, / And sprinckled frost vpon his deawy beard," and when he captures Florimell his presence so benumbs her "faint heart . . . with the frozen cold . . . that her wits nigh fayld, / And all her senses with abashment quite were quayld." He does kiss her—but only "softly"—and while he does "the cold ysickles from his rough beard, / Dropped adowne vpon her yuorie brest" (3.8.30–35). The predominant characteristic is moist coldness, and John Huarte reminds us of Galen's observation (ultimately Aristotle's) that "coldnesse is apparantly noysome to all the offices of the soule." Huarte also says that eunuchs are cold and moist, that when a man loses his cods he loses his forces and his natural heat and that "from the wit and manners of a man we coniecture the temperature of his cods."[8] Proteus's cods are cold. Unlike Ariosto, who contrasted Proteus to his element, Spenser incorporates the waters "salt and cold" into his Proteus; and the result is a character who is the very antithesis of those, like Britomart and Florimell, who are moved by sexual energy, by a superabundance of seed in their testicles, to find their loves.

Proteus's behavior toward Florimell expresses his inner state. The fisherman, who has some of the characteristics of Ariosto's hermit and some of Ariosto's Proteus, is old; but Florimell's presence refreshes him, and he feels "in his old courage [sexual desire] new delight / To gin awake, and stirre his frozen spright" (3.8.23). The sight of Florimell "Infixt such secret sting of greedy lust, / That the drie withered stocke it gan refresh, / And kindled heat" (3.8.25). Nothing similar happens to Spenser's Proteus, and given Spenser's openness about sexuality, its absence must be significant. All of Proteus's attempts to win Florimell's "liking vnto his delight" (3.8.38) are nonphysical. When he takes her to his bower, he first offers flattering words and gifts and then, failing to achieve his objective with pseudokindness, tries various oppressive ways to subvert her will. He tries to awe her with his divinity, he threatens her, and, finally, using his power to transform himself into monstrous forms, tries to frighten her.

That Proteus's is not a healthy physical desire is clearly indicated when we come back to the story in Book IV and are reminded how "Vnlouely *Proteus* ["lovely" could mean "amorous," "loving," as well as "attractive" in the sixteenth century], *missing to his mind* / That Virgins loue to win by wit or wile," threw her into his dungeon (4.11.2; my emphasis). The efficient cause of Proteus's desire is the *idea* of possessing Florimell—it is in his mind that he misses having her. His desire is not the product of natural affection; it does not stem from testicles full of hot seed. And his efforts to win her, by "wit or wile," are directed toward dislodging the image of Marinell from her mind and heart rather than by drawing her affections to himself or even by raping her. Healthy courtship is an outward expression of the inward "kindly flame," not an intellectually conceived strategy deriving from an at least predominantly psychological need. Proteus, like Malbecco, is male but not masculine. Proteus is the epitome of those who, unlike Scudamour, lack the courage, both in a sexual sense and in the related senses of force and purpose, to confront Daunger in the Temple of Venus:

> Againe some other, that in hard assaies
> Were cowards knowne, and litle count did hold,
> Either through gifts, or guile, or such like waies,
> Crept in by stouping low, or stealing of the kaies.
>
> (4.10.18)

Everything about Proteus implies the negation of healthy physical desire: his age, his coldness, his manner of courtship, his desires, his bower where besides himself only the old nymph, Panope, lives, and particularly his dungeon, where Florimell, like Persephone, is kept from the life-giving, male and masculine, sun. Proteus is, allegorically, everything that would prevent the natural fruition of life and love. In his protean nature, he is winter, he is chaos, he is death, he is coldness, he is darkness, and he is even the rich and powerful old man, like Malbecco, who would, by taking a young woman, keep her from finding a young man to share with her the springtime of life. Proteus does not appear in the marriage pageant with its celebration of love and fertility. Significantly, Nereus, an old prophetic deity like Proteus who does appear in it, "takes great ioy / Ofttimes amongst the wanton Nymphs to sport and toy" (4.11.19).

Also significant is that Proteus's perception of Marinell's impending defeat should manifest itself in a warning to Cymoent to keep Marinell from womankind

(3.4.25–28). Proteus accurately envisions the danger as being from a "stout" virgin who will either "dismay" or "kill" Marinell, but his warning that Marinell should be kept from "womankind," although not gratuitous, is misleading. In this instance the moist coldness of Proteus's complexion relates him to the eunuch's intellectual deficiency. As Huarte says, even if a man before castration had "much wit and habilitie," as soon as "his stones be cut away, he groweth to leese the same, so far foorth as if he had receiued some notable dammage in his very braine" (*Examination of mens wits*, 279).

Cymoent's understanding that "hart-wounding loue" is the danger envisioned by Proteus also reflects her psychology. She has ears only for Proteus's warning to keep Marinell from womankind, and, consequently, like Proteus, completely misses the import of Proteus's vision of the threat to Marinell as a "stout" virgin. Perhaps Spenser wishes us to understand that Cymoent's possessiveness predisposes her to see the danger to her son in the form of another woman's love. Most significant, however, is not that she misreads the prophecy but that she should follow her interpretation of it. Herein is the real distortion in her vision of life.

Perhaps Cymoent means well, but she is unable to see that life, whatever the dangers, must be lived and that to avoid one kind of danger is to embrace another. And so, the distorted view of life that caused Cymoent to think she should govern Marinell's life in the first place causes her to conclude that he must live apart from love. The message in Cymoent's efforts to control her son's destiny, to control fortune, is clear. The "termes of mortall state" are "tickle . . .[,] full of subtile sophismes, which do play / With double senses, and with false debate." And those whose lives are misaligned will, as did Cymoent, "vainely . . . expound" those terms (3.4.28). The "termes of mortall state" are not something to be figured out; they are to be lived through. Proteus and Cymoent together present a complex of conditions and attitudes that militate against the forces of life, that would prevent life from being lived as "faire endeuour." In every way Spenser makes clear that Proteus is a principle of evil that would destroy natural affection. Proteus represents all that which prevents love, courtship, and marriage in the first place; and he is to be compared with Busyrane, who represents all that which operates in society to destroy the expression of love after marriage. Both these central evil characters are enemies of constancy; their chief purpose is to destroy constancy in love and thereby destroy constancy in all human affairs. Both are finally images of death-in-life and are analogous to the death-in-life figures appropriate to Books I and II, Duessa and Acrasia.

A. Bartlett Giamatti finds reflections of Proteus in Archimago (1.2.10), Duessa (4.1.18), Malengin (5.9.16,17), Death (6.11.16), and finally in Mutability, the ultimate evil figure of change, who Giamatti says, "is Proteus writ large." Giamatti's argument, which fits neatly within Renwick's seminal understanding of constancy and mutability in *The Faerie Queene*, is that because these Proteus figures are "completely unfettered" they "lead to shapeless evil and horrible dissolution." They are, Giamatti says, to be contrasted with "two superb versions of the restraint of change, where order and energy are wed in a perfect whole": the Garden of Adonis and the Marriage of the Medway and the Thames.[9] Translated into terms appropriate to the love quests, Giamatti's phrases describing the Proteus figures apply to the enemies of love such as Malecasta, Malbecco, Busyrane, Radigund, and Proteus himself; and those describing the allegorical cores describe the traits of those who truly love. "Restraint of change" and "order" become constancy, and "energy" becomes sexual desire. The wedding of "order" and "energy" in the characters becomes chastity, as chastity is defined by Britomart's love for Artegall. Perpetuity in the body politic depends upon the bonding of monarch and subject by true love. And true love in the commonwealth is not possible without true love between individual males and females. Finally, when the middle books are read cumulatively and retrospectively, the ordered energy of the virtuous is the ordered energy necessary to the health of the commonwealth and consequently to corporate perpetuity.

Through the constancy of her love, Florimell is more powerful than Proteus and all that he represents, and she enables Marinell to become more powerful than Cymoent and all she represents. Like Persephone who lives through the winter, Florimell endures her imprisonment without losing her strength. Her love for Marinell, expressed in her poignant lament, touches his "stony" heart, mollifies his "mighty courage," and causes him to fall in love and to suffer the sacrificial death that represents the destruction of his immaturity. Neptune's judgment that he, as "the seas sole Soueraine" (4.12.30), has control over life and death resolves the conflict between those who would deny life and those who would live. His decision, as god of the sea, which is the source of all life, the birthplace of Venus, and the "womb" where the waters of the Medway and the Thames mingle—and also as he is, allegorically, the liver that produces the blood that the testicles concoct into seed (Crooke, *Microcosmographia,* 282)—means that the lives of the young are to be lived as expressions of the energies of youth. It means that finally Florimell and Marinell will be able to share the kind of love that comes so naturally and effortlessly to the Medway and the Thames. The Marriage of the Medway and the Thames presents order and harmony and fullness of life in the natural world. Proteus and others represent forces that would prevent Florimell and Marinell from achieving the kind of life that is presented in the pageant. However, the two have the capacity within themselves to achieve order and harmony and fullness in their own lives because they are able to channel the energy of their lives into virtuous endeavor. By so living they not only express their innate capacity to resist evil and to pursue good, but they by the same effort align themselves with Providence and are thereby able to prevail against the accidents of fortune.

When Florimell and Marinell come together, Marinell is resurrected

> As withered weed through cruell winters tine,
> That feeles the warmth of sunny beames reflection,
> Liftes vp his head, that did before decline
> And gins to spread his leafe before the faire sunshine.
>
> (4.12.34)

Here at last, associated with Marinell, are the images of spring and growth and life that manifest themselves so naturally and spontaneously in the figures of the Medway and the Thames. After an initial life of narrow, fragile, unsubordinated masculinity, Marinell finally subordinates himself to love. A defective character when we meet him, he undergoes no character development or moral regeneration other than that implied by his falling in love. But by falling in love and by subordinating himself to love, he enables Florimell as well as himself to join the dance of life. The heroes need not be paragons of virtue; they need only be basically virtuous and love properly—just as those who are to be shaped by the reading of this allegory of love need not be perfectly virtuous in order to be proper members of the commonwealth. They must, however, subordinate themselves as males and females, nobles and commoners, monarch and subjects, etc., to their proper roles in that commonwealth.

3

Scudamour's Quest for the
Love of Amoret

WHEN the middle books of *The Faerie Queene* are read as a social vision in which
the ordered energy of chaste love provides the ordered energy fundamental to
the health of the commonwealth, the fact that the Florimell quest takes place in
the natural world of forest, shore, and sea focuses the implications of that quest
on the lives of men and women as natural creatures. Scudamour's quest for
Amoret enlarges the scope of Spenser's vision through episodes that, in addition,
focus the implications on men and women as social creatures. Florimell, Amoret,
and Britomart are all creatures of nature in that they are "buxome . . . and
prone" to the god of love; all express the operation of inborn, natural forces.
Scudamour's progress through the Temple of Venus is also moved by a most
natural force. Spenser understood that a healthy society depends upon the proper
direction of the self-love that moves us to preserve ourselves; and, next to preserving our very selves, self-love is expressed most fundamentally in that complex of desires that leads us to reproduce ourselves. But the obstacles to
Scudamour's progress through the Temple are expressive of social conventions
as well as the natural tendencies of a buxom, pubescent female to delay; and
Busyrane's later attempt to subvert Amoret's love for Scudamour is not only an
attack on Amoret as an individual but also an attack on one who represents the
expression of love within the social institution of marriage.

The focus of Scudamour's quest for the love of Amoret is on the object of
the quest rather than on the quester. The important episodes trace Amoret's
progress from her birth to her rescue from the House of Busyrane and her reunion with Scudamour. We simply cannot make sense of Scudamour's quest
without assuming that when Spenser published the 1596 installment, he intended
to come back in some later book to the discarded 1590 ending of Book III in
which Amoret and Scudamour are reunited. A Renaissance psychophysiological
reading of the sequence of highly allegorical episodes that constitutes Amoret's

progression reveals an Amoret not defective, as most previous studies understand her, but an idealization of that portion of the female sex that is to lead the generative life, an even more feminine female than Florimell, an Amoret who is a proper object for Scudamour's quest.

The essential Scudamour, the Scudamour who wins Amoret to the generative life in the Temple of Venus, is consequently revealed as an idealization of the masculinity necessary to win a pubescent female to her proper role in life. That Scudamour is less than ideal elsewhere reinforces a central theme in these books: Spenser's "ensamples," especially the males, are not models of perfection, just as perfection is not the goal toward which Spenser attempts to fashion his readers. Spenser's vision for Elizabethan England requires only that members of that commonwealth subordinate themselves to their proper roles in the commonwealth. I suggest that the central critical problem in Scudamour's quest is not, as in the debate between Thomas Roche and A. Kent Hieatt, whether Amoret or Scudamour is the defective character. The problem is the extent to which the Maske of Cupid is to be read as a projection of Amoret's internal state, as in modern psychological readings, among which are Roche's and Hieatt's, or an external threat that Busyrane has imposed on Amoret, as Lewis reads it.[1] My Renaissance psychophysiological reading of Amoret's progression to the House of Busyrane leads me toward Lewis. I read the Maske as a spell that Busyrane *is attempting* to impose on Amoret. No explanation answers adequately all of the questions one can ask of the episode, but I believe Renaissance science provides a better frame of reference within which to pursue answers than does modern science.

Amoret's Birth and Adoption

Spenser's initial description of the birth of Amoret and Belphoebe "of the wombe of Morning dew, / And . . . the ioyous prime [i.e., sunrise]"; the description of the sun's "fruitfull ray" on Chrysogonee, whose body has been mollified by the water of the fountain; and the allusion to the generative power of the sun on the muddy banks of the Nile—all these allegorize basic forces essential to generation in human beings (3.6.3–6). The energizing force in the seed, the male seed especially, is, like the sun, a form of vital heat; and the nourishing power of the seed, the female seed especially, is in its moisture. Aristotle's comment, "Man and the sun generate man," which John Hankins traces through a number of medieval and Renaissance authorities, makes a similar point.[2] But a more explicitly physiological definition of the roles of vital heat and moisture in generation is contained in Hippocrates' dictum, "The Soule creepeth into man being made of a mixture of fire and water." Helkiah Crooke explains Hippocrates: "By the Soule he m[e]aneth the Seed . . . by Fire hee meaneth the spirits and the in-bred heat . . . by Water he meaneth the Alimentary moysture which is bloud" (*Microcosmographia*, 259). After the mixture of male and female seeds "sprouts" and forms the spermatic parts, the white parts of the body (bones, nerves, gristle, etc.), the addition of the maternal blood provides the material for the sanguine, the fleshy parts of the body. The specific act of generation responsible for Amoret and Belphoebe, however, bypasses sexual processes and involves only the most fundamental, underlying forces of vital heat, seminal principles, and moisture:

> The sunne-beames bright vpon her body playd,
> Being through former bathing mollifide,
> And pierst into her wombe, where they embayd
> With so sweet sence and secret power vnspide,
> That in her pregnant flesh they shortly fructifde.
>
> (3.6.7)

The obvious point of the episode is that the conception of Belphoebe and Amoret is as far from sin and guilt as is the conception of creatures in the banks of the Nile, where the sun and the moisture operate directly on the *rationes seminales*. Belphoebe's (and surely Amoret's) creation is exempt from "all loathly crime, / That is ingenerate in fleshly slime" (3) and on a more psychological note: "Vnwares she them conceiu'd, vnwares she bore: / She bore without paine, that she con-ceiued / Withouten pleasure" (27). Since women loosed seed orgasmically, they could not conceive in the ordinary way without pleasure—Crooke allows only women with "impure, mucous and moyste" bodies, those who could loose seed without pleasure, to be able to conceive without pleasure (*Microcosmographia*, 295).

David Lee Miller draws on Hankins's presentation of Aristotelian genera-tion theory in order to relate the generation of the twins to the generation of Errour's brood. This relationship provides the basis for Miller's argument that "Spenser's most positive images of the feminine are organized by a scheme that apprehends femininity apart from the masculine origin as an object of nausea."[3] For Aristotle—and for Hankins and Miller Aristotle's *is* Renaissance generation theory—both sexual and spontaneous generation are initiated by an act of de-composition comparable to that initiated by rennet in the "setting" of milk, causing it to coagulate. As Hankins summarizes the Aristotlelian tradition, the mixture of male seed and female menses lies motionless in the womb for seven days, at the end of which time it begins to "work," to ferment, or putrefy, or coagulate—to use terms employed by several commentators [Scaliger, Pico, and Paracelsus]. Aristotle compares the process to the curdling of milk and makes clear that it is a form of corruption, which is followed by generation.[4]

In Galenic sexual generation theory, however, which was universally accepted by physicians and anatomists, there is no hint of decomposition, just as there is none in this episode. The sunbeams effect their purpose through "sweet sence and secret power," words that evoke the opposite of corruption. Crooke never understands normal sexual generation to include processes such as decay or corruption. The following quotations, which emphasize the sanctity of life, the nobility of the womb, and the wholesomeness of the process by which life is actuated out of potentiality, are typical. In the first, for example, the basic analogy is to the creation of the macrocosm; and the images are of brooding, knitting and weaving, and nourishment:

> We begin with the seed which is like the *Chaos*. Vpon which as the Spirit of God moued whilst it was without forme, first to preserue it & after to distinguish it, so it is in this masse of seed [male and female]; the Formatiue spirit broodeth it first. After as a Spider in the center of her Lawny Canopy with admirable skil weaueth her Cipresse web, first hanging it by slender Ties to the roofe, and after knitting her enter [entire] braided yarn into a curious net; so the spirit first fastneth the seed to the womb with membranes and ligaments, after distinguisheth it into certaine spermaticall threds which we call *Stamina corporis*, the warpe of the bodie. To these when the second principle which is the Mothers blood accrueth, it filleth vp their voyde distances and so amasseth them into a solid body, which euery day is nourished and encreased into all dimensions, furnished also with motion, sense and finally with a reasonable soule. Then as impatient of so close imprisonment, as vnsatisfied with so slender allowance, it instantly striues till this Little world arriues into the great. (*Microcosmographia*, 257)

Again,

> This mingling of the seeds is the first worke or indeuour of Nature in generation. And presently after the seeds are thus mingled, the womb, which is the most noble and almost diuine Nurse, gathereth and contracteth it selfe, and that I may vse the words of the Arabians, is so corrugated that there is no empty or void place left therein. And this it doth as being greedy to conteyne and to cherish, we say to Conceiue the seed. . . . Then the wombe rowzeth and raiseth vpp the sleepy and

lurking power of the seeds, and that which was before but potentiall, it bringeth
into act. (262–63)

In fact, the only time Crooke associates corruption with normal generation in
human beings is when he contemplates the possibility that the seeds could end
up elswhere than in the womb:

> The place is the wombe, which by a naturall disposition looseneth the bondes
> wherein the spirit of the seed is fettered, and withal helpeth to adde vigour and
> efficacy thereunto. For if the seed should be powred into any other part of the
> body it would not be as we use to say, Conceiued but putrified, not preserued, but
> corrupted. (271)

And so, if we follow Galen and the physicians, there is no justification for
Miller's dramatic statement, "The [Renaissance] womb, in other words, is a place
where life emerges out of rot."[5] Of course, the womb was thought to be more
susceptible to disease than any other part of the body. The suffocation of the
uterus could be caused, for example, by a lack of blood, a surplus of blood, or by
seed that had been retained in the womb and consequently corrupted.[6] Also,
because of its location, humors could flow into the womb, corrupt the menstrual
blood, and cause various diseases (Crooke, *Microcosmographia,* 288–93). And defective offspring could result from various moral and physiological causes. My
purpose here is not to deny the general frailty of the flesh or the especial frailty of
the womb; but Chrysogonee does not suffer from disease, and Amoret and
Belphoebe are certainly not defective. Not only were the twins "enwombed"
differently from "other wemens commune brood," but they were not, "As other
wemens babes," nourished "with commune food." They "sucked vitall blood"
(5). There are different possibilities here. Crooke refers to Hippocrates' dictum
that the fetus nourished first on the mother's "pure blood" and later took in
milk that flowed from the breast to the womb. Crooke also quotes Galen: "[T]he
small and tender Infant drawes in the first months the purest of the Blood, but
when he is growne greater, he draweth the pure and impure together" (316). At
another place, Crooke explains that the arteries distribute the "spiritous and
vitall blood" from the heart to the various parts of the body so as to "transmit
heate and the vitall faculty perpetually into the whole body, to cherish the inbred
heate of the particular part, to moderate and gouerne their vitall functions and to
defend their life" (859). The veins, on the other hand, carry "a thicker blood and
a more cloudy spirit: the veins haue an inbred faculty to alter and boyle the
blood; the arteries haue no such faculty, because their blood attaineth his vtmost

elaboration and perfection in the heart" (825). Whatever the physiological referent, it is clear that the nourishment supplied to Amoret and Belphoebe contributes to the purity, the vigor, and the nobility of the generative processes that
produced them.

The common reference to the Nile generation myth in the birth episode and
in Errour's den is central to Miller's thesis. And here also he draws on Hankins.
Hankins's treatment of the myth is not comprehensive, however, because his
project, namely, Hamlet's phrase, "For if the sun breed maggots in a dead dog,
being a god kissing carrion," limits his interest to the spontaneous generation of
creatures out of putrescence, and so he does not distinguish between the variet-
ies of spontaneous generation that have been found in the myth. Although only
maggots are generated by the operation of the sun on putrescent flesh, the operation of the sun on the Nile mud was believed to produce perfected as well as
monstrous creatures. Of C. W. Lemmi's sources for Spenser's "Monster-Spawning
Nile-Mud," only Albertus Magnus says genuine monsters are generated out of
the mud. Both Mela and Diodorus Siculus thought normal animals emerged if
the process was brought to completion, the monstrous being merely incomplete
creatures—in Mela's words, "animals that, not yet perfect but rather in the act
of receiving life, appear partly formed and partly still of the earth."[7] Clearly the
accounts of generation in the mud of the Nile provide a latitude within which
Spenser could appropriately allude to the myth in an episode in which there is a
healthy spontaneous generation as well as in one in which there is generation of
monsters.

Like Maureen Quilligan, Miller also assumes that Errour's brood was generated in her womb; but the words of the poem associate them with the mid and
upper levels of her digestive system and, particularly appropriate to her allegorical significance, with her mouth. The creatures who are nursing at beginning of
the episode go into Errour's mouth when Redcrosse appears. (The monstrous
brood of Milton's Sin, appropriately to her allegorical significance, reenter their
mother's womb when they choose [PL 2.654–67; 799–801].) Later Errour spews
out of her "filthy maw" various objects—gobbets, books, blind toads and frogs,
etc. And when Errour perceives their stink to cause Redcrosse's courage to fail,
she vomits "serpents small, / Deformed monsters, fowle, and blacke as inke"
(1.1.15, 20, 22). I believe we can best understand the generation of Errour's
monsters by seeing it as analogous to the generation of worms in the stomach
and guts out of "a putrid and rotten humour" (Crooke, Microcosmographia, 297).
And in that case, Errour's brood would say nothing at all about wombs in women.
Quilligan says the episode evokes "nauseated horror at the facts of monstrous
female creation" and images "our subterranean terror at the very slime of origin."

(Both Quilligan and Miller make a lot out of the word, "slime," responding to the word according to its connotations of stickiness and repulsiveness. "Slime" had those connotations in early modern England, but more applicable to the context here is the word's association with fertility. All of the sixteenth-century OED citations are to passages about fertility. There is a particularly relevant fifteenth-century citation that points out that God did not make woman, as he did man, out of "slime.") A reading of the episode as evoking nauseated horror at the facts of spontaneous generation out of putrescent humors ameliorates the misogyny that Miller and Quilligan find in the den. I find no misogyny in the birth of the twins.[8]

A specific reference to worms in the stomach is not essential to my argument. I understand Spenser's use of the Nile story in the separate episodes to focus on different aspects of spontaneous generation. In Errour's den, there is no sun and the products of the generation are "loathly frogs and toades, which eyes did lacke," "Deformed monsters," etc.; and so the generation is more like the generation in rotting wood, or dung heaps, or putrescent humors. Significantly, I believe, the sun is not mentioned in this reference to the Nile myth. In the birth of the twins, the sun plays upon a living female body, and two perfect female babies are consequently "enwombed in the sacred throne" of that "chaste bodie" (3.6.5). Generation here is like normal generation in human beings, except that the elemental forces in generation—vital heat, moisture, and seminal reasons—are divorced from the matter in which they are incorporated when generation is sexual.

A physiological interpretation of the birth reintroduces into Spenser's allegory of love the elemental physiological forces inherent in self-love as the instinct for self-preservation. It also emphasizes that those physiological processes in themselves are innocent and, consequently, that the physiology of sexual desire in Amoret and the physiology that provides the potentiality for sexual desire in Belphoebe are to be perceived in the same light as the physiology of sexual desire in Britomart. The vegetal soul operates apart from considerations of good and evil; only when the higher, voluntary faculties play their part is there a basis for moral judgment, a basis for separating the chaste love of a Britomart or an Amoret from the lust of a Malecasta.

The following episode, in which Belphoebe is adopted by Diana and Amoret by Venus, differentiates the roles of the physiological from the higher, voluntary psychological faculties in human sexuality through its differentiation of the complementary roles of Venus and the armed Cupid. Lewis's attempt to get at the Cupid complex by associating the unarmed Cupid with true love and the armed Cupid with false love has influenced, if not determined, most of the subsequent discussions of Cupid in *The Faerie Queene*.[9] But Lewis understood manifestations of love without a sexual basis as true love—as in the proem to *The Faerie Queene*, in the angel's guarding Guyon (2.8.6), and in the House of Alma. Lewis also understood the idealized sexual love in the Garden of Adonis as true love. But true love in the middle books is better understood as Britomart's, Florimell's, and Amoret's kind of love: love expressed through a fallen but virtuous psyche in a fallen world. The love that takes place in the Garden and the "love" that moves the Medway and the Thames to their inexorable union are expressions of purely physiological forces, of the vegetal soul, apart from any possibility of psychic dislocation, and so are better understood as neither true nor false.

A better way to differentiate the armed from the unarmed Cupid is to associate the armed Cupid with the psychological, with all that causes a member of the other sex to be sexually attractive (other than one's own testicles being full of seed) and to identify the unarmed Cupid with Venus, who is identified consistently throughout *The Faerie Queene* with the physiological causes of sexual desire, with testicles full of seed. In *An Hymne in Honovr of Love*, the unarmed Cupid suffices for the lower creatures, who are moved "without further care, / To quench the flame, which they in burning fynd." But "man" has higher faculties, "hauing yet in his deducted spright, / Some sparks remaining of that heauenly fyre," and seeks "Beautie." Consequently, for human beings, Cupid tips arrows with beauty, arrows "Which glancing through the eyes with countenance coy, / Rest not, till they haue pierst the trembling harts, / And kindled flame in all their inner parts" (100–124). In *The Faerie Queene* sexual attractiveness is a more useful term than beauty, because in Faeryland there is false as well as true beauty, both of which are attractive. And there are false psyches that respond to true beauty only as if it were mere sexual attractiveness, as with Braggadocchio's response to Belphoebe (2.3.42). This distinction between the Cupids will hold true whether sexual desire consequent to psychological instigation leads to true or to false love. The armed Cupid is true when both the beauty and the psyche that perceives that beauty are true; and he is false when either is false. The weapons of the armed Cupid include the enticements, the messages of love, such as the "firie dart, whose hed / Empoisned was with priuy lust" (3.9.28), which Hellenore willfully fires at Paridell; but they also include the "vnwary dart, which did rebound / From . . . [Belphoebe's] faire eyes and gracious countenance" and wound Timias (3.5.42). The armed Cupid's weapons include the attractiveness of the learned lover, Paridell, but they also include the attractive image of Artegall that enters Britomart's eyes, an image that is equated with the "arrow" shot by the "false Archer" (3.2.26).

Arthur's recounting of the love that brought him to Faeryland makes the same distinctions. Arthur says that when he was in the "freshest flowre of youthly yeares," when "the coale of kindly heat appears / To kindle loue in euery liuing brest" (1.9.9)— i.e., when through the agency of the unarmed Cupid or Venus he came of age sexually and began to produce and to accumulate seed—he had defended himself psychologically even though "Their God himself, grieu'd at my libertie, / Shot many a dart at me with fiers intent" (10). What Arthur was finally unable to resist was the armed Cupid as he operated through the beauty of the Faery Queen, her "face diuine" (15) and the "Most goodly glee and louely blandishment" that "She to me [Arthur] made" (14). Then that "proud auenging boy [Cupid] / Did soone pluck downe, and curbd my libertie" (12).

In most cases, whether Cupid is to be depicted as armed or unarmed is uncomplicated. When Spenser fictionalizes the impact of sexual attractiveness through Cupid, he has Cupid to shoot his arrows and so describes him in one way or the other as an "armed" Cupid. When Spenser has Cupid rather than Venus figure the cosmic forces of love—among which are the forces that operate through the vegetal soul—the shooting of arrows would be incongruous, and so we get an unarmed Cupid by default. This does not mean, however, that the psychological and the physiological components of sexuality are completely isolable, that the armed Cupid can be separated absolutely from Venus and the unarmed Cupid. Cupid is armed in the Maske of Cupid, but he also is presented there as embodying those powers that are generally relegated to Venus. On the level at which femaleness itself is attractive to males and maleness itself attractive to females, there is little difference between the operation of testicles full of seed and attractiveness in the other sex. And so there cannot be, in conception, a completely "unarmed" Cupid. Nor can there be an "armed" Cupid who operates independently of the seed-filled testicles, without which there is no sexual desire to be aroused. Crooke's explanation that erection is both "Naturall" (of the vegetal soul) and "Animall" (of the sensitive soul) makes clear that the roles of the psychological and the physiological intertwine. Erection is "Naturall" because it is not voluntary as are the movements of our arms, legs, etc.; its "efficient cause is heate, spirites and winde, which fill and distend these hollow bodies [in the penis]." But it is also "Animall," because the penis is "not distended vnlesse some luxurious imagination goe before" (*Microcosmographia,* 247–48). As a practical matter, whether Spenser's Cupid is armed or unarmed depends upon whether there is emphasis on the psychological or on the physiological.

In the meeting of Venus and Diana, Diana's comment that Cupid gives "good ayd"—I would say psychological incitement—to Venus's "disports" supports the foregoing distinction, as does Venus's fears that he has hidden himself among

Diana's nymphs and will "turne his arrowes to their exercize" (3.6.21, 23). Venus fears that Cupid will forsake his part in the instigation of sexual desire and live the virgin life of the hunt, thereby severely curtailing her influence among human beings. The incitements to sexual desire would then be limited to the natural functions of the vegetal soul unaided by the higher, psychic faculties. The loss of the armed Cupid would deprive Venus of the power she exercises through the capacity of the imagination to embroider the physical act and would thereby impoverish her beds, bowers, "banckets," and feasts (22).

Diana's fear of, and consequent anger at, the prospects of Cupid's hiding among her nymphs and arousing them to sexual desire is indicated by her aversion to his influence: "we scorne his foolish ioy, / Ne lend we leisure to his idle toy." The nymphs have the physical potentiality for love, but they arm themselves psychologically against love. They "scorne," they consciously and deliberately reject Cupid's "foolish ioy" (24). Spenser does not present a change of affections in the nymphs from desire to scorn, because they have always been of the same mind; but it is clear that they live a strenuous life that uses up the psychic energy through which the armed Cupid operates. They, in modern jargon, sublimate their sexuality, psychic and physiological, into the strenuous life of the hunt. The vehemence of Diana's threat to send Cupid to the shores of the Styx and to clip "his wanton wings" (24), keeping him from flying about and exercising his power, expresses the danger that Cupid poses to her minions. Belphoebe demonstrates a commitment to the virgin life essentially the same as that of Diana and her crew. Belphoebe's initial Venus-like description in Book II indicates that she is a physiologically complete young woman, as does the elaborate description of her sexual attractiveness, which emphasizes her "daintie paps . . . which like young fruit in May / Now little gan to swell" (2.3.29). However ready for love physiologically, Belphoebe rejects any attempt to move her psyche toward physical love. She responds to the attempts of "the blinded god" to kindle "lustfull fire" in her eyes by breaking "his wanton darts" and thereby quenching "base desire" (2.3.23).

Venus and Diana have opposite fears of the consequences of Cupid's hiding among Diana's nymphs, fears that reflect the aversion each goddess has to the life of her counterpart. Especially when one emphasizes its implications for the adventures of Belphoebe and Amoret, the episode is one of separation rather than reconciliation or even truce.[10] Belphoebe, reared by Diana, and Amoret, reared by Venus, come to live completely different lives; the pair is not only never reconciled but at their only meeting Belphoebe threatens to kill Amoret with the same arrow with which she had killed Greedie Lust. Even though as twins they are to be perceived as identical physiologically, their psychological makeup causes an absolute polarity. Our focus for the moment is on Amoret, the girl destined to lead the generative life.

The Garden of Adonis

When the middle books are read as a social vision in which the sexual energy in individuals is elemental, the physiological rather than the cosmic implications of the Garden of Adonis become the focus.[11] And although the Garden as physiology is not a place of perfection, it is as good and as healthy a place as can be the source of life for physical creatures who live in time. I mention the obvious because some who understand the House of Busyrane and its faulty images of love as a projection of or reflection of Amoret's psyche have sought to support their position by finding a deficiency in Amoret's education in the Garden. Amoret does not figure largely in the Garden, but that she is adopted by Venus and brought to the Garden indicates that her generative powers are, unlike Belphoebe's, to be expressed according to the natural inclinations of the female and consequently are in themselves neither good nor bad, neither proper nor faulty. But that she is given to a Psyche recently reconciled to Cupid to be lessoned not just in "the lore of loue" but also in "goodly womanhead," "trained vp in true feminitee" (3.6.51), indicates clearly that her psychology is to be perceived as that appropriate to idealized womanhood. Amoret's education, the results of which are to be found in her depiction in the Temple of Venus, takes place off to the side. In its major movements, the Garden is neither good nor bad. It simply is.

The basis for the analogy of the Garden of Adonis and generation in human beings is that both give form to matter. According to Crooke, who gathered the best evidence from the most renowned physicians, Renaissance and ancient, generation begins with nutrition, with the assimilation of the nourishing blood by the various parts of the body. That assimilation is effected by the blood's taking on the idea, or form, of the various parts to which it comes. Although Crooke does not go into such matters, those ideas or forms are the physiological manifestations of Augustine's seminal reasons, a concept that has, since Robert Ellrodt, largely supplanted souls or Platonic forms as the closest equivalent to the shapes and forms in Spenser's seminary.[12] When a part of the body does not need all of the blood that comes to it, the remainder, now imprinted with the idea of that part, enters the veins, joins other surplus blood also imprinted with the idea of the part of the body from which it comes, and falls back through the veins to the testicles (*Microcosmographia,* 198). At another place, Crooke says the spirits, "which being firie and aery substances wandering and coursing about the whole bodye doe conteine in themselues the Idea or forme of the particular parts," are brought by the "spermaticall" arteries to mix with the surplus of blood before that mixture reaches the testicles (278). In both male and female testicles, the surplus blood, when concocted into seed and stored, becomes the physiological cause of sexual desire. During coitus the female seed is loosed into the womb through the Fallopian tubes, and the womb draws the male seed from the vagina into itself. In both sexes the loosing of the seed causes the pleasure. The two seeds, containing potentially all of the parts of the bodies of both prospective parents, are mixed and then actuated by the combined influence of the womb and the vital heat in the seeds, thereby generating a new creature. When that new creature comes of age, the ideas, mixed with those from one of the other sex, are passed on to the next generation (277–79).

The final stages of generation in human beings were viewed as analogous to the observable aspects of generation in plants. Unaware that seeds contain an already conceived new plant, and so confusing germination with conception, the authorities understood plant seed to conceive life when the vital heat from the sun and the warmth of the earth actuated the potentiality of life inherent in the seed. Consequently they concluded that when the two seeds of human beings combine in the womb, conception takes place through the action of the spirits in the seed, which contain the vital heat analogous to the power of the sun, and the forming faculty of the womb, which is analogous to the warmth of the earth. Again, from Crooke:

> For as in the seed of a Plant, the power of the whole tree is potentially included & contained, which not withstanding neuer breaketh into act, vnlesse that act be stirred vp by the heate of the earth; Right so, the seeds of the Parents conteining in them the Idea or forme of the singular parts of the body, are neuer actuated, neuer exhibite their power and efficacy, vnlesse they be sown and as it were buried in the fruitfull Field or Garden of Nature, the wombe of the woman. (270–71)

Important to the analogy of the Garden and generation in human beings is that both were perceived to operate animistically, all kinds of powers and spirits and faculties being essential to the Renaissance understanding of the operation of the body. Besides the vegetal, sensible, and rational faculties of the soul, each part of the body functioned by means of its faculty, or spirit, or propriety— Crooke uses a number of terms, seemingly interchangeably. During coition, for example, the womb has a *desire* to conceive; it "hath a kinde of Animal motion or lust to be satisfied" (223) and, "being desirous and longing after the seed," draws the seed from the vagina into itself (296). After conception, the vegetal soul of the embryo, the chief overall agent in the development of the embryo, needs an "organ" or "instrument" in order to implement its needs:

> [The soul] setteth vpon her worke, and buildeth her selfe a habitation fit for the exercise and performance of all hir functions. But because shee could not performe this so great a worke without an organ or Instrument, she vseth the spirit (where-with the froathy seede swelleth) as hir Painter or drawer to score out and delin-eate all the particular parts. . . . This spirit . . . gathereth all of the particles of a kinde together, extendeth them, and as a glass maker holloweth or boreth them by blowing into them. (263)

All in all, in Renaissance physiology the womb is not so much an organ where biological processes are caused by the interaction of materials as it is an arena where various personified powers and forces operate on materials. It is just as Crooke describes it: like a "Garden of Nature" where different and inevitably personified agents are required to effect generation and growth. Physiologi-cally, Spenser's Garden of Adonis is, however, more than a womb. In human beings, the whole body is a seminary in that all parts of the body are sources of the ideas in the seed, and, consequently, the collective bodies of human beings make up the seminary for the human race. And, just as the production of seed in human beings is only a part of a whole complex generative process, when the Garden of Adonis is approached physiologically, it is more than a seminary and its locus is not an area—the womb or even the genital organs of both sexes. The Garden of Adonis is to be found in that complex of actions by which the seminal reasons, which shape matter into the life forms of the various species, are passed from generation to generation.

Read physiologically, the Garden of Adonis comprises three "locales" or aspects: the seminary, in which there are babes and shapes and in which time functions beneficently; the pleasure garden, in which there are birds, plants, and the pairs of lovers and in which time is both beneficent and destructive; and the Mount of Venus, which subsumes the other two.[13] That the Garden is not to be perceived as a single entity is first indicated in the argument for canto 6, where the phrase is *Gardins* of Adonis, not *the Gardin* of Adonis, and in the introductory stanza, which seems to refer to two parts of the larger Garden. The first three lines of stanza 30 point to the garden of pleasure as a separate part of or aspect of the larger Garden through reference to the flowers, not shapes or forms of flow-ers that would be found in the seminary, but the actual flowers with which Dame

Nature beautifies herself and decks the "girlonds of her paramoures." And these flowers are fetched *into* the Garden, not fetched *from* it as they would be if they were found in the seminary. The second part of the stanza can also be read to point to the seminary as a separate part of the Garden: "there," [i.e., as a part of the overall Garden] . . . is the first seminarie / Of all things, that are borne to liue and die, / According to their kindes" (3.6.30).

The succeeding stanzas, 31–35, describe the seminary, "sited in fruitfull soyle of old," much of which is reminiscent of the "life" of the seed and its ideas and the faculties that govern and prompt the development of the fetus, as well as the fetus itself. The permanent existence of the shapes and forms in the Garden is similar to the permanent existence of the ideas of the parts of the bodies. Both the shapes and forms in the Garden and the ideas of the body have a cyclical existence requiring them to be, in Crooke's words, "sown and as it were buried in the fruitfull Field or Garden of Nature" (*Micromosmographia,* 271). The ideas of the parts of the bodies must move to the womb, the "Garden of Nature," in order to form the new parts of the new creature, and then, when that new creature has entered the great world and has matured sexually, the cycle begins anew. Thus the ideas in the seed of mankind are transmitted from generation to generation undiminished. I do not mean to imply that the individual ideas in the parts of the bodies have a permanent existence like Platonic ideas. They die with the body, but, having replicated themselves in the surplus blood and consequently in the seed, they have the kind of permanent existence that Augustine's seminal reasons and Spenser's Adonis have.

The shapes and forms are said to "grow" in the seminary (33, 34, 36), and, using the appropriate definition of "grow" to mean "sprout" rather than to increase in size, the development of the ideas in the seed from the parts of the body is comparable to the "growth" of the shapes and forms in the seminary. And since the ideas in the separate human bodies can be understood to increase and multiply as do the numbers of human beings in the world, we can understand how the shapes and forms in the seminary can increase and multiply when they clearly are not in themselves generative creatures. Also reflecting the development of the ideas in the seed into new creatures is that the forms and shapes in the seminary, which seem to exist at first much as plants or seedlings in rows, can be seen to go through a kind of development into the more fetuslike "thousand thousand naked babes" (32). These "babes" seem to be more "alive" than the shapes and forms in that they cluster about Genius like fetuses in Renaissance physiology, each of which, "impatient of so close imprisonment, as vnsatisfied with so slender allowance," strives to enter into the great world (*Microcosmographia,* 257). A crucial point of comparison is that time is beneficent and comparatively distant both in the cycle from the seminary in the Garden to the world and back to seminary again and also in the generative cycle in human beings, in which the ideas move from flesh to seed and then to flesh again in the real world. In both cases the focus is on what is permanent. Both the shapes and forms in the Garden and the ideas in the human body exist in time the way we today would perceive genes to exist in time were it not for Darwin, and if we perceived the "life" of genes to be a cycle of burial and regeneration like plant seeds. Insofar as the seminary in the Garden is the womb, the babes leave the Garden to go into the real world to live the transitory life of physical creatures. Insofar as the seminary is the repository of the ideas that form the human race out of the dust of the earth and, consequently, is the collection of bodies comprising the human race, those ideas move from one generation to another to the end of the world.

In its introduction of the union of form and matter necessary for the babes to live real lives, stanza 36 initiates the transition from the seminary to the garden of pleasure, from that aspect of generation in which form is permanent to that in which matter is permanent. I do not mean that the babes in the poem leave the seminary to go to the pleasure garden. The babes leave the seminary to go into the world. The creatures in the pleasure garden are all sexually mature, and so the pleasure garden allegorizes an aspect of life in the real world that is different from that aspect of life in the real world allegorized by the seminary.

> Daily they grow, and daily forth are sent
> > Into the world, it to replenish more;
> > Yet is the stocke not lessened, nor spent,
> > But still remaines in euerlasting store,
> > As it at first created was of yore.
> > For in the wide wombe of the world there lyes,
> > In hateful darknesse and in deepe horrore,
> > An huge eternall *Chaos*, which supplyes
> The substances of natures fruitfull progenyes.

(stanza 36)

The word "stocke" seems at first to refer back to the store of permanent shapes and forms in stanza 35, but as we read on, it becomes clear that it looks forward to the matter necessary for the actualizing of those forms into real creatures. And, as we move to that aspect of generation—the generation of an individual creature—we move toward the garden of pleasure where form, in its Aristotelian sense, is temporary and matter is permanent:

> For formes are variable and decay,
> By course of kind, and by occasion;
> And that faire flowre of beautie fades away,
> As doth the lilly fresh before the sunny ray.

(stanza 38)

The transition to the garden of pleasure is completed in stanza 39 with the intro-duction of Time, both the great friend and the great enemy of mortal creatures, who mows "the flowring herbes and goodly things, / And all their glory to the ground downe flings." When form in its Aristotelian sense decays, the matter that that form has organized returns to the dust from which it came. Time, however, had also brought those "goodly things" to fruition in the first place.

The pleasure garden (stanzas 41–43) captures in all its poignancy the double blessing and curse that we experience as individual creatures of formed matter existing in time. The blessing is that the creatures in the pleasure garden are mature and sexually active lovers in a place of movement, of real life, of "goodly meriment, and gay felicitie," "laughing blossomes," "fresh colours," and "ioyous birdes" flitting back and forth between the trees. Unlike the shapes and forms and babes in the seminary, they are completed creatures, among whom "sweet loue" throws "gentle fits," those gentle fits being the product of testicles, male and female, full of seed. The curse is that the same transitory bond that enables matter to live makes one a creature of time and causes one, as time moves, to decay "By course of kind and by occasion" (stanza 38).[14] Crooke explains that

> This forme we call Life . . . continueth so long therein, as it is supplied with nourishment, which nourishment is the radical moysture of the spermaticall parts. Nature therefore being not able to generate anie part of seede whose moysture shoulde not in time bee exhausted, could not produce any particular creature eternall or immutable." (*Microcosmographia,* 198)

The forms and shapes in the seminary, we remember, do not need the "water of the ford . . . For in themselues eternall moisture they imply" (stanza 34). In a physiological reading, the problem of time in the Garden is not a problem posed by there being a destructive force in an episode in which there are indestructible life forms. The problem is to account for both cycles of time, one of which is essentially beneficent and the other both beneficent and destructive. Real human beings take part in both cycles; and the Garden of Adonis, read physiologically, reflects both cycles. Amoret, a representative of that portion of females who are to live the generative life, is also to take part in both cycles, as are Florimell and Britomart.

The pleasure garden is distinct from the seminary, but it is just as necessary to the generative cycle as is the production of and combination of the male and female seed. For without sexual desire and the pleasures attendant upon coition, both of which are the product of seed, there would be no mixture of the seed in the womb. When one has a hierarchical rather than an evolutionary view of humankind, justifications of physicality seem appropriate, even necessary. Crooke's typical Renaissance patriarchal understanding of male and female sexuality makes the point:

> And indeede this sting of pleasure was very necessary, without which man (especially the one sexe) in scorne and detestation of so brutish and base a worke, the other sexe for feare of payne and trouble, would haue abhorred this worke of Nature. (287)

Spenser puts the matter more acceptably: his narrator says, "But well I wote by tryall, that this same / All other pleasant places doth excell" (29).

In this particular episode, however, the sexual pleasures experienced by the lovers are purely physiological and so are free from any possible mismanagement of sexual desire. The lovers share a love purified of that which taints actual loves between those unlikes, male and female, but not in the Neoplatonic way in which love has been abstracted from the flesh. Attraction in the Renaissance was between likes, not unlikes, as in Du Bartas's account of the creation when, at God's spoken word, "Fire flew to Fire, Water to Water slid, / Aire clung to Aire, and Earth with Earth abid."[15] The Neoplatonists would, by moving up the ladder, leave behind the differences between male and female and so, finally, have love to be an attraction of likes. Spenser's hints of Neoplatonism, however, as in his description of Britomart's love having been "ykindled first aboue," connects that love with higher forces without etherealizing its physicality. The supernatural origin of love relates Venus's power to unite the unlikes, male and female, with God's power to unite the discordant elements into the cosmos. At the Creation the like elements flew to each other and formed the four separate, essentially unlike levels of the cosmos, but those unlike spheres could not have been joined together by other than God's spoken word. Comparably, those unlikes, male and female, could never be united apart from the power of Venus. As Crooke says of the physical union of male and female, without the "sting of pleasure" males and females would "haue abhorred this worke of Nature" (287).

The move from the seminary to the pleasure garden, where there are completed creatures—plants, birds, and pairs of lovers—involves a change from the view of the generative cycle in which form is permanent and substance temporary to a view in which form is temporary and substance permanent. In the seminary the cycle is presented from the point of view of the ideas, the forms; in the pleasure garden, the cycle is presented from the point of view of the individual creature, for whom time is finally destructive. Another of the advantages of the physiological approach to the Garden is that the physiology of generation involves both cycles. Consequently, the stanzas describing the pleasure garden do not constitute an intrusion of the real or material world into a place of immaterial forms; nor do they constitute a digression in which we leave the Garden and look ahead to the lives of creatures when they reach the real world. Physiologically, both the seminary and the pleasure garden are parts of or aspects of the whole in that they are both analogous to particular parts of or aspects of the generative cycle. The seminary allegorizes what happens in the material world, just as does the pleasure garden.

On the Mount of Venus, the coition of Venus and Adonis subsumes both pleasure garden and seminary, just as does the fruitful union of human beings. Venus, as Helkiah Crooke and the mythographers point out, is allegorically the seed (259); and she is present in the seed as the physiological cause of sexual desire, as the pleasure in coitus, and as the cause of generation. The coition of Venus and Adonis contains both the seminary and the pleasure garden less allegorically in that she, in Spenser's words, "when euer that she will, / Possesseth him, and of his sweetnesse takes her fill" (46), a copulation that is not only reflective of the pleasures of the sexual life but that also augments the world. Adonis's part in this copulation also reflects both seminary and pleasure garden because he also is a source of the seed ("sweetnesse"), and he is, allegorically, the sun and consequently the vital heat necessary for the seed to "germinate" in the womb.

As long as the Garden is viewed only cosmologically, Lewis is correct in concluding that, despite its name, it is really the "Garden of Venus," because Venus, not Adonis, is the central deity of generation.[16] However, insofar as the Garden is analogous to generation in human beings, it is appropriately named because, while both Venus and Adonis, as male and female seed, bring both form and matter to conception, the matter of both seeds providing the material for the spermatic parts of the body (Crooke, *Microcosmographia,* 259), Adonis is *more* the formal principle than is Venus because male seed is *more* active than female seed (219). Much more important, unlike Venus, Adonis is both mortal and immortal. He is permanent in the same way as are the shapes and forms in the seminary and as are the ideas in human seed; and he is also transitory as are the plants, birds, and lovers in the pleasure garden and as are the individual creatures here on earth. Throughout the stanzas on Adonis the emphasis is on his ambiguously mortal-immortal nature. The flowers growing around the mound—hyacinth, narcissus, and aramanthus—are the subjects of myths of death and rebirth. And although his function is to copulate with Venus and thus give life to the world, his description is funereal: "Lapped in flowres and pretious spycery, / By her hid from the world" (46). Here Venus and Adonis are reminiscent of their Egyptian equivalents, Isis and Osiris, as Osiris is cared for by Isis after his second death. In Spenser's Adonis are both cycles of time, the pre-Darwinian cycle in which species are immortal and the cycle that applies to all of us creatures who are composites of the eternal life principle and matter.

A physiological reading of the Garden answers the objections that Lewis posed to the identification of the Adonis in the Garden with the sun, an identification with us at least since Warton. Scholars since Lewis have continued the identification but have not answered his objections. How can we, Lewis said, equate this particular Adonis in this particular episode with the sun when he inhabits a secret place within a gloomy grove in a garden on earth that is full of moisture, where he is hidden from the world, where, if he were the sun, his own beams could never reach him? "Its darkness, foliage, dampness, shelter from the wind (44) seem . . . the antithesis of the shining mountain top."[17] However, when the Garden is viewed anatomically *and* physiologically, the role of the sun is to be found in the vital heat, which is also hidden from view. Adonis can be identified not only with the testicles, whose "irradiation or beaming influence," Crooke informs us, concocts the blood into seed (279), but also with the seed itself. Crooke explains Hippocrates' statement that seed is composed of fire and water by identifying the "fire" as the spirits or inbred heat of the seed and identifying the "water" as the nourishing moisture of the seed (259). Both Hippocrates and Aristotle equate the role of the vital heat of the sun on plant seeds with the role of vital heat in the male seed.

I argued earlier that the role of the testicles in Galenic physiology as "another hearth [besides the heart] as it were of the inbred heate" (Crooke, *Microcosmographia,* 241) accounts for Britomart's extraordinary energy and sexual presence. The ultimate source of as well as the basic purpose for Britomart's, Amoret's, and the others' energy and sexual presence is to be found in the Garden of Adonis. If we are to understand Books III, IV and V as a hierarchy of love quests that comprise a social vision, we must understand the principles that enable the gardens in the loins of the virtuous to bear fruit in an evil world seemingly governed by fortune. Whatever the cosmological significance of the Garden of Adonis, its significance as the next stage in Amoret's progress to the House of Busyrane is twofold. Not only is she to take into the world a fully functional

Garden of Adonis within herself, but that Venus commits her to Cupid and Psyche to be "trained vp in true feminitee" and "lessoned / In all the lore of loue, and goodly womanhead" (51) means exactly what it says: Amoret's femininity is true femininity, and she is properly prepared psychologically for love and not just womanhood but *goodly* womanhood. The attempts to find a problem in Amoret's upbringing are attempts to read into the Garden a basis for internalizing the Maske of Cupid in Amoret. Her role in the Garden, as in the Temple of Venus and the House of Busyrane, is to be an ideally feminine female.

The physiological approach does not provide an entrée to the larger cycle of the Garden in which the "infinite shapes" return to the Garden and remain there "Some thousand yeares" before leaving again. This larger cycle does, however, reinforce the perception that in *The Faerie Queene* the important human and natural progressions are circular. Only God's Providence is linear, and that Spenser's larger natural cycle is only a thousand years rather than the pagan Platonic cycle of some thirty thousand years is perhaps designed to fit the natural cycle more properly into a larger, providential order.

The Temple of Venus

The depiction of Amoret's "true feminitee" begins with the "beuie of fayre damzels" representing the feminine virtues who surround her in the Temple of Venus: "goodly *Shamefastnesse*," "sweet *Cherefulnesse*," "sober *Modestie*," "comely *Curtesie*," "Soft *Silence*," and "submisse *Obedience*" (4.10.48–51). At the heart of the virtues are passivity and subordination; and the epithets, "goodly," "sweet," "sober," "comely," and "soft," indicate that the reader is to see such passivity and subordination as good. A comparable "true feminitee" is also found in Womanhood's "sad semblant," "demeanure wyse," and eyes "stedfast still." Womanhood's steadfast eyes that "Ne rov'd at randon after gazers guyse, / Whose luring baytes oftimes doe heedlesse harts entyse" (49) compare with Canacee's (4.2.36). They contrast directly with Malecasta's "wanton eyes, ill signes of womanhed," which "Did roll too lightly, and too often glaunce" (3.1.41), and the "light eye-glance" of the false Florimell (4.2.9). These descriptions of good and evil femininity reinforce the perception that, for purposes of creating an idealized femininity, Spenser endorsed in large measure the constraints upon the public expression of female sexuality that were considered proper in the Renaissance. Amoret's reluctance and delay when Scudamour takes her hand are also part of this idealized femininity:

> She often prayd, and often me besought,
>> Sometime with tender teares to let her goe,
>> Sometime with witching smiles:

(4.10.57)

Her behavior, a form of inhibition and modesty, is like that hinted at in the Medway's prolonged delay of the Thames (4.11.8) and is psychologically similar to the perception of Milton's Eve that her future mate is not as pleasing to her as her own image in the pool, a reaction that reflects her desire to remain in the unattached virginal state (*PL* 4.460-91). With the Temple of Venus we move from the world of nature, from the purely physiological, to the more social aspects of love, to the roles of males and females as social creatures. The subordination of the individual to his or her role in society, here the subordination of an individual female's sexual instincts to what was considered proper social behavior for females, will loom larger and larger as we move up the hierarchy in Spenser's allegory of love.

In the chapter on Florimell's quest I examined the way in which the difference between the hotter male seed and the colder female seed determined not only sexual but gender differences, differences that today are understand to be determined largely, if not exclusively, by social pressures. Apparently, however, the simple distinction between the hotter male and the colder female seed was not sufficient to account for the gradations of masculine and feminine qualities in males and females; and so it was determined that each sex produced two kinds of seed, a hotter masculine seed in the right testicle and a colder feminine seed in the left. Hippocrates, Crooke says,

> acknowledgeth in either Sex a double Seed, the one Masculine hotter and stronger, the other Feminine that is colder, out of the diuers permixtion of which, both Males and Females are generated. He therefore thus distinguisheth a three-fold generation of Males and females. If both the Parents yeeld a Masculine Seed they breed Male Children of a noble and generous disposition . . . nobly minded & strong of body. If from the Man there issue Masculine Seed [and] from the Woman Feminine [seed] and the Masculine prevaile a Male will be generated, but lesse generous & strong then the former. If from the Woman there issue Masculine Seed, from the Man Feminine and the Masculine [i.e., the seed from the man] ouercome[,] a Male will be generated, but womanish, soft, base and effeminate. The verie like may be said of the generation of Females: for if from both the Parents doe issue Feminine Seed a Female will be procreated most weake and womanish. . . . If from the Woman proceed a Feminine Seed and from the Man a Masculine and yet the Feminine ouercome, Women are begotten bold and mod-

erate. If from the Man proceed Feminine Seed and from the Woman Masculine, and the Womans Seed preuaile, Women are begotten . . . fierce and mannish. (308)

The Renaissance need to understand as polarities the principles underlying gender differences, the principles of masculine and feminine powers in male and female seed, is clear in that the physiology of the time did not logically support the idea but was forced to. The passage quoted clearly implies that one of the seeds necessarily dominates completely; however, in order to explain how children can bear physical resemblances to both parents, a matter toward which society was indifferent, Crooke describes the necessary partial victories of male and female seed. Children are "like vnto their parents,"

> wholly to the Father if the Fathers Seed doe alwayes and totally ouercome; and altogether to the Mother if the Mothers seed haue the victorie: In some parts to the Father, in others to the Mother if any part of the Seed of either be ouercome by the other. For though the Seed appeare to the view *Homogenit* yet hath it some parts more thicke others thinner. (310)

While the random inheritance of physical traits was acceptable and while gradations of masculine and feminine were too obvious to ignore, a tangle of masculine and feminine in each person, especially the male, was not, because it would violate what was considered to be an essential duality, not of male and female, but of masculine and feminine.[18]

Besides reinforcing the centrality of seed in all matters sexual—differences in temperament also derived from humors other than the blood from which seed is concocted, and that the other humors are unimportant to the middle books is another indication of the importance of seed theory in this part of *The Faerie Queene*—a sixteenth-century understanding of typical masculinity and femininity provides a starting place for an understanding of Amoret and Scudamour in the Temple of Venus as idealized femininity and idealized masculinity, respectively. My view is that gradations of masculine and feminine are missing from characterization in these books and that, consequently, there are only two kinds of masculinity in Spenser's allegory of love: subordinated and unsubordinated. Although initially incomplete, the essentially virtuous Marinell and Artegall are finally able to express their masculinity appropriately by subordinating themselves to love. The archetypically vicious Paridell, on the other hand, is unable to or refuses to subordinate himself to love in any of its forms, whether chaste love between the sexes, friendship, or (in his Book V appearance as one of Duessa–Mary

Stuart's henchmen), justice. Characters like Malbecco, Proteus, and Busyrane are male but are not masculine. Malecasta, Hellenore, and Radigund exemplify unsubordinated femininity, but only a minor unsubordinated female character, Poeana in the story of Amyas and Placidas, learns to subordinate herself to the proper male. The important virtuous feminine females, Florimell and Amoret, and the feminine-masculine Britomart seemingly subordinate themselves automatically to the males with whom they fall in love. Although Florimell's and Amoret's femininity has been generally understood by Spenser scholars as weakness, both these characters should be perceived as heroic *and* feminine. Neither is an Amazon, yet the phrase Crooke reserves for the male, "his mind should be stout and invincible to undergo dangers" (274), describes exactly the quality of mind that enables these heroines to resist their captors.

Scudamour's masculinity, more than Amoret's femininity, has been the focal point of the discussions of the Temple of Venus.[19] A. Kent Hieatt compares Scudamour's courtship of Amoret unfavorably to Artegall's courtship of Britomart, in that Artegall does not attempt, in Hieatt's word, to "master" Britomart.[20] A look at some terminology is necessary here. Dame Helen Gardner, in what seems to be a rejection of Hieatt's general notions about Amoret and Scudamour, distinguishes between "winning" a young woman and "wooing" her. She points out that Amoret's reluctant response to Scudamour after he takes her up by the hand (4.10.57) is natural to a young girl, who "having been won, must now be wooed"; that is, if I understand Dame Gardner's distinction, Amoret, having been won, must now be so treated as to make her feel comfortable in her new state.[21] But since the interval between the "winning" and the wedding is not depicted, there is no way to compare the two courtships. I believe the most serious problem with Hieatt's comparison of Scudamour and Artegall is that the situations are entirely different. When Britomart and Artegall meet, Britomart has already been won, yea, "mastered," by Artegall's forceful masculine image. The Amoret we first see in the lap of Womanhood, surrounded by the abstractions that represent her femininity, is like Britomart before Britomart looks in the mirror, and so is yet to be won, much less wooed.

The best argument that we are to see in Scudamour an idealized masculinity is that the contrast developed in his progress through the Temple of Venus is not between his and a more appropriate mode of winning a woman, but between the masculine Scudamour and those who lack masculinity. The Temple is "seated in an Island strong . . . And wall'd by nature gainst inuaders wrong" (4.10.6), "inuaders wrong" being those unmanly men who would attempt to bypass the plain with the twenty knights and the bridge on which there is the gate guarded by Doubt and Delay and also the gate guarded by Daunger. Scudamour's initial encounters with the twenty knights and with Doubt, Delay, and Daunger allegorize the generalized sequence by which a male properly wins a female. He must first prove himself worthy; he must then overcome in himself the tendencies toward hesitance—"Faint heart ne'er won fair hand," etc.,—and, finally, he must overcome in the female the corresponding tendencies toward reluctance and delay (Daunger). Hieatt claims that Scudamour's boldness is appropriate in the beginning of the episode but excessive at the end.[22] A more likely reading is that his taking of Amoret toward the end of the episode enacts in plainer fiction his earlier, more allegorical encounters with Doubt, Delay, and Daunger.

Scudamour's encounter with Doubt provides the first of the comparisons with those who lack manliness, here those who lack the courage to contend with doubt and have consequently "lost great hope." Scudamour moves past Doubt with no trouble and would "by no meanes . . . forslow" his way for the female, Delay. The contrast between Scudamour and those who lack masculinity becomes even clearer with those who are daunted by Daunger, whose purpose is to guard the gate from "fearfull cowards" and "faint-heart-fooles, whom shew of perill hard / Could terrifie from Fortunes faire adward" (17). Daunger's significance in this episode is clarified by distinguishing between those meanings appropriate to an experienced woman and those appropriate to a young virgin such as Amoret. In general, Daunger signifies the difficulty raised by a woman being courted. With an experienced woman, meanings of the word such as "difficulty," "hesitation," "reluctance," "chariness," "stint," "untowardness," and "uncompliant or fractious conduct" could be applicable either as tactic or as the reflection of an inner state. All these words could apply, for example, to the behavior of Arcite's "newe lady": "Her daunger made him bothe bowe and bende, / And as her liste, made him turne or wende" (*Anelida and Arcite*, 186–87). But for a young and inexperienced but buxom virgin like Amoret, Daunger would be the behavior and/or state of mind resulting from the reluctance natural, or at least appropriate, to a virtuous female on the way to leaving the virginal state. In both cases, however, the defeat of Daunger requires manliness. Spenser makes clear that the faintheartedness of the "faint-heart-fooles" (17) who are daunted by Daunger is purely sexual, for

> many doughty warriours, often tride
> In greater perils to be stout and bold,
> Durst not the sternesse of his looke abide,
> But soone as they his countenance did behold,
> Began to faint, and feele their corage cold.

(18)

These warriors with "corage cold"—and "corage" here clearly means "sexual vigour and inclination," because the "doughty warriours" are, in other perils, "stout and bold"—are contrasted with Scudamour, who resolves to assault Daunger with "manhood stout" (19). I do not think we are to visualize a tumescent Scudamour proceeding through the temple, but the words of the poem do remind us of the physiology of desire and, consequently, reinforce the explicit purpose of the stanza, which is to condemn those whose lack of manliness keeps them from winning a woman and also to condemn those whose lack of manliness results in an unmanly, though successful, courtship:

> Againe some other, that in hard assaies
> Were cowards knowne, and litle count did hold,
> Either through gifts, or guile, or such like waies,
> Crept in by stouping low, or stealing of the kaies.
>
> (18)

One such villain is Malbecco, whom we are surely to understand as having won Hellenore with his wealth and who later tries to "master" her, to use Hieatt's term, solely through his position as husband and for his own purposes. Busyrane and Proteus, with their nonsexual attempts to "master" Amoret and Florimell for their own purposes, are representative of evil in Books III and IV of *The Faerie Queene*, not those, like Britomart and Scudamour, with strong sexual drives that are bound to the image of one virtuous person of the other sex.

After defeating Daunger, Scudamour stays right on course to Amoret, not letting any of the delightful sights in the Temple delay him (29). When he spots Amoret on the lap of Womanhood, he shakes off "all doubt and shamefast fear, / Which Ladies loue I heard had neuer wonne"—words reminiscent of those earlier about "faint hearts" and "faint-heart-fooles." Scudamour steps near to Amoret, takes her hand, and is rebuked by Womanhood for being "ouer bold." Womanhood's phrase is central to Hieatt's argument that Scudamour is responsible for Amoret's plight in the House of Busyrane. Hieatt argues that these sentiments are "part of Spenser's pattern," that "Scudamour has obeyed the injunction in the House of Busyrane to be bold and bold; but he has now been 'too bold.' He has overstepped the bounds of love in asserting a passionate mastery incompatible with . . . a happy marriage. . . ."[23] I submit that his boldness in taking Amoret by the hand and leading her away, despite the reluctance reflected in Amoret's prayers and tears—perhaps her "witching smiles" are to be viewed as encouraging his boldness—is identical to the boldness necessary to get past Doubt, Delay, and Daunger. All in all, a psychophysiological reading of the Temple supports Roche's position on Scudamour but not Roche's position on Amoret.

Also weakening Hieatt's position are the strong indications that Womanhood's argument is to be considered fallacious. She claims it is an "vnseemely shame" to lay hands on a virgin "That vnto *Venus* seruices was sold" (54). But insofar as a virgin can properly be in the services of Venus, her virginity must be a temporary state; to be a virgin otherwise is to be, like Belphoebe, in the services of Diana. Scudamour sees the fallacy:

> To whom I thus, Nay but it fitteth best,
> For *Cupids* man with *Venus* mayd to hold,
> For ill your goddesse seruices are drest
> By virgins, and her sacrifices let to rest.
>
> (54)

Never is Scudamour's boldness brought into question except by Womanhood, and her objection is, at the very least, questionable. Womanhood, not Amoret, is terrified by Scudamour's shield of Cupid; and Womanhood's response is that of a protective adult who sees what she perceives as an immature female being treated as a woman.

Venus's approval of Scudamour does not necessarily imply social approval, because Venus approves of all sexual behavior that augments the species; nevertheless, we must remember that in Books III and IV the main enemies of love, Busyrane and Proteus, have sexual tendencies that work against such augmentation. Concord's approval does have social overtones. Concord, a condition rather than a force, is even more basic than Venus: she "vnto *Venus* grace the gate doth open right" (35). And, quite significantly, Concord allows Scudamour to go into the Temple and then to depart *with Amoret*, both times on the side of Loue. She does so because she is the state in which the polarities of love and hate are properly subordinated, i.e., hate is subordinated to love. Cosmologically she is the state in which the hatred that would otherwise cause the elements to devour each other has been mastered by the bond of God's love, "Else would the waters ouerflow the lands, / And fire deuoure the ayre, and hell them quight" (35). Without the animosity of the elements toward one another, however, the cosmos would be static. The difference or "hatred" between the elements activates the cosmos, and the difference between male and female activates mankind. Concord arises from discord or potential discord through proper subordination; in this episode, it is Scudamour's subordination to love and Amoret's subordination both to love and to Scudamour. Both Scudamour's masculine boldness and Amoret's feminine submissiveness are good and both are physiologically based. What Crooke only implies, Galen states outright. Not only does seed determine the basic temperament of male and female at birth, but the continuance of sexual and gender differences is fueled by the testicles: "[A] certain power is distributed from the testicles . . . to the whole body. . . . [and this] power is in males the cause of strength and masculinity; in females it is the cause of their very femininity."[24]

Although seed theory provides an entrée to the relatively simple character-izations of Scudamour and Amort, Britomart's would pose a problem if the as-sumption was that Spenser worked from a recipe. Britomart's characterization includes all three of the possibilities for females described by Crooke: she is, at least to a degree, "weak and womanish" in her response to Talus's report of Artegall's capture by Radigund; she is elsewhere (especially in more social mo-ments, as in Malbecco's castle) something like "bold and moderate"; and when confronted in battle, she is "fierce and mannish." She is also described by Glauce as having a masculine physique, as tall and large of limb (3.3.53). That she has from the beginning a potentially masculine temperament is first indicated when Glauce's stories of valorous women "so deepe into the mynd / Of the young Damzell sunke, that great desire / Of warlike armes in her forthwith they tynd, / And generous stout courage did inspire" (57). Although the characterization of Britomart is too complex to fit into the rigid confines of seed theory, that charac-terization does not violate basic Renaissance assumptions about male and female and masculine and feminine. The problem with Britomart's characterization is to reconcile her masculine and feminine qualities: "Faire Lady she him [to Redcrosse] seemd, like Lady drest, / But fairest knight aliue, when armed was her brest" (3.2.4). That reconciliation is better understood as a complementarity in which the two remain separate and distinct rather than through an amalgam-ation of the two, through androgyny.

The House of Busyrane

The critical problem in the episode at the House of Busyrane is the relation-ship of the image of the wounded Amoret to the context provided for that image by the House of Busyrane. Lewis's solution is that the image represents Christian marriage wounded by the traditions of courtly love, which are symbolized by the works in the House.[25] The modern psychological approach, which has domi-nated post-Lewis attempts at the House, understands the works of the House as projections of a damaged psyche, which is symbolized by Amoret's wounds. In 1971 Helen Cheney Gilde described a consensus, still largely intact, "that Amoret's problem is internal and is partially the consequence of her education, that it is fear of sexual passion in marriage, and that both the House and Busyrane are objectifications of that fear."[26] My Renaissance psychological approach leads me toward Lewis's position in that I understand the works of the House to reflect a social evil with which Busyrane *is attempting to* corrupt Amoret rather than a reflection of a psychological condition within Amoret.

A Renaissance psychological analysis offers the means for a closer look at the works of the House than Lewis provides, and it offers the means for an understanding of the relationship of the works of the House to the image of Amoret that is consonant with the Amoret we have followed since her birth. The key to such a reading is progression, not within Britomart as she moves through the House but the progression of the rooms themselves. Roche says that Britomart's "entry through the wall of flame gives her an intimate knowledge of the House of Busyrane, and her understanding finally allows her to release Amoret from her fears." He says that she "learns something about the transforming power of love" in each of the rooms and "Without describing the process by which Britomart comes to this knowledge Spenser informs us that she has seen the mask as an idle show, the product of a false charm."[27] I see no evidence that Britomart learns anything from any of her experiences in Book III. At Malbecco's Castle she is the same innocent who saw Malecasta's advances in the best possible light. Unaware that Paridell is recounting his history only as a way of strutting before Hellenore, she is hesitant to ask him to go over his history again because she thinks the remembrance would bring him pain. What Britomart exhibits through all her trials are not understanding and a point of view but the qualities she is given in her first appearance in the poem: a "constant mind," "stedfast courage and stout hardiment," and innocence: "Ne euill thing she fear'd, ne euill thing she ment" (3.1.19). Britomart does not understand the sequence of Busyrane's cryptic "bold" signs, but "She was no whit thereby discouraged / From prosecuting of her first intent, / But forward with bold steps into the next roome went" (3.11.50). It is clear, at least to me, that Britomart manifests the same naïveté in this episode as she does throughout Book III. The words in the poem that articulate her response to the rooms as well as to the Maske of Cupid add up to little more than wonderment (3.11.49, 53; 12.5). And her response to the opened door on the second night—"in went / Bold Britomart . . . Neither of idle shewes, nor of false charmes aghast" (3.12.29)—is so much like her attitude toward the riotous life in the Castle Ioyous and toward Marinell's treasure (3.4.18) that it would seem to be a matter of virtue, not education.

I find progression in the depiction of the power of Cupid in the several rooms and then in the reunion of Amoret and Scudamour outside the House. That power is, as I read it, simply *presented* in the outer room. It is neither corrupt nor incorrupt. However, the bas reliefs and the Maske of Cupid in the second room clearly depict the corruption of Cupid's power. In the inmost room

Britomart forces Busyrane to reverse a new, partly completed spell and thus defeats Busyrane's continuing attempt to corrupt the operation of Cupid's power within Amoret. Amoret and Scudamour are then reunited in chaste love.

The tapestries in the first room depict the power of Cupid—an armed Cupid, clearly, because his idol at the upper end of the room is described as armed and three of the gods whom he victimized are described as being struck with arrows. The emphasis, then, in the first room is on Cupid's power to inflame the psyche. First are the "faire pourtraicts," "all of loue, and all of lusty-hed," which treat of "*Cupids* warres" and victories over the gods (3.11.29). And then, briefly mentioned, are the other tapestries depicting the kings, queens, lords, and ladies who were "mingled with the raskall rablement . . . To shew Dan *Cupids*" powre and great effort [power]" (46). Underneath the idol of Cupid is a dragon with a shaft through each eye, a shaft "That no man forth might draw, ne no man remedye" (48). Lewis rightly identifies the dragon as a dragon guardian of chastity, such as that in Alciati which keeps girls safe from the snares of love before marriage. But this guardian is, as Lewis says, "mutilated in the very organ that qualified it for guardianship."[28] The identification does not, however, identify this armed Cupid as the Cupid of false love. Alciati's emblem is about the maintenance of virginity, not chaste love, and to maintain virginity is to ward off Cupid's arrows, as Belphoebe does. After the arrows hit their mark, as they do with Britomart, Florimell, and Amoret, the dragon can no longer function as guardian. Just as no one can reconstitute the pristine virgin state that exists before the initial onslaught of love, no one can remove the shafts from the dragon guardian's eyes. The chaste loves of Spenser's heroines are protected by the constancy of their affections, their psychological integrity, and by Providence, not by a dragon guardian. When approached within the contexts of Britomart's adventures in Book III and of Amoret's progression to the House of Busyrane, that Cupid has destroyed the capacity of the dragon to protect girls from the snares of love should be understood, as the tapestries should be understood, to reflect the power of the armed Cupid to cause human beings to fall in love. Cupid, like Venus, is not concerned with moral questions. Venus-as-seed moves the satyrs to mate with Hellenore, just as she moves Britomart to seek Artegall. Cupid shoots his arrow into Britomart's heart just as he shoots it into Paridell's. The psyche of the individual determines the way both Venus and Cupid are expressed in that individual's life. As the narrator says, "Ah man beware, how thou those darts behold" (48). If we are to love properly, we must be able to see the falseness of a Malecasta's or a Paridell's attractiveness, just as we must be able to see the trueness of a Britomart's or an Artegall's. And that the people in the House of Busyrane commit "fowle Idolatree" before the image of Cupid means that they misconceive or misuse the power of Cupid; it is not a condemnation of the power of Cupid himself, whether he is armed or not. Busyrane, not Cupid, is the enemy; Busyrane corrupts Cupid.

The theme of the second room, the corruption of Cupid's power, is first revealed in the description of the gold reliefs as "wilde Antickes" in which a "thousand monstrous formes therein were made, / Such as false loue doth oft vpon him weare" (51). The bas-reliefs are not described, and so the specifics of the room's depiction of false love appear only in the Maske of Cupid, where false love is translated into psychological states. Nevertheless, we must not neglect these "Antickes," or, to use the later term, "grotesques." Vitruvius complained about the "decadent critical principles" that dictated such grotesques as pediments with "numerous tender stalks and volutes growing up from the roots and having human figures senselessly seated upon them; sometimes stalks having only half-length figures, some with human heads, others with the heads of animals."[29] But the grotesques here are specifically sexual in nature; and since Spenser treated rather casually the copulations of satyrs and human beings, the Romans' favorite "monstrous formes of loue," we would need to stretch our imaginations in order to visualize Spenser's grotesques. Another humanizing touch in Britomart's characterization is that she spent the day earnestly beholding the ordinance of this room, "ne could satisfie / Her greedy eyes" (53).

And it is in the second room that we get the first of the images of the wounded Amoret as she is paraded about in the Maske of Cupid. Her bleeding heart, having been extracted from her breast and pierced by a dart, lies in a silver basin. As with Britomart's experience at the Castle Ioyous, scholars have attempted to work outward from the wound in order to explain the episode. Clearly Amoret's wounds invite response, but it is the kind of response Harington had in mind when he said that "infinite Allegories" can be picked out of "Poetical fictions," the kind of allegorical interpretation reflected in Puttenham's definition of a "full allegorie" as that in which interpretation is left to the reader's "iudgement and coniecture."[30] How are we to decide among interpretations of the wound such as a fear on Amoret's part of "physical surrender" (Roche), a fear of the consequences of her own sexual passions (Nelson), the torment characteristic of all human love (Alpers), a tendency toward lesbianism (Hankins), a tendency toward frigidity (Gilde), and a painful ambivalence in Amoret between constancy and "adulterous temptations" caused by Scudamour's attempt at mastery (Hieatt)?[31] Besides, all of these interpretations read fairly modern, more or less Freudian concerns back into a period that had an attitude toward female sexuality much different from the notions about female vulnerability popular in the nineteenth and earlier twentieth century. What I find in Renaissance literature and Renaissance science generally are not concerns about female inhibitions but concerns about the lack of them, concerns about the capacity of females for constancy and fidelity. In medical circles, the debate was whether women are more wanton than men because their temperament is by nature hotter or because they lack the higher faculties necessary for them to inhibit their own appetites (Crooke, *Microcosmographia,* 276). The indications elsewhere are that Spenser subscribed to the traditional restrictions designed to impose inhibitions on the expression of female sexuality; and so, as a general proposition, it is not likely that he would focus a climactic episode in his masterpiece on the inhibitions with which a bride may anticipate her wedding night or would see as serious concerns either such inhibitions or the male assertiveness that could cause them. Also, those who say the House is a reflection or projection of Amoret's psyche never argue that the tapestries in the first room, which also disappear when Britomart forces Busyrane to undo his spells, are reflective of Amoret's psyche. I suggest that such interpretations of the episode would be much more soundly based if, upon the reversal of the spells, Britomart and Amoret suddenly found themselves outside with the building and Busyrane gone. Helen Gardner is right to say we "weaken our response" to the House of Busyrane "by puzzling over Amoret and trying to find some explanation of her torment," insofar as she means we should not narrow the significance of the episode by restricting its application to Amoret's psyche.[32]

When the characters are approached as fictional personages created within the framework of Renaissance psychology, the wound, instead of providing the focus for an attempt to get at Amoret's own particular psychological state, symbolizes the threat that Busyrane poses to humankind generally. The threat is the concept of false love that Busyrane is attempting to impose on Amoret. Previous explications of the episode assume that Amoret has been captured psychologically. Roche, for example, says that Busyrane's conveyance of Amoret "quite away to liuing wight vnknowen" (4.1.3) means allegorically that he "has got possession of Amoret's mind."[33] But does it? Busyrane certainly attempts to "win" Amoret, to inform her imagination with the images of corrupted love that constitute the second room. But does he succeed, even temporarily? The indications are that he does not. Specifically, *after* she appears in the Maske and just as Busyrane is working up another spell, we are told that "A thousand charmes he formerly did proue; / Yet thousand charmes could not her stedfast heart remoue" (3.12.31). Amoret never shows signs of being psychologically captive. Her weakened condition as she is paraded about in the Maske is not psychological but physical and results from a loss of blood that causes her "vitall powers" to fade (21). Nor does she ever evidence any of the states of mind represented in the Maske, such as doubt, dissemblance, suspicion, cruelty, or fury. When we see her tied to the brass pillar in the inmost room, she is not faint or bewildered or even unsure. She is alert and she desires to escape. Were she Busyrane's psychological captive, I would think her behavior would reflect that psychological captivity, just as Redcrosse's behavior in the Cave of Despair reflects despair and Scudamour's behavior in the House of Care reflects the impact of that allegorical place. And those who think that one of the phrases that indicate the large number of "maladies" in the confused rout at the end of the Maske of Cupid—"So many moe, as there be phantasies / In wauering wemens wit"—is descriptive of Amoret's psyche are also on shaky ground. This is one phrase of three designed to indicate a large number, the other two being "paines in loue" and "punishments in hell" (26); and so the phrase should not be considered, even as a theoretical possibility, any more applicable to or revealing of Amoret's psyche than are the other two. If there is one quality that Amoret possesses in strength, it is constancy under duress. She is never "wauering."

As with Britomart's passage through the House, progression is also the key to the Maske of Cupid. Read as a whole, it is an allegorical depiction of the psychological states typical of an affair of false love from beginning to end. The Maske is introduced by a puzzling figure who is described as a "graue personage," "Yclad in costly garments, fit for tragicke Stage" and who puzzlingly presents a dumb show, which is for some reason not described (3–4). Clearly though, his name, Ease, announces the theme of the Maske: that a life of ease, idleness, or sloth initiates the corruption of sexual desire. The theme is reinforced by the introductory music, a "delitious harmony" that "The feeble senses wholly did confound, / And the fraile soule in deepe delight nigh dround" (6), which is similar to the "sweet Musicke" that "did diuide / Her looser notes with Lydian harmony" in the Castle Ioyous (3.1.40). Renaissance psychologists were as convinced of the corrupting effects of luxurious music as are modern moralists,[34] and apparently so was Spenser.

But that the Maske in and of itself is an allegory of the corruption of sexuality caused by the psychic dislocation inherent in a life of ease, idleness, and luxury is most clearly indicated by the first couple— Fancy and "amorous *Desyre*." Reminiscent of Malecasta's "flit fancy," Fancy is "vaine and light" and tainted by the allusions to the "louely" boys fancied by Jove and Alcides; and he is also the sire of "amorous *Desyre*." That "Amorous *Desyre*" represents a passion cultivated voluntarily for its own sake by the higher faculties of the psyche is evident because "amorous *Desyre*" is fathered by the fancy and not by the natural operation of the vegetal soul. Also, the first "few sparkes" are blown upon and "kindled busily / That soone they life conceiu'd, and forth in flames did fly." This is self-love expressed as autoerotism. We should remember the way Malecasta vexed her "falsed fancy" so that her "fickle hart" would conceive "hasty fire" (3.1.47) and the way Paridell willfully opened his heart to the dart fired by Hellenore. Why such "love," as with Malecasta, is actually "hate" (3.1.50) is the theme of the Maske.

The primary characteristics of the corrupted, unsubordinated self-love in Malecasta and Paridell are weakness and inconstancy. Similarly, inconstancy and the resulting false, unstable, and finally self-destructive inner state are emphasized in the figures that follow Fancy and Desyre. Doubt is in his Romish garments and is full of mistrust, walking as if thorns were in his way and leaning on a broken reed. Daunger, in turn, has a knife for his foes and a net "to enwrap" his friends. The next couple, Hope and Fear, are not the good passions of hope and fear that cause us to move toward good and away from evil in order that we may experience true joy rather than grief. These corrupt passions result when evil is mistaken for good, and so both the false hope and the false fear lead to grief. Hope's initial cheerfulness and amiability are characteristic of all hopes, good and bad, because hope is always in itself a pleasing anticipation of a good. But that Hope is without substance is reflected in her suspiciously Catholic "holy water Sprinckle" and in her "Great liking vnto many, but true loue to feowe." The true nature of Hope's companion, Fear, is immediately apparent. This fear is self-generated. It is the projection of an unstable interior. Although armed, Fear does not feel safe, and even the glittering of his own armor, among other things, frightens him.

Dissemblance and Suspect are another pair that reflect the false, tentative, and threatened inner state created in both sexes by inconstant love, by love unsubordinated to a virtuous other. Surely no reference other than to life is necessary to understand the appropriateness of the male Suspect's lowering at Dissemblance and the female Dissemblance's laughing at Suspect. Dissemblance is much like the false Hope in her pleasing exterior and underlying falsity. Not only is that exterior "painted, and purloynd" but that she is "seeming debonaire" is belied by the tension that causes her continual twining of the two clews of silk. Suspect, a form of fear, contains an interesting complexity. Although he clearly shows his nature to others by lowering at Dissemblance and by his rolling, suspicious eyes, he indicates his own blindness to that obviousness by peeping through a lattice that he holds before his face. When one translates the allegorical image into an imagination of human behavior, the sharpness of Spenser's depiction of the interior state caused by suspicion is impressive.

Dissemblance and Suspect, like Hope and Fear, reflect another pattern in the Maske; they as well as the following pairs are in conflict with each other.

Renaissance psychologists believed that simultaneous, conflicting passions cause serious internal damage, both psychic and physical.[35] Scudamour's desperate condition outside the House of Busyrane reflects such an inner conflict in plain fiction. He is in despair caused by grief for Amoret and hatred for himself. The next pair, Grief and Fury, are passions that incapacitate in radically conflicting ways. Griefe is expressed inwardly in "wilfull languor" and "inward wounds of dolours dart," both forms of idleness resulting from psychic dislocation. Fury is the opposite—a frenzy of external gyrations like a "dismayed Deare in chace embost," a form of ungoverned activity completely foreign to heroic endeavor. It was the internal conflict caused by these two diametrically opposed passions that drove Malbecco's transformation into Gealosie. Displeasure's wasp and Pleasance's "hony-lady Bee" signify that although the personifications are radically differing states of mind, each has its sting. Pleasance, however, like the earlier Hope and Dissemblance, conceals its sting under a falsely agreeable exterior. Perhaps this pair could also be thought to break up a developing progression from less to more severely disordered interior states and help make the point that there is no order at all in the disorder of a psyche corrupted by false love. Finally, Despight and Cruelty, although not described, indicate a deeper corruption than do those which are described. The earlier personifications are self-contained states of mind, but Despight is the attitude that leads to Cruelty, and so they combine to create the state of mind that is expressed in abuse, physical and/or psychological.

The "Antickes" depict false love and the Maske of Cupid depicts false love, but what is Cupid's part in the depiction? Can one come to Lewis's conclusion that this is the determining image for the House of Busyrane? In the Maske, after Amoret,

> the winged God himselfe
> Came riding on a Lion rauenous,
> Taught to obay the menage of that Elfe,
> That man and beast with powere imperious
> Subdeweth to his kingdome tyrannous:

So far this image, like the images in the tapestries and the idol in the first room, figures the power of Cupid, Cupid here being even more powerful than the Cupid in the first room because he includes the power of Venus to instigate sexual desire in animals as well as in human beings, and in so doing includes the powers of both the armed and the unarmed Cupid.

> His blindfold eyes he bad a while vnbind,
> That his proud spoyle of that same dolorous

Faire Dame he might behold in perfect kind;
Which seene, he much reioyced in his cruell mind.

Here, one might say, must be a false Cupid, that cruelty in love which makes love false. But "cruel" also meant "fierce" in the Renaissance, and we cannot be sure what Cupid rejoices in. If he rejoices in Busyrane's attempt to capture Amoret's psyche, we could say he rejoices in false love and so is a false Cupid, but clearly specified is that he unbinds his bandaged eyes to behold "his proud *spoyle* of that same dolorous / Faire Dame" (my emphasis). Not only does the separating out of his "spoyle" from the whole figure of Amoret indicate that it is her heart that he wishes to behold but that it is her heart that is his "spoyle" is indicated by the traditional depiction of Cupid with a string of hearts representing the spoils of his wars. But such a distinction only brings up another problem. If Amoret's heart is Cupid's "spoyle," it is either because Amoret is in love with Scudamour, in which case Cupid is "true" and is properly taking delight in someone in love in the way that gods take delight in their "children." But perhaps her heart is his "spoyle" because Busyrane has removed her heart, in which case we are back to a false Cupid. The image of Cupid is, in and of itself, ambiguous; it is the Maske as a whole that is a depiction of false love.

The figures that precede Amoret and Cupid reflect the mental and emotional states during an affair of false love; the three following Amoret and Cupid—Reproch, Repentance, and Shame—are the residue of such an affair. All three involve self-inflicted, self-defeating punishment: Reproch with "sharpe stings," Repentance with "whips entwind," and Shame with "burning brondyrons." Repentance, who is "feeble, sorrowfull, and lame," has none of the cleansing qualities of Christian repentance and so is more like unrelieved guilt or regret. The final consequences of a life governed by corrupted love appear in a catalog of afflictions: "sterne *Strife*," "*Anger* stout," "Vnquiet *Care*," "fond *Vnthriftihead*," "Lewd *Losse of Time*," "*Sorrow* seeming dead," "Inconstant *Chaunge*," "false *Disloyaltie*," "Consuming *Riotise*," "guilty *Dread* / Of heauenly vengeance," "faint *Infirmitie*," "Vile *Pouertie*," and "lastly *Death* with infamie." This final group in the pageant makes clear that those who corrupt sexual desire corrupt the very energy of their lives and at the same time deprive themselves of the direction that constancy in love gives to the virtuous. Hence their lives are unstable, filled with strife and inconstant change—lives governed by fortune. By living evil as well as unhealthy and unstable lives, they live in "guilty *Dread* / Of heauenly vengeance," depriving themselves of providential guidance, and so die with "infamie."

Continuing the progression from the outer to the second to the innermost room, we reach the instigator of false love, the villain, Busyrane, conjuring up another of his spells. And the best way to understand Busyrane himself is to see him as defined by his house. He has attempted to convert his victim by informing her imagination with the images of false love in the gold bas-reliefs and in the Maske of Cupid. Proteus represents all that which, on an elemental, natural level, threatens and opposes constancy and integrity, and so Florimell's resistance of Proteus is a reflection of the strength necessary to lead a virtuous life in an unstable world. Busyrane represents a threat to constancy and integrity on a higher, societal level. The Maske, one of Busyrane's charms, presents modes of thought and feeling that are destructive to love and marriage as social institutions. The Maske allegorizes those expressions of self-love that have the potential to cause physiological, psychological, and moral chaos. And Amoret's resistance to Busyrane's attempts to impose upon her psyche the images of false love that make up the Maske of Cupid allegorizes her resistance to that tradition of false or inconstant love. The constancy of the lesser heroines, Amoret and Florimell, is fictionalized as the defense of their virginity, the traditional virtue of women, but in these stories chastity is more than abstinence; it must be seen as reflecting a larger sense of constancy as the only resource that human beings have to combat mutability. When we understand Amoret's role in the Maske of Cupid to be the same role she has in both the Garden of Adonis and in the Temple of Venus— she represents that part of virtuous womankind which is to live the generative life—the Maske can be seen to present a comprehensive view of what Lewis referred to as "the whole tradition of polite adultery."[36] And only true, chaste, constant love, love as it is embodied in Britomart, can save one from such a tradition.

The hermaphroditic embrace of Amoret and Scudamour in the discarded 1590 ending of Book III, the joining of the male and female partners at the conclusion of a dance of love, is a fitting conclusion to Amoret's rescue. The dance necessarily takes place in a chancy world where powerful forces separate the pair but, because virtue as expressed in Britomart is more powerful, those forces are unable to prevent the dance from concluding properly. The exterior setting of the reunion contrasts significantly with the interior of the house: its murkiness, the monstrous physiology in the gold bas-reliefs, and the monstrous psychology in the Maske. Scudamour runs to Amoret with "hasty egernesse," like a deer that "greedily embayes / In the cool soile, after long thirstinesse." Such language reflects the very same masculine "greediness" with which he had formerly attempted to accost the flames (and for which he has been most severely criticized by scholars); the language reflects his masculine love for and hunger for Amoret. Amoret, after she is "lightly . . . clipt . . . twixt his armes twaine," responds just as physically but, being the ideal, yielding female, responds receptively and internally. Her body, which was "late the prison of sad paine," is now "the sweet lodge of loue and deare delight"; and she, "overcommen quight / Of huge affection, did in pleasure melt, / And in sweete rauishment pourd out her spright." All of the impediments that Busyrane attempted to impose between Amoret and Scudamour are now gone and Amoret is now able to melt into Scudamour so that they, metaphorically at least, become one flesh.

The allusion to the statue of the hermaphrodite in a rich Roman's bath is puzzling because such statues, as Donald Cheney explains, were of a single bisexual figure rather than of the joining of a male and a female figure.[37] I cannot explain away the allusion to the rich Roman, but surely the power of the visual image is so much greater than any power exerted by the allusion that it would effectively cancel out or at least marginalize the kind of response that Cheney explores. Besides, Roman baths were almost always enclosed within buildings and so the scene in the poem is more like a garden bath of the Middle Ages. There is an illustration of such a bath in a manuscript of Ovid's *Metamorphoses* that is much closer to what is visualized in the scene than any Roman bath of which I am aware. In it is a typical Ovidian hermaphrodite, a naked man and woman embracing. They are standing hip deep in a hot-tub-like bath in front of a towerlike building, which is also in the bath and is consequently totally out of proportion. The bath itself is situated in a gardenlike setting.[38] If Spenser had such a visual image in his mind, it would explain the curious comparison of Scudamour to the deer embayed in the "cool soile," a pool of water in which a deer seeks refuge from the chase. Amoret and Scudamour are not, of course, standing in water, but if such a hermaphroditic image was in Spenser's mind, it would account for the simile.

Lewis's impression of the House with its "vast, silent rooms, dazzling with snake-like gold," and his depiction of false love there in all its "heartbreaking glitter, its sterility, its suffocating monotony" does justice to the House of Busyrane as one of Spenser's important visions of the corruption of love.[39] Those who attempt to understand the episode as an expression of psychological problems in Amoret do not. The House of Busyrane is better understood as the attempt of an evil magician to impose a social evil upon a virtuous maiden than as a reflection of a sexual difficulty within that maiden. And, as far as I can tell, only a Renaissance psychophysiological approach to the middle books enables an understanding of the episode not simply as emblematic of a victory of Christian marriage over courtly love but as an important episode in a allegory of love in which healthy love between male and female is essential to a healthy commonwealth.

4

Timias's Quest for the
Love of Belphoebe

WITH Timias's quest for Belphoebe we move away from the hierarchy of quests that celebrate chaste love as the proper expression of the generative powers to a quest that celebrates virginity as a proper expression of those powers—Belphoebe's virginity, just as Florimell's, Amoret's and Britomart's chastity, is an active, dynamic state, an immanent virtue. And we move to the quest most closely allegorical of Elizabeth in her Body natural. In the poem as we have it, Mercilla, not the Faery Queen, most clearly expresses Elizabeth in her Body politic, but Belphoebe fulfills the role she is given in the Letter to "shadow" Elizabeth as a private person, as "a most vertuous and beautifull Lady." These two are crucial to Spenser's metaphorical restructuring of what Kantorowicz would call an "organological whole," the Elizabethan commonweal.[1] Spenser does not, however, simply apportion one of the two "bodies" to each character. Although only briefly characterized, Mercilla evidences passions, products of the Body natural. And, as a "vertuous" lady, Belphoebe allegorizes the Elizabeth who, according to Camden, had, as a private person, chosen virginity as a way of devoting herself to God's service.[2] But Elizabeth's choice of virginity also had political implications, for by so choosing she wed herself to the nation and became the mother exclusively of her subjects and not of naturally born children. As a "beautifull" lady, Belphoebe allegorizes the Elizabeth to whom her courtiers were bound by romantic love, but the conclusion to Timias's quest clearly signifies that love for the queen in her Body natural transmutes into love for her in her Body politic. Such an understanding of Timias's quest for Belphoebe's love enables a unified view of the psychological and the physiological aspects of Belphoebe's characterization, aspects that have their mythological equivalent in her identification with Venus and Diana. Also, that love for Elizabeth in her Body natural is only the first stage of love for her in her Body politic enables the incorporation of the Elizabeth and Raleigh allusions in the allegory—no matter what problems those allusions cause to the story line.

Belphoebe's story, like Amoret's, begins at birth. Lewis captures the essence of the separation of the two: "Diana took the one twin into a quasi-divine, unchangeable life. Venus plunges the other into the world of generation: the world, that is, of pleasure, spontaneity, and sexuality, but the world also of mutability and chance."[3] As a consequence, the twins have psyches, complexes of higher faculties, that enable virtuous but contrary expression of the natural processes idealized in their shared birth. Amoret's schooling prepares her for a metamorphosis from innocent virgin to married lover. Her virgin psyche causes her to resist Scudamour's efforts to raise her up by the hand and lead her off to a life of love, but Scudamour's masculine forcefulness brings out an incipient womanhood and a consequent commitment to love and to the generative life. Belphoebe's upbringing gives her a psyche that commits her to lifelong virginity, to the expression of her self in the strenuous life of the hunt. As with those virtuous characters who are moved psychically toward sexual love, Belphoebe is a self primarily as she gives expression to the urgings of sexual desire; but for Belphoebe there is only the transmuted expression of those urgings, the desire for honor that prompts noble deeds.

However relevant or irrelevant Belphoebe's conspicuous appearance in Book II may be to the adventures of Guyon, her characterization there as a physical Venus with a Diana psychology initiates her allegorization of Elizabeth in her Body natural. The full description indicates the importance of the physiology as well as the psychology of virginity. Praises of and glimpses at the other heroines' beauty abound; but only the paragon of virginity, she who is later to be filled with indignation and wrath at the sensual affection that Timias shows the injured Amoret, is given the full treatment, beginning with her flowing hair. Diana's hair, we remember, is braided for the chase (3.6.18), but Belphoebe's, even though she is on the hunt, is "scattered" like that of Venus and also adorned with "sweet flowres . . . fresh leaues and blossoms"—emblems of life and sexuality (2.3.30).

All in all, Spenser's modeling the first appearance of Belphoebe on Venus's appearance to Aeneas and Achates is a direct way of identifying Belphoebe with the attractiveness and sexuality of Venus.[4] The allusions to Dido as Diana and to Penthesilea can be seen to serve the same purpose because, although dressed as Diana, Dido is a woman of powerful physical passions. In Spenser's source for this appearance of Penthesilea, she comes to Troy out of love for Hector. Throughout Belphoebe's initial appearance, Spenser presents us with a young woman who has all of the physical attributes found in one who is ready for the sexual life. Just as important, Belphoebe's beauty and sexuality are juxtaposed to other qualities that reflect a psyche committed to virginity. The sexuality of the Graces that sit on her eyelids, "Working belgards, and amorous retrate" (2.3.25), contrasts with the "dredd Maiestie, and awfull ire" with which she broke Cupid's "wanton darts, and quenched base desire" (23). Most pointedly juxtaposed are her weapons—the tools of, as well as the emblems of, the Diana-like life of virginity and the hunt—and her breasts. The baldric for her quiver "forlay / Athwart her snowy brest, and did diuide / Her daintie paps; which like young fruit in May / Now little gan to swell, and being tide, / Through her thin weed their places only signifide" (29). Clearly Spenser wishes his paragon of virginity to be perceived as a young woman with the same physicality found in one who is ready for the sexual life but just as clearly committed psychologically to the virgin life of the hunt. Belphoebe is female, but she certainly is not feminine.

Given the physical description, it is most understandable that the base Braggadocchio, moved by Cupid and capable of responding only to Belphoebe's sexuality, would wonder why she is not at court, "where happie blis / And all delight does raigne" and would react, not to the sense of her explanation that honor is found with peril and pain and sweat and "wakeful watches," but to her "sweet words" and "wondrous beauty" and try to rape her. It may even be that we are to see his attempt at rape as a base misapplication of her statement that the doors to "pleasures pallace" "to all stand open wide." And, also most appropriate to her characterization, when Braggadocchio makes the attempt at rape, what he thought was a Venus responds Diana-like with her boar spear (39–42). Readers must, however, pay closer attention than does Braggadocchio to her words. Her speech on honor and the necessity of sweat is a variation on the necessity of "faire endeuour," a theme that is applied to and uttered by the virtuous throughout *The Faerie Queene*. Only when manifested as virtuous activity is virginity a virtue; and Diana-like virginity, even though expressed in the strenuous life of the hunt, could be a way of separating oneself from one's obligation to bring God's will to fruition in human affairs. But Belphoebe's rescue of the wounded Timias, occasioned by "Prouidence heauenly" (3.5.27), is an exercise of *caritas*: "We mortal wights, whose liues and fortunes bee / To commun accidents still open layd," Belphoebe says, "Are bound with commun bond of frailtee, / To succour wretched wights, whom we captiued see" (36). Her response is that enjoined by the admonition to love our neighbors as ourselves and, by reminding us of the Pauline gift of virginity that enables a commitment to the spirit not possible in the generative life, reminds us of Elizabeth's report of her original choice of the virgin life. Belphoebe's care of Timias allegorizes Elizabeth's love for those of her subjects—such as Sir Walter Raleigh—under her immediate supervision.

Belphoebe's reflection both of Venus and Diana is a part of her reflection both of Elizabeth's Body natural and her Body politic. Belphoebe's characterization is similar to Elizabeth's characterization in the "Rainbow" portrait, probably done when Elizabeth was sixty-eight, which also depicts both her persons. Elizabeth's outer cloak, covered with the eyes and ears of her loyal subjects, symbolizes the extension of her royal presence and power, her Body politic. Inside the cloak, her dress, which is covered with flowers emblematic of youth and spring and has an embroidered serpent of wisdom mastering the emotions of an embroidered heart, brings us closer to an idealized version of her Body natural and reminds us of Belphoebe, the "beautifull" as well as "vertuous" lady. Elizabeth herself is depicted as a relatively young, sexually desirable female with loosened hair, softened, "beautifull" features, and young breasts exposed almost to the nipples. She is depicted as a young woman so desirable as to cause those subjects with personal access to her to love her in her Body natural and consequently to serve her both in her Body natural and in her Body politic.

That portrait contrasts significantly with the "Armada" portrait, in which her face is not flattered and she is almost all symbolic clothing, almost all Body politic, almost all, in *Faerie Queene* terms, Mercilla-Elizabeth. Belphoebe, with her budding breasts, is a much younger Elizabeth than that in the "Rainbow" portrait, and she expresses an active as well as a desirable Elizabeth. Both Belphoebe's choice of the virgin life of the hunt and her desirability are at heart sexual, the energy for her strenuous life being a product of her sublimated sexuality. These two motifs—virginity as an expression of the generative powers and beauty as the moving force to love—cause Belphoebe's physical beauty and her potentiality for the sexual life to be as important to her allegorization of Elizabeth as is her choice of the virgin life.

Belphoebe brings the wounded Timias to her dwelling in a kind of Wood of Diana (as opposed to a Garden of Diana) appropriate to Belphoebe's Venus physiology and her Diana psyche. In it are both Venus's myrtle trees and the laurel, and the birds sing "their loues sweet teene" as well as "gods high prayse" (3.5.40). Belphoebe tends Timias's wounds, Timias falls passionately in love, and the story of Belphoebe and Timias ensues. The story is Timias's quest for the love of Belphoebe, a quest fulfilled when he becomes worthy through a subordination of self and a consequent attainment of a love exclusively for Belphoebe-Elizabeth. But even Timias's initial passion is appropriate to the romantic love of courtier for his queen because, although it is clearly physical and, when unrequited, is internally destructive, he never evidences any really carnal thoughts, or any really carnal reasons for the physical attraction. For Timias, even Belphoebe's beauty inheres in such things as her "excellencies" and a "celestiall hew." And his attempts to renounce his passion are always for reasons of differences in states of life, her sovereignty and honor and heavenly light as opposed to his villainy (44–47). Like Elizabeth, Belphoebe is to be the object of a romantic and exclusive but rarified love; and, like Elizabeth, she is to accept that love and to return it in the form of grace.

The celebration of Belphoebe's "dainty rose" invokes a kind of *mons Dianae* in Belphoebe's sylvan garden. Both her physicality and her commitment to virginity are reflected in this passage. Belphoebe spares neither pains nor expense to treat Timias's wound,

> But that sweet Cordiall, which can restore
> A loue-sick hart, she did to him enuy;
> To him, and to all th'vnworthy world forlore
> She did enuy that soueraigne salue, in secret store.
>
> (50)

The implied fiction is that although Belphoebe searched the woods for plants from which she made medicines for Timias's wound, she would not in any circumstance make a "Cordiall" (heart medicine) for Timias's "loue-sick hart" from the appropriate plant, because the flower of that plant symbolizes her honor:

> That dainty Rose, the daughter of her Morne,
> More deare then life she tendered, whose flowre
> The girlond of her honour did adorne:
> Ne suffred she the Middayes scorching powre,
> Ne the sharp Northerne wind thereon to showre,
> But lapped vp her silken leaues most chaire,
> When so the froward skye began to lowre:
> But soone as calmed was the Christall aire,
> She did it faire dispred, and let to florish faire.
>
> (51)

The physical allegory of the first three lines is clear: whether the symbolism of the rose flower was based on physiology or the physiology derived from the symbolism, Helkiah Crooke says the parts of the hymen, the four fleshy caruncles with interconnecting membranes, "make the form of the cup of a little rose halfe blowne" (*Microcosmographia*, 235). The rest of the stanza, concerning Belphoebe's protective care of the plant, is appropriate to the story; but it evokes the physical allegory so curiously as to cause Thomas Roche to declare that the rest of the stanza marks an immediate shift to the "spiritual aspects of virginity."[5] David Lee

Miller, on the other hand, associates this image of concealment and display not only with that of Diana surprised at her bath but with that of the "Virgin Rose" in the Bower of Bliss, an image that suggests invitation and delay. I understand Belphoebe's care of her rose, both plant and membrane, to evoke (rather unsuccessfully) the innocence and protectiveness she reveals in her encounter with Braggadocchio. Like Miller, I emphasize the physicality of Belphoebe's characterization but do not accept his treatment of her demeanor as coyness.

My reading differs from Miller's most clearly, however, in that he understands the episode to reflect an ambivalence toward Elizabeth's choice of the virgin life because he believes it disrupts an important emphasis of Book III, the "congruence of natural and cultural forms of perpetuity." I would have the episode evoke the love that is to bind Elizabeth and her courtiers, a love essential to perpetuity in the body politic and necessarily predicated on her virginity. The image that informs stanza 52 is not of generation but of propagation by grafting. God planted the flower of virginity in heaven; and then "to make ensample of his heauenly grace" he fetched it out "of her natiue place, / And did in stocke of earthly flesh enrace" so it could bear fruit "of honour and all chast desire" (52). Throughout the passage the image of the plant remains constant, with "spire" (to produce, or put forth, as a plant) and "ympes" (grafts) used to describe the young women. Miller sees this part of the passage as ambivalent because "it makes an image of natural propagation signify a moral idea that, in the present context, denies propagation." But the propagation here is not "natural"; it is asexual; and the perpetuity of virginity is achieved by example and emulation, not by generation. As is explained to the young ladies: "To youre fair selues a faire ensample frame, / Of this faire virgin, this *Belphoebe* faire . . . For thy she standeth on the highest staire / Of th'honorable stage of womanhead, / That Ladies all may follow her ensample dead" (54). Thus the word "stocke," which Miller reads as evoking, among other things, the penis, should be understood in its plain sense of that onto which something is grafted; and "dead," instead of undercutting the praise of Belphoebe, should be taken in its less-than-usual sense of "unrelieved, unbroken, absolute, or complete." All in all, instead of being implicitly critical of Elizabeth's refusal to marry and bear children and thus disrupting the natural perpetuity on which the perpetuity of the nation depends, I understand this passage to contribute to the overall theme of Spenser's allegory of love: the necessity of the various forms of earthly love to perpetuity in the body politic. Miller's reading illustrates the difficulties caused by removing episodes from their contexts within quests.[6]

Coming immediately after Timias yields himself to love and is wasted internally by its effects, the celebration of the rose serves the fiction by precluding any

notions that a love story like the others is to develop. The passage also reinforces
the idea that Belphoebe's virginity is not just the absence of sexual behavior or a
reflection of supramundane concepts of love but is a positive, fruitful expression
of that basic self-love which is the source of the energies of life. And her characterization in the Book IV episodes that conclude Timias's quest is largely consonant with that in the earlier books. That Greedie Lust flees Belphoebe, "Well
knowing her to be his deaths sole instrument" (4.7.29) and that she dispatches
him with an arrow through the throat could reflect a virginity totally separated
from sexuality; but that, having dispatched Greedie Lust, she stands over him,
"long gazing" at his dead body and wondering at his monstrous shape, continues
her characterization as a personage whose commitment to the virgin life governs
a potentiality for the sexual (32). If, as so many believe, Greedie Lust is to be
perceived as phallic, we are to be reminded of the innocent but sexually inclined
Britomart gazing at the shapes of "monstrous loue" in the House of Busyrane.

The conclusion to Timias's quest for Belphoebe's love takes place when,
after having been rejected by Belphoebe for his too sensual attentions to the
wounded Amoret, Timias is received back into Belphoebe's grace, a state allegorically appropriate to that of a courtier who subordinates himself to his queen
in her Body natural. That Timias is accepted into such a state rather than achieves
it through virtuous endeavor sets this story apart from the others, but perhaps
that was, in Spenser's mind, necessary to allegorize the proper relationship of
any courtier to his queen. However, that Timias later maintains that he was
wrongfully banished in the first place obviously derives not from the story line
but from Spenser's desire to support Raleigh. One can understand Timias's dec-
laration that he had been misdeemed as a statement of Raleigh's continuing loyalty to Elizabeth in her Body politic despite the betrayal of his love for her in her
Body natural through his marriage. But if Spenser's description in the Letter of
Belphoebe's role as Elizabeth the "most vertuous and beautifull Lady" is, as I
have found it to be, fictionalized in Timias's quest for Belphoebe, then loyalty to
Elizabeth in her Body politic is only the end result of his love for her in her Body
natural, a love obviously betrayed by an attachment to Amoret.

But there is another way to account for the disparities in the story. I cannot
read the story of Belphoebe and Timias without feeling that it contains relics of
an earlier fiction that was a true romantic love story.[7] There is external evidence
of such a story in the curious reference in *The Ruines of Time* to a "Paradize" by
implication "Full of sweete flowres and daintiest delights," which Merlin made
"for the gentle squire, to entertaine / His fayre *Belphoebe*" (519–25). Such a
paradise would be most unsuited to the Belphoebe we know, a Belphoebe not
his, i.e., Timias's, or anyone else's, for that matter. The argument to canto 8 can

be read to mean that Timias loves Amoret, and Timias is depicted, however shadowily, in the following episode as expressing that love. This could remind us of a rivalry over Amoret, referred to cryptically when Amoret left the Garden of Adonis and came to the Faery Court, where "many one . . . found / His feeble hart wide launched with loues cruell wound" (3.6.52). Such a rivalry is also hinted at in the younker's claim that "fairest *Amoret* was his by right" (4.1.10) and in the quarrel between Blandamour and Scudamour in which both lay claim to Amoret (4.1.47). In that same episode Blandamour expresses hatred for Scudamour "Both for his [Scudamour's] worth . . . And eke because his [Blandamour's] loue he [Scudamour] wonne by right" (4.1.39). However one may regard the specifics of Josephine Bennett's theory about the poem's evolution, the puzzling references to the knights of the maidenhead that she identified do imply the existence of an earlier stage of some kind.[8] Could an earlier Timias have been romantically in love with an earlier Belphoebe but have strayed in his affections?

The conclusion to Timias's quest can be related to Spenser's larger purpose to create a story that allegorizes the courtier's love for the queen in her Body natural and through that love his subordination to her in her Body politic. But allowances must be made for the disparities. The argument to canto 7, which returns us to the story, can be read to forecast an episode in which Timias betrays his commitment to Belphoebe through a romantic love for Amoret:

> Amoret rapt by greedie lust
> Belphoebe saves from dread,
> The Squire her loves, and being blam'd
> his dayes in dole doth lead.

In the third line, "her" can be read to refer to either Amoret or Belphoebe. If we read the argument to forecast a story in which Timias loves Amoret, "blamed" is to be understood in the sense of "censured" rather than "accused." I so read it because the fictional situation in canto 7 clearly implies that Timias has an attachment for the wounded Amoret that violates that romantic attachment to Belphoebe, which can be expressed only through a commitment to the virgin life.

That Timias comes upon Amoret being attacked by Greedie Lust while Timias is with Belphoebe indicates that he had committed himself to the virgin life—especially since Belphoebe is hunting, as was her wont, "to banish sloth." This indicates that Timias has committed himself to the virgin life of the hunt. That Belphoebe condemns his lack of "faith" indicates that he failed the first test.

When Belphoebe returns from killing Greedie Lust, she finds Timias with Amoret, described as a "new louely mate" (35). Of the definitions of "mate," only "lover" is appropriate here, and that Amoret is a *new* lovely mate indicates a switching of affections on Timias's part. Timias's fight with Greedie Lust, with the suggestive details of Amoret's body taking the brunt of Timias's "intended stroke," the consequent staining of immaculate dress with blood, and the tender solicitations afterwards—Timias wipes the tears from her eyes, kisses her "atweene" the eyes, and softly handles her hurts (26, 27, 35)—can be read to allegorize an initial sexual encounter in the marriage bed and would consequently seem to shadow the marriage of Raleigh and Elizabeth Throgmorton. The allusions do not serve, however, merely to remind us of that marriage or to hint at Elizabeth's neurotic jealousy about the charms and lives of her ladies in waiting. Any affection for a woman other than Elizabeth, if the professed love of the courtiers for Elizabeth in her Body natural had been taken with absolute seriousness, would have inhibited their love for her in her Body politic. In Raleigh's case, however, since the marriage was contrary to the wishes of his sovereign it constituted a clear betrayal of his love to Elizabeth in both her persons and was consequently an expression of self-love destructive to the social fabric. Belphoebe's intensity of feeling—the "deepe disdaine, and great indignity" and "wrath" that inclines her to kill both Timias and Amoret with the same arrow that killed Greedie Lust—can be understood fictionally as Belphoebe's condemnation of any deviation from the virgin life or allegorically as an entirely appropriate jealousy of Elizabeth in her Body natural about the love of her courtiers. And so, whether Belphoebe's response to Timias's ministrations to Amoret is seen to reflect her indignation at Timias's change of love from her to Amoret, or indignation at the expression of an untoward physicality toward any female, her rejection of Timias is justified. However we are to understand Timias's declarations of fidelity later, a reading of this episode would not lead us to think that Belphoebe "misdeems" Timias; and her parting question, "Is this the faith?" (36), is properly inclusive of the lapses of both Timias and a courtier such as Raleigh. The story, the topical allusion, and the larger allegory all seem to be in phase here.

Timias's behavior after his rejection continues Spenser's treatment of the courtier's love for Elizabeth in her two persons. Timias suffers from a love melancholy appropriate to his rejection by Belphoebe and consequently appropriate to a courtier's rejection by Elizabeth in her Body natural. When Arthur reads Belphoebe's name, which Timias had written on the trees, Timias kisses the ground where he had also written it (4.7.39–8.13). Timias sighs and laments, and he has what Burton described as the "biting cares" (728) of the lover. His fellow feeling for the dove's loss of its mate is also pure love melancholy, as is his treasuring the heart-shaped ruby. (However, that Belphoebe gave him such a gift is appropriate to the relationship of Elizabeth and Raleigh, but not to that of Belphoebe and Timias. Belphoebe expresses affection toward no one—pity and concern, yes; affection, no.) Timias falls into a fit of slothfulness appropriate to love melancholy but also reflective of any subject's repudiation of his love to his queen in her Body politic. Timias goes where there is gloomy shade, where one cannot "see bright heauens face," where there are mossy trees, indicative of a life of inaction, and where he breaks his weapons and vows not to use them more. His intention is to "wast his wretched daies in wofull plight; / So on him selfe to wreake his follies owne despight." Timias deplores "his hard mishap in dolor," language reminiscent of Scudamour's psychological state outside the House of Busyrane, and he is described as "wearing out his youthly yeares, / Through wilfull penury." Numerous stanzas are devoted to Timias's rejection of the active life. And surely that Arthur, by contrast, is on an adventure when he happens to see Timias is a way of contrasting Arthur's active life with that of Timias, as is Belphoebe's resting after weary toil when the dove finds her. Belphoebe's speech to Timias on sloth emphasizes that such a life is a defective manifestation of self-love.

The concluding episode of the story contributes to Spenser's larger purpose of allegorizing the love that the courtier must necessarily have for the queen in her Body natural, a love that transmutes into love for her in her Body politic; but the presence of Raleigh and Elizabeth is especially heavy. Canto 8 begins with the comment that "displeasure of the mighty is / Then death it selfe more dread and desperate" and that the only cure for such displeasure is time. All of this is most appropriate to the topical allusion, but Belphoebe is "mighty" only "allegorically" in the sense that we are to substitute Queen Elizabeth for the fictional character.

Belphoebe's characterization in the reconciliation scene (4.8.1–18), except for her having given Timias the love token, is consistent with that in her earlier rescue of Timias. The dove finds her resting after "saluage chase" (9), and when she is led to Timias she pities his desperate case. Belphoebe's appearance enables the final focus on Timias's present state as a violation of the life of "faire endeuour," a refusal of a subject to play his proper role in the commonweal. The whole of Belphoebe's speech—or query—about the cause of Timias's condition, whether it is from "heauens hard disgrace," "wrath of cruell wight," or especially "selfe disliked life," is a way of relating the episode to the necessity of a life in which the basic energies that derive from self-love are subordinated to a higher good. As she says, "For he whose daies in wilfull woe are worne, / The grace of his Creator doth despise, / That will not vse his gifts for thanklesse nigardise" (15). These lines clearly relate the story of Belphoebe and Timias and the correlative story of Elizabeth and Raleigh to the central conception in Merlin's speech to Britomart on the importance of her virtuous quest to find Artegall, to Britomart's similar speech to Scudamour outside the House of Busyrane, to the sloth inherent in the life Marinell led before his defeat by Britomart, to the virtuous quest of Florimell to find Marinell, and so forth. Timias's subservient yet stubborn defense of himself—that it was through "misdeeming" that her "high displesure" was wreaked on such a "worthlesse wight"—and his placing himself at her mercy strikes a tone that supports Raleigh and at the same time recognizes the supreme majesty of the Queen. The "mightie hart" of Belphoebe-Elizabeth accordingly "did mate"

> With mild regard, to see his ruefull plight,
> That her inburning wrath she gan abate,
> And him receiu'd againe to former fauours state.
>
> In which he long time afterwards did lead
> An happie life with grace and good accord,
> Fearlesse of fortunes chaunge or enuies dread,
>
> (17–18)

The whole story is thus wrapped up in six or seven lines, depending on the way one counts, and without even a period at the end. And none of the problems of the narrative are resolved. Does Belphoebe forgive Timias his trespass, and if she does, why does she? Would that forgiveness be appropriate to her characterization? Timias does not repent his attachment to Amoret; he merely defends himself and denies that he *really* betrayed his love for Belphoebe.

Nevertheless, the final statement that Timias is now "Fearlesse of fortunes chaunge" reiterates the theme of Spenser's allegory of love: the control of fortune through love. Constancy as expressed in the virgin life is different from constancy as expressed in the generative life, but both are ways of controlling fortune. And the love expressed by Timias-Raleigh's subordination of himself to Belphoebe-Elizabeth and Belphoebe-Elizabeth's return of that love in the form of grace is the means by which fortune in the life of the kingdom is controlled. The perpetuity of the body politic is possible only in a kingdom united by love. This theme will become clearer with the introduction of Mercilla-Elizabeth in Book V, but that Spenser allegorized the queen's two bodies in a quest that is woven into Books III and IV is a clear indication that the adventures in Book V are to be read as the culmination of those in Books III and IV. As with the other quests, however, Timias's quest in some ways ends ambiguously and inconclusively, indicating again that Spenser's theme is a statement of faith rather than an observable operation.

5

Social Concord in Miniature

APPROACHING the middle books of *The Faerie Queene* by sorting the episodes into the quests of which they are a part isolates important elements of Book IV, the so-called "friendship" stories of Cambell and Triamond and Amyas and Placidas and the Ate and Duessa false-friends episodes, because neither the stories nor the episodes are parts of a larger quest. Both are, however, important to Spenser's allegory of love. They occupy a midpoint in the allegory between the love that unites the different sexes and the love that unites the commonwealth, but they do not do so merely as they illustrate friendship and the absence thereof. Each of these "concord" stories concludes in the creation of a little concordant community of four united by both friendship and chaste love; and the creation of those true communities requires God-like sources of power and authority— Cambina in the story of Cambell and Triamond, and Arthur in the story of Amyas and Placidas. The creative and sustaining power found in these two characters will reappear with larger contours in Book V as the power by which Mercilla sustains the larger community of the commonwealth. Spenser did not envision communities, large or small, either emerging from or being maintained merely by an interaction of individuals, any more than he envisioned the cosmos emerging from or being maintained by a Lucretian interaction of primal bodies. Spenser's concordant communities, large and small, are possible because those capable of subordinating their self-love can be united by the exercise of or even the presence of authority. And that these same principles are found both in the English nation as symbolized by the relationship between Mercilla and her true subjects in Book V and in the stories of concord in Book IV, where the connection with Elizabeth is distant, indicates that Spenser's idealization of power and authority was heartfelt. From time to time I bring up a Spenserian conservative, even medieval outlook. I certainly do not mean, however, that Spenser was in sympathy with the specifically English medieval notion, still influential during the Tudor years, of the mixed government. As John Aylmer noted in 1559, "[T]he regiment of

Englande is not a mere Monarchie as some for lack of consideracion thinke, nore a meere Oligarchie, nor Democrate, but a rule mixte of all these wherein ech one of these have or should have like authorite."[1] In his attitude toward authority, Spenser was more than up-to-date; he was looking forward to Stuart notions of monarchical absolutism.

The concord complex at the entrance to the Temple of Venus, in which Concord is depicted as enforcing a union of Love and Hate, provides the symbolic center for both the concord stories and the discord episodes by allegorizing principles of power-as-authority and subordination, principles that are crucial to Spenser's social vision. I quote the passage in full so as to draw attention to such words as "maystred," "tempered," "forced," "commaundmant," "subdew," "contained," "ordained," "bound," and "holds."

> On either side of her [Concord], two young men stood,
>   Both strongly arm'd, as fearing one another;
>   Yet were they brethren both of half the blood,
>   Begotten by two fathers of one mother,
>   Though of contrarie natures each to other;
>   The one of them hight *Loue*, the other *Hate*,
>   *Hate* was the elder, *Loue* the younger brother;
>   Yet was the younger stronger in his state
> Then the elder, and him maystred still in all debate.
>
> Nathlesse that Dame so well them tempred both,
>   That she them forced hand to ioyne in hand,
>   Albe that *Hatred* was thereto full loth,
>   And turn'd his face away, as he did stand,
>   Vnwilling to behold that louely band.
>   Yet she was of such grace and vertuous might,
>   That her commaundmant he could not withstand,
>   But bit his lip for felonous despight,
> And gnasht his yron tuskes at that displeasing sight.
>
> *Concord* she cleeped was in common reed,
>   Mother of blessed *Peace*, and *Friendship* trew;
>   They both her twins, both borne of heauenly seed,
>   And she her selfe likewise diuinely grew;
>   The which right well her workes diuine did shew:
>   For strength, and wealth, and happinesse she lends,
>   And strife, and warre, and anger does subdew:

Of litle much, of foes she maketh frends,
And to afflicted minds sweet rest and quiet sends.

By her the heauen is in his course contained,
    And all the world in state vnmoued stands,
    As their Almightie maker first ordained,
    And bound them with inuiolable bands;
    Else would the waters ouerflow the lands,
    And fire deuoure the ayre, and hell them quight,
    But that she holds them with her blessed hands.
    She is the nourse of pleasure and delight,
And vnto *Venus* grace the gate doth open right.

                                        (4.10.32–35)

The subordination of "love" and "hate" through authorized power is common-place Renaissance cosmology. The overall stable universe was formed when God separated what had been a confusion of elements in Chaos into the familiar levels of earth, water, air, and fire. But the relationship between these essentially stable levels involves a potentially destructive "hate," the inclination in the elements to destroy the differing and therefore antagonistic qualities in the other elements, as well as an attractive "love." In Du Bartas's commonplace explication, the hot and dry fire would destroy the cold and dry earth were it not separated from the earth by both the hot and moist air and the cold and moist water. There is also conflict and therefore the potential for change within order in the different strata of elements. Differing levels of heat in the air caused by proximity to the elemental fire, for example, account for the winds of various temperatures that blow in the different seasons and also account for the different temperatures of moistures shed from the air (*Devine Weeks*, 45–46).

But it is on Earth that Concord becomes a kind of proto-Venus. On Earth she is the force that orders the elements into the sublunary world of change— the world of life and love and decay—and thus is "the nourse of pleasure and delight, / And vnto *Venus* grace the gate doth open right" (4.10–35). Earth was conceptualized as composed of compounds, mixtures of the four elements in which love or attraction provides a temporary coherence within which hate or repulsion creates a dynamic instability. Life proceeds from the interaction of love and hate. From Du Bartas:

        Sith then the knot of sacred Mariage,
    Which ioynes the Elements, from age to age

> Brings-forth the Worlds Babes : sith their Enmities
> With fell diuorce, kill whatsoeuer dies:
> And sith but changing their degree and place;
> They frame the various Formes, wherewith the face
> Of this faire World is so imbellished:

(40)

And both "love" and "hate" are but differing expressions of the elemental self-love, the God-given inclination of each creature to conserve itself, in Thomas Wright's words, to "procure what it needeth" through love and by means of hate to "resist and impugne whatsoeuer hindereth it of that [which] appertaineth vnto his good and conservation." We see, Wright says, that fire "continually ascendeth vpward, because the coldnesse of the water, earth, and ayre much impeacheth the vertue of his heate : heauie substances descend to their centre for their preseruation. . . ." The difference between the behavior of the elements and the behavior of the characters in Spenser's stories is that the elements act through what Wright described as a "naturall inclination" and the characters are moved by "voluntary affection" (*Passions of the Minde*, 12).

Previous examinations of the tetrads in Book IV by Alastair Fowler, James Nohrnberg, and A. Kent Hieatt follow Plato and Pythagoras and consequently focus on the patterns of four created when the characters are treated as mathematical and/or geometrical counters. Thus, in his *Spenser Encyclopedia* article on the tetrad, Hieatt comments on the square formation created by the titular heroes of Book IV, namely, Cambell (1) and Triamond (2), as they ride along with their loves, Cambina (3) and Canacee (4): "1 and 3 are bound by love; so are 2 and 4. 1 and 2 are bound by friendship; so are 3 and 4," etc.[3] My purposes require an understanding of the roles of the power and authority figures that are essential to the creation of the concordant as well as the discordant communities of characters understood as fictional personages. And so when Empedocles is Christianized—Spenser's purposes with cosmic as well as social harmony cannot be fully understood apart from Christian views on subordination to God and to God's viceroys here on earth—Empedocles' views on primal love and hate are more congenial to my purposes than are Plato's views on mathematical means.

The social and cosmic implications of the false-friends episodes are clearer than those of the concord stories, and they are especially clear in the episode that continues the falling out of the false friends Paridell, Blandamour, Satyrane, and Erivan over the False Florimell that began at the tourney for Florimell's girdle. The descriptors of these representations of antecosmic forces in romance figures—"sterne *Druon*," who leads the single life; "lewd *Claribell*," who "loued out

of measure"; "Loue-lauish *Blandamour*," who would change his liking "at pleasure"; and "lustfull *Paridell*," who "lusted after all" (4.9.20–21)—focus attention on their eccentric expression of sexual desire, on their unsubordinated self-
love that leads to the chaos of lust. That there are four false friends with opposing
natures and that the movement is from the temporary bonding of pairs of knights
to the dissolution of those bonds and then to the forming of other temporary
bonds clearly relates the false friends to the warring elements in chaos. And the
comparison of this little false community of four to the four winds that "Dan
Aeolus" marshaled against Neptune in order to "tosse the deepes, and teare the
firmament, / And all the world confound with wide vprore, / As if in stead thereof
they *Chaos* would restore" (4.9.23) relates them to the instability of the stratum
occupied by the air and the general instability within strata occupied by water
and by earth. The shifting of their attack from Britomart to Arthur continues the
basic image through the comparison to a storm that hovers round about, here
and there, and finally descends on Arthur. Crucial to an understanding of this
episode is that the cessation of hostilities is effected by the godlike power and
authority of Arthur, not through any internal dynamics operating within the false
friends. Nor had it been merely a lack of virtue that initiated the discord of the
false friends at the tourney. They fell out through the "lewd vpbraide" of those
two principles of discord, Duessa and Ate. Always integral to the actions in
Spenser's allegory of love are such representations of the basic forces of love and
hate.

Ate is pure hate. Her ultimate purpose is "that great golden chaine quite to
diuide, / With which it blessed Concord hath together tide" (4.1.30), and she
functions within the narrative action as the "mother of debate [i.e., "strife"] /
And all dissention" (4.1.19). Ate should remind us that the conflict that today
we see as a clash of forces that initiates natural, historical, and social processes
was, in orthodox Elizabethan thought, perceived to be divisive and destructive
discord. Ate serves to augment the forces of social mutability. Her description,
after the inevitable "fowle and filthy," is a composite of unresolvable contrarie-
ties: "squinted eyes," a lying tongue that is divided into two parts (and so her lies
are not simple lies but contentious lies), and a "discided" heart "That neuer
thoght one thing, but doubly still was guided" (27). There are also the unmatched
ears, the "vnequall" hands, one reaching out and the other pushing away, and the
feet pointing in different directions (28–29). She is a collected disparity.

Ate's general influence in human affairs is reflected in her dwelling, a collection of images of brokenness, repulsion, aversion, and repugnance. The interior
is comprised of "ragged monuments" and "relicks" adorning her "riuen walls":
"rent robes," "broken scepters," "Altars defyl'd," "Disshiuered speares," "shields

ytorne in twaine," "cities ransackt," and so forth (21). Outside her dwelling, in the images of the "wicked weedes, / Which she her selfe had sowen all about," are her weapons, "The seedes of euill wordes and factious deeds" that breed "Tumultuous trouble and contentious iarre, / The which most often end in bloudshed and in warre" (25). Explication of the passage is not difficult. The problem is to appreciate the orthodox belief that "euill wordes and factious deeds," "debate" or strife, are destructive to frail human beings when those frail human beings are not ordered by legitimate authority.

Ate is the "mother of debate" and "all dissention, which doth dayly grow / Amongst fraile men, that many a publike state / And many a priuate oft doth ouerthrow" (4.1.19). The overthrow of the private state is the focus of the false-friends episodes, and overthrow of the "publike" is the focus of the justice episodes in Book V. Ate exploits the false pride, or unsubordinated self-love, that allows the overthrow of the private person, the pride that leads to the discord in the Blandamour and Paridell episodes. Duessa plays a minor role in the false-friendship episodes, but in Book V, as Mary Stuart, she exploits the false pride that leads to the discord of sedition, rebellion, and anarchy.

Ate's function, "to trouble noble knights, / Which hunt for honor" (19), accounts for the characterization of Paridell and Blandamour as bona fide knights, but sufficiently frail to be vulnerable to her and Duessa's machinations. Blandamour and Paridell will engage in combat for what they consider worthy purposes, such as maintaining their perceptions of themselves as worthy knights, fighting for their ladies, and fighting for the temporary bonds that are, for them, friendship. Blandamour is described as "a jollie youthful knight, / That bore great sway in armes and chiualrie," a man "of mickle might" (32). And both Blandamour and Paridell later participate in the tourney for Florimell's girdle along with the other knights. Their strength and willingness to exercise that strength in knightly combat is important to their reflection in human form of the energy, the combativeness, and the self-destructiveness of the elements in Chaos. Such qualities contrast them with true knights and also with the unknightly Braggadocchio, who refuses to fight Blandamour for the False Florimell and is immune to Ate's attempts to stir his passions: "But naught he [Braggadocchio] car'd for friend or enemy, / For in base mind nor friendship dwels nor enmity" (4.4.11). Unlike Braggadocchio, who lacks pride and also combativeness, both Blandamour and Paridell have concepts of self and honor, however false, that Ate can corrupt, and so both are suitable victims.

That Blandamour and Paridell "hunt for honor," however imperfectly, describes the only positive aspect of their characterizations. Blandamour, whose

name, "did descrie / His fickle mind full of inconstancie" (4.1.32), is inconstant
to the point of mental instability; his vacillation between extreme emotional states
approximates the manic-depressive. When Paridell refuses to fight Britomart
again, Blandamour, the "hot-spurre youth," impulsively gives Ate to Paridell and
takes after Britomart so fast "that one him scarce could see" (35). His defeat at
the hands of Britomart plunges him from exhilaration into a state "as sad, as
whilome iollie" (36) and he becomes depressed "with wondrous griefe of mynd,
/ And shame" (37). Blandamour's false pride is such that he is either unable to
see things as they are or is compelled to misrepresent them. Wounded from his
fight with Britomart, he urges Paridell to fight Scudamour on the ground that he,
Blandamour, had just fought for Paridell's sake, when he had done no such thing;
he had fought to win the "louely ladie," Amoret. Blandamour also accuses
Scudamour of taking advantage of Paridell when the fight between the two was
clearly fair (44) and then shortly thereafter shows his own flawed sense of fair
play by impulsively unhorsing Ferraugh without even giving him fair warning.

The direct influence of Ate on the false friends is more apparent in the next
episode, in which Blandamour wins the False Florimell. Blandamour, in a manic
phase brought on by his cowardly defeat of Ferraugh, begins to gloat over his
victory and to berate Paridell for not rising to the occasion (4.2.7); and Paridell,
just as consumed by unsubordinated self-love and consequently just as faulty in
his "hunt for honor," envies Blandamour's possession of the False Florimell. Ate
urges Paridell on by stirring in him a mix of passions that gives expression to his
envy. She reminds Paridell of Blandamour's boastfulness and also appeals to
Paridell's sense of his "owne more worth" (12). Paridell then reminds Blandamour
of their pact to share in the spoils, causing Blandamour to go into a rage. The
problem with the friendship as well as with the psyches of both Paridell and
Blandamour is the inconstancy expressed in their inability to control self-love by
subordinating themselves to external bonds, here the bonds of friendship. They
fight and they fight with strength and knightly skill, but their physical prowess
does not make them virtuous, because their combat is caused by hate: "So mortall
was their malice and so sore, / Become of fayned friendship which they vow'd
afore" (18). Throughout the false friends episodes Spenser deliberately and effectively turns upside down commonplaces about friendship from such as Sir
Thomas Elyot (ultimately from Cicero and Aristotle): "[F]rendship can nat be
without vertue" and "[I]n them that be constante is neuer mistrust or suspition,
nor any surmise or iuell reporte can withdrawe them from their affection, and
hereby frendship is made perpetuall and stable."[4]

Neither Paridell nor Blandamour is entirely evil, but both are weak. Both, like ordinary human beings, need a structuring force that could buttress their virtues and stem their errancies; instead, the influence of Ate and Duessa, as in the encounter of the false friends with Scudamour, prevails. Ate's carefully crafted lies about Britomart and Amoret not only worsen the relationship between Scudamour and Blandamour and Paridell, but they stir up such powerful discord within Scudamour that he is ready to kill Glauce (4.1.52). The initiating comment of the following canto describes discord as the "Firebrand of hell," a power "whose small sparkes once blowen / None but a God or godlike man [like Orpheus or David or Menenius Agrippa] can slake." In *The Faerie Queene*, the efforts of such "godlike" men are matched by Arthur, Cambina, and Mercilla-Elizabeth, among others. However, when Glauce, who obviously lacks godlike power, attempts to bring peace to the group, both Blandamour and Paridell, moved by the "Ate" within them, attack her:

> Both they vnwise, and warelesse of the euill,
> That by themselues vnto themselues is wrought,
> Through that false witch, and that foule aged dreuill,
> The one a feend, the other an incarnate deuill.
>
> (4.2.3)

The false friendship of Blandamour and Paridell is a dance in the sense that the discordant elements in Chaos danced. And Ate is ultimately the evil that ordinary human beings, those in whom self-love dominates, work "by themselues vnto themselues" when they yield to their own inner impulses and thus fail to subordinate themselves to the structuring force of an ordered society. Ate and Duessa, unlike Cambina and Arthur, have no actual powers in themselves; they can operate only through the tendencies toward self-love in others and are consequently limited to inciting the passions of those incapable of subordinating themselves to rightful ways. The celebrated use of Renaissance social and political commonplaces by Shakespeare's Ulysses makes the point that when society is threatened, individuality is a form of insubordination, inconstancy, and/or instability (*Troilus and Cressida*, 1.3.101–26). Spenser's Blandamour and Paridell make a similar point.

The antithesis of the chaos created by the false friends appears in the conclusions of the concord stories of Campbell and Triamond and Amyas and Placidas, stories that create little true communities of four united both by friendship and by chaste love: the male pairs are friends, the female pairs are friends, and the appropriate male-female pairs are in love, each of the groups "linckt in louely bond" (4.2.31). The stories are designed in part, but only in part, to illustrate the commonplace Renaissance idea that friendship, as found in Cicero and later in, say, Sir Thomas Elyot, is founded on virtue and similitude:

> For as Tulli saieth, Nothinge is more to be loued or to be ioyned to gether, than similitude of good maners or vertues; where in be the same or semblable studies, the same willes or desires, in them it hapneth that one in an other as moche deliteth as in him selfe. (*The Boke Named the Gouernour*, 2:161)

This understanding of friendship, fictionalized over and over as "one soul in bodies twain," is more clearly the basis of the friendship of Amyas and Placidas; the twinlike identity of Cambell and Triamond, besides being more or less implied, is not revealed until the occasion for their animosity toward one another is over. The appeal of such stories is to be found in Cicero's analysis of the audience's response to the grand moment in a play about Orestes and Pylades when each attempts to sacrifice himself for the other:

> The herers that stode aboute, preised it with clapping their handes, beying but a matter feigned. What thinke we then thei would have doen in a true matter. Here nature her selfe did soone bewraie her own ernestenesse, when these men judged the same to be well dooen in another, whiche they could not doe them selfes. (*The Booke of Freendeship*, trans. John Harington of Stepney, 151)

Through perfect friendship, both Orestes and Pylades accomplish that ultimate victory over self-love which is denied to real human beings, as do the twinlike heroes in Elyot's story of Titus and Gysippus, one of the pairs of friends who make their appearance in Spenser's Temple of Venus. Gysippus, although himself truly in love with and about to marry Sophronia, recognized that Titus's love for her was greater than his own and, out of friendship, arranged for Titus to substitute himself for Gysippus in the wedding bed, thereby making Sophronia Titus's wife. That Sophronia apparently just shifts her affections to Gysippus when he gives her the ring and "looses the girdle of her virginity" is another of the typical views of relationships between the sexes published in the Renaissance. Cicero makes the same connection between such friendships and the necessary harmony of society as we are asked to make about the concord stories in *The Faerie Queene*. Without friendship

> neither any citie be able to continue, no not the tillage of the land can endure. And if this can not be understand herebi, yet of strife and debate it maie wel be percieved, how great the power of concorde and freendship is. For what howse so

stedie, or what cities standes so faste, but thorough hatered and strife, it may be utterlie overthrowen? (*The Booke of Freendeship*, 150)

However, Spenser's stories of Cambell and Triamond and Amyas and Placidas are not, in theme, friendship stories. In true friendship stories, friendship is demonstrated to be the prime virtue by prevailing over some other form of love, usually love between the sexes. Spenser's goal is a concord achieved by a combination of chaste love between those of different sex and friendship between those of the same sex. Spenser heartily promoted a complementarity achieved by the subordination of the female to the male and the subordination of the male to the love that unites the two sexes. However, at least in the middle books of *The Faerie Queene* he did not view society from the typically Renaissance narrow male point of view, as found in Elyot's story of Titus and Gysippus. In that view society is perceived to consist essentially of relationships between males and consequently the relationships between males and females, while necessary to the continuation of the human race and crucial to the well-being of both males and females, occupy a lower place in the hierarchy of love.

And that the two observations in Book IV on the nature of friendship are consonant with the commonplace view of the superiority of friendship to other forms of love does not alter in any significant way Spenser's overall views on the relationship of the sexes. Prompted by the true friendship of Amyas and Placidas, the narrator evaluates the "three kinds of loue" and says that "zeale of friends combynd with vertues meet" surpasses both love of kin and chaste love because "loue of soule doth loue of bodie passe / No lesse then perfect gold surmounts the meanest brasse" (4.9.2). But friendship is not presented in the action of that story as superior to chaste love between the sexes and there is no love of kin treated in the story. The stanzas on friendship that interrupt Scudamour's progression through the Temple of Venus provide another anomaly. After describing the chaste lovers who "together by themselues did sport / Their spotlesse pleasures, and sweet loues content," Scudamour describes "another sort"

> Of louers lincked in true harts consent;
> Which loued not as these, for like intent [inclination],
> But on chast vertue grounded their desire,
> Farre from all fraud, or fayned blandishment;
> Which in their spirits kindling zealous fire,
> Braue thought and noble deedes did euermore aspire.

If the intention were to contrast true friendship with the general run of other relationships between human beings, these stanzas would be appropriate to

Spenser's allegory of love, but the stanzas interrupt the progress of the sexually driven, faithful, and virtuous Scudamour toward the winning of the sexually receptive, faithful, and virtuous Amoret. Scudamour's love is also based on "chaste vertue" and is "Farre from all fraud, or fayned blandishment." In the action of the middle books of *The Faerie Queene,* it is chaste love between the sexes, not friendship, that, "kindling zealous fire," inspires "Braue thought and noble deedes." Besides, the continuity here would be improved if the two stanzas on friendship were left out. The lines immediately preceding those on friendship refer to the lovers who "did sport / Their spotlesse pleasures, and sweet loues content"; and in the stanza immediately following the two on friendship, Scudamour, who had "neuer tasted blis," is described as envying the "endlesse happinesse" of the chaste lovers: "That being free from feare and gealosye, / Might frankely there their loues desire possesse" (4.10.28), a reference that skips back over the friendship stanzas as if they were not there. I believe these friendship stanzas, as well as those just previously discussed, were simply inserted at this point so as to give a friendship coloration to the fiction.

These difficulties of incorporating traditional notions about friendship into the narrative stream do not, however, diminish the role of friendship, love based on virtue and similitude, in Spenser's overall allegory of love. The union achieved through friendship is analogous to the union of the elements into the four strata of the cosmos by means of similitude. The overall stable cosmos was created when God caused the four, essentially stable levels of earth, water, air and fire to come together, partly through the inherent attraction of like to like. As Du Bartas would have it,

> when the Mouth *Diuine*
> Op'ned, to each his proper Place assigne,
> Fire flew to Fire, Water to Water slid,
> Aire clung to Aire, and Earth with Earth abid.
>
> (41)

Further, even the bonding of the adjacent, antagonistic elements is by means of the like qualities of those elements—Du Bartas would have the like qualities to join the different strata as country maidens join hand in hand in a May Day dance—just as Spenser's Concord has Love and Hate join hands. And the joining of the likenesses also apparently serves in Du Bartas to separate the discordant:

> Water, as arm'd with moisture and with cold,
> The cold-dry Earth with her one hand doth hold;

> With th'other th'Aire: The Aire, as moist and warme,
> Holds Fire with one; Water with th'other arme:

(42)

This Lucretius-like physics of attraction and repulsion is, of course, only subordinately operative in both the creation of and the maintenance of the cosmos. God's spoken word, in Du Bartas's inimitable metaphor, provided the essential force. Nothing would have happened,

> Saue that the Lord, into the Pile did poure
> Some secret Mastike of his sacred Power,
> To glew together and to gouerne faire
> The Heau'n and Earth, the Ocean, and the Aire,

(12)

The bonding of the friends is thus important to the macrocosmic implications of the poem. A cosmological analogue for a permanent bond that can unite virtuous males and females, a bond that is as important to the little concordant communities as is friendship, is another matter, because there is nothing physical, nothing *within* unlikes that can account for a permanent bond. The sting of lust and the pleasure in its satisfaction serve to bring males and females of whatever virtue together temporarily, but not permanently. However, something on the order of God's uniting the disparate bands of elements is supplied by the power of chaste love. Spenser understands chaste love between the sexes as a "sacred fire . . . ykindled first aboue, / Emongst th'eternall spheres . . . And thence pourd into men" (3.3.1) because chaste love bonds males and females permanently. As I indicated earlier, I believe this passage, rather than evoking Neoplatonic notions, relates the love that unites those unlikes, Britomart and Artegall, to the love by which God formed the cosmos from the unlike elements. The chaste, rather than the Heavenly, Venus is a force in Spenser's allegory of love that is analogous to that by which God created the cosmos.

It is clear that Spenser would have the reader to accept the story of Cambell and Triamond as at least *a* major component of Book IV. He features it in the title of his book of Friendship, just as he features the story of Red Crosse in Book I; and he introduces the group of true friends, Cambell and Triamond and Cambina and Canacee, "linckt in louely bond," as a clear contrast to the false friends, Ate and Duessa and Blandamour and Paridell (4.2.31). Yet, for the most part, the story is more like an "accident" than an "intendment." In the first place, although it is the title story of Book IV, it has no relationship to the Faery court, nor is it, as are the structuring stories in the middle books, a quest in any plain sense of the word. Scudamour leaves the Faery court on a quest authorized by Gloriana to rescue Amoret; Artegall leaves the Faery court on an authorized quest to rescue Irena; Florimell leaves the Faery court on her own to find Marinell; Britomart is on a quest, entirely unrelated to the Faery court, to bring Artegall back to England; and Arthur is on a quest to find the Faery Queen. Indeed, Spenser seems to have seen the need to focus the attention of the reader on the friendship theme in the Cambell and Triamond story by introducing it at a point when the group is "linkt in louely bond" and in contrast to the false friends, instead of beginning at the chronological beginning of the story, where other themes such as mortality, fate, brotherly love, and chaste love between the sexes would have misled the reader.

Spenser also clearly intended the Amyas and Placidas story to complement that of Cambell and Triamond, because it also concludes in the creation of a little community united by friendship between members of the same sex and by chaste love between the appropriate members of the different sexes. And it also is set beside a false-friends episode so that the final proper subordination of self-love by the virtuous is contrasted with the inability or refusal of the false friends to subordinate themselves. In addition, the story contributes a fuller treatment of friendship as the attraction of similitude, Amyas and Placidas being more clearly than Cambell and Triamond the traditional twinlike friends whose friendship is paramount in their lives. The comparative poverty of the fiction, however, is apparent when one looks in the major studies for discussion of the story and finds only brief references. And, indeed, my interests are not in exploring the fiction, per se, but in examining the implications of what I see as Spenser's manipulation of story materials so that Arthur, like Cambina, can function as the central source of power and authority essential, in Spenser's mind, for social concord.

More pointedly, I am convinced that Spenser removed the heart of this friendship story, the voluntary substitution through which one friend demonstrates the paramount value of the friendship, so as to give Arthur a role in the story necessary to the allegory. Placidas recounts how he went to Corflambo's castle where Amyas was prisoner and, being mistaken for his friend, was imprisoned and reunited with him. Here are the beginnings of a scheme whereby the substitution of one friend for another is, one would think, to be the means for working out the problem of the story. Amyas is aggrieved when he sees that Placidas is now also imprisoned because, as one would expect in a friendship story, all his joy is in his friend and in his loved one, Aemylia, and, again as one would expect, his greater love is for his friend, Placidas. Placidas then counters Amyas's grief:

But I with better reason him auiz'd,
  And shew'd him how through error and mis-thought
  Of our like persons eath to be disguiz'd,
  Or his exchange, or freedome might be wrought.

(4.8.58)

But no such substitution takes place. Released from prison by the dwarf so he can go to see the enamoured Poeana, who believes he is Amyas, Placidas inexplicably picks up the dwarf who was watching over him and takes off, abandoning his friend and leaving him in prison. However incongruous in a friendship story, this act of betrayal provides the means for working the Arthurian rescue into the story through Arthur's intercepting Corflambo's pursuit of Placidas. Another indication that a story involving a substitution is buried in the present one is Placidas's puzzling explanation of his seizing the dwarf: "Finding no meanes how I might vs enlarge, / But if that Dwarfe I could with me conuay" (61). Nothing emerges from this act either, although one can infer that the dwarf's keeping the keys to the prison would have had something to do with a scheme involving Placidas's substitution for Amyas.

In any event, Arthur's power and authority, not the interaction of characters within the bonds of friendship, resolve the conflicts of the story. The problem, after Amyas is rescued from Corflambo's prison, is to effect a concord of the foursome of Amyas and Placidas and Poeana and Aemylia comparable to that which unites the foursome of Cambell and Triamond and Cambina and Canacee. There is no problem with Aemylia and Amyas, since they are already truly in love; and there is no problem with Amyas and Placidas, because they are true friends throughout the story. The problem is to effect concord between Poeana and the others. Poeana is in love with Amyas, and now that Amyas and Aemylia have been reunited, she is grieved by the loss of her love, "the hope of her desire." She is also grieved by the loss of her father—Arthur had killed Corflambo—and her lands. Poeana had also not been the kind of young lady she should have been. Although she "were most faire and goodly dyde [complexioned?], / Yet she it all did mar with cruelty and pride" and had also defaced her beauty "with lewd loues and lust intemperate" (4.9.13–16). Arthur smooths out all of these difficulties through the force of his rhetoric:

But her the Prince through his well wonted grace,
  To better termes of myldnesse did entreat,
  From that fowle rudenesse, which did her deface;
  And that same bitter corsiue, which did eat
  Her tender heart, and make refraine from meat,

> He with good thewes and speaches well applyde,
> Did mollifie, and calme her raging heat.
>
> (14)

Moreover, Arthur is able to move Placidas to love Poeana with similar dispatch: "That trusty Squire he wisely well did moue / Not to despise that dame, which lou'd him liefe [we do not get Poeana's change of affection from Amyas to Placidas], / Till he had made of her some better priefe, / But to accept her to his wedded wife" (4.9.15). The result of Arthur's rhetoric is that the foursome lives happily ever after: "From that day forth in peace and ioyous blis, / They liu'd together long without debate, / Ne priuate iarre, ne spite of enemis / Could shake the safe assuraunce of their state" (16). The foursome is now bonded in the perfect state of concord that binds the foursome of Cambell and Triamond and Cambina and Canacee. And, as with the Cambell and Triamond story, the union achieved is the product both of the bonds of chaste love and those of friendship.

But the bonds of friendship, as in the story of Cambell and Triamond, are not created within the story, nor do they function importantly in the story. That friendship is a union of similitude and consequently is conceptually a more noble force than is chaste love is developed not in narrative action—there are no grand moments in which the bonds of friendship prevail over the bonds of chaste love—but in more expository moments, in comments such as the "zeale of friends combynd with vertues meet" surpasses both love of kin and chaste love because "loue of soule doth loue of bodie passe, / No lesse then perfect gold surmounts the meanest brasse" (4.9.1,2).

In the past two or three decades, little attention has been paid to the seams that Josephine Bennett uncovered in *The Faerie Queene*.[5] As long as one maintains that Spenser was essentially uninterested in story or that the story becomes meaningful only through analogy to higher realms of being, then one can agree with Roche that Bennett's findings do not trouble one's sense of the poem.[6] However, when one attempts to follow the story, difficulties are apparent and troublesome.

6

Toward Mercilla's Castle

ARTEGALL'S quest in Book V focuses Spenser's allegory on the love that unites the commonwealth, the love that forms the apex of Spenser's hierarchy of sublunary love. In Spenser's overall vision of social harmony, justice is, in part, the product of chaste love and friendship and, in part, the social order necessary for chaste love and friendship. For the nation to be united in true social harmony, both true friendship and true sexual love must flourish; and neither friendship nor sexual love can truly flourish without social order. The adventures of Artegall, Arthur, and Britomart in Book V complete this reciprocal relationship and so complete the vision begun in Book III. The controlling theme of all the adventures in Book V, including the episodes at Isis Church and Mercilla's Castle, is the necessity of subordination; and Britomart's appearance in Book V, including her stay at Isis Church, serves to reintroduce into the overall allegory of love the healthy subordination of the sexes that is the continuing concern of the adventures in Books III and IV.

My endeavor in this chapter will be to counter the consensual view that while Artegall's adventures in Book V focus on the suppression of disorder, *true* justice is expressed in the iconography of equity and mercy at Isis Church and Mercilla's Castle. When understood as part of an overall allegory of love, Spenser's ideas about social order are not limited to the suppression of disorder. However, the attempts to separate a true justice—a merciful, equitable, Christian justice—from justice as the maintenance of order distorts Spenser's social vision.[1] Clemency is never exercised in Book V except perhaps for the faithful in Mercilla's Castle who are being dealt "righteous doome" (5.9.23). Although we may read the iconography in Isis Church so as to associate Britomart with clemency, she never once restrains Artegall's "sterne behests" or "cruell doomes." Britomart's appearance in Book V, instead of softening Spenserian justice, reinforces the grand principle of subordination, in part by her removal of Radigund's head.

And equity is a minor theme in Book V, illustrated clearly only in the Amidas and Bracidas episode. What is missing from Spenser's *Legend of Artegall or of Iustice* is the sense that each of us needs understanding and mercy, that none of us, if judged according to our "desert," would escape a whipping. As to be expected of one emotionally committed to the status quo, Spenser's sympathies are with the police; and my thesis does not require me to downplay those sympathies.

Christian principles are essential to Spenserian justice, but they apply differently to those who subordinate themselves and those who do not. The children of God are not to be judged Polonius-fashion. But, on the other hand, in orthodox sixteenth-century Christian thought those who do not properly subordinate themselves to their heavenly father are so judged and are to be treated at least as severely as Artegall, Talus, and (despite her *expression* of compassion) Mercilla treat those who fail to subordinate themselves to proper earthly authority. True justice as expressed in the actions of Book V is like God's justice. Even at Mercilla's Castle, justice as a positive expression of love is found only in the voluntary subordination of the virtuous and in the reciprocated grace by which the queen responds to the love expressed in voluntary subordination. Justice to outsiders is administered first of all by the personified Awe, who, by preventing those moved by "guyle, and malice, and despight" (5.9.22) from entering the castle and receiving "righteous doome," marginalizes the undeserving, those guilty of thought crimes, whether or not they have committed criminal acts. Within the castle we get the punishment of the convicted: Malfont, the scurrilous poet who blasphemed the queen, has his tongue nailed to a post and Duessa-Mary Stuart is condemned to die.

I begin the final chapter as I began the first, with a reference to Cardinal Pole's commonplace equation of love with civility, order, and justice: "[I]n a cuntrey, cyty, or towne, ther ys perfayt cyuylyte, ther ys the true commyn wele, where as al the partys, as membrys of one body, be knyt togyddur in perfayt loue and vnyte." The deficiencies in such a system derive from the tendencies of fallen creatures toward self-love and their consequent inability or refusal to subordinate themselves voluntarily to proper order. The difference between Starkey and Spenser is in the intensity with which each identifies himself with the need for social order. Unlike Spenser, Starkey communicates a sense of proportion, an understanding that the society works but could work better if people were not so governed by self-love: "For me semyth," Starkey has Lupset say, "playnly wyth vs euery man, vnder the pretens[e and] colour of the commyn wele, regardyth the syngular, by the reson whereof our cuntrey lyth rude, no thyng brough[t] to such cyuylyte as hyt myght be by gud pollycy."[2]

The vision of hierarchical harmony in middle books of *The Faerie Queene* contrasts with that in Ben Jonson's vision of Penshurst, where the lord and lady, "in restraining their own self-love . . . provide the moral capital on which the whole productive community is based."[3] Mercilla expresses this ideal by subordinating herself to the good of the commonwealth and so serving as the godlike source of power and authority in the trial of Duessa as well as the center of reference for Artegall's and Arthur's exercises of force. But the middle books focus on the threat to order and the removal of threat rather than on the benefits of order. In the middle books Spenser is relaxed about social order only in moments when the demonic other is defeated, in moments of unthreatened stability, such as that after Arthur destroys Geryoneo and Geryoneo's monster and the common folk join in a celebration much like the one after Redcrosse kills the dragon. Elsewhere in the middle books the common folk, rather than members of a productive community, are perceived as a threat. Their ignorant self-love makes them willing dupes of the Leveler Giant, who transforms them into a "rascal crew" (5.2.52) bent upon destroying the social hierarchy; and they are also easy victims of Ate when, in her attempt to destroy all harmony, she manifests herself as "false rumors and seditious trouble / Bred in assemblies of the vulgar sort, / That still are led with euery light report" (4.1.28).

The tone of Book V derives from a fear for social stability comparable to that in the homilies on obedience and the tone in both is, in part, the product of the same fear of the energies set free by disorder. From "An exhortation concerning good order and obedience to Rulers and Magistrates":

> For where there is no ryght order, there raigneth all abuse, carnall libertie, enormitie, sinne, and Bablonicall confusion. Take awaye Kynges, Princes, Rulers, Magistrates, Judges, and such estates of Gods order, no man shall ride or goe by the high way vnrobbed, no man shall sleepe in his owne house or bed vnkylled, no man shal keepe his wife, children, and possessions in quietnesse, all thynges shalbe common, and there must nedes folow al mischiefe, and vtter destruction both of soules, bodyes, goodes, and common wealthes. . . .

Today, we understand our universe to be held together by forces inherent in the very particles by which it is constituted, and we have developed social theories appropriate to that understanding. As a result, we have difficulty appreciating the fears for social stability in those who lived in a cosmos that was created by the imposition of order on mutually repellent particles and continues to exist in a state of tension only because the attractive, cohesive love is stronger than the repelling, destructive hate. I do not mean to imply a pervasive fear on the part of Spenser's contemporaries that God might withdraw his love—that would be a solution. The problem was whether the bonds of society that were the product of the mutual love of monarch and subject would hold. Those bonds were produced by voluntary and moral acts; and Elizabethans were no more deluded about the extent to which human beings are governed by proper moral considerations than are we.

We should also remind ourselves that things *were* unstable in Spenser's England. There was serious uncertainty caused by the problem of succession to an aging virgin queen. Whatever views Spenser may have had on the specifics, whether succession should follow the Stuart or the Suffolk line, are not, as far as I can tell, detectable in *The Faerie Queene*. Spenser apparently was obeying his queen's edict not to discuss the succession. He was, however, vitally and observably concerned with the larger question of corporate perpetuity. I explore in the middle books of *The Faerie Queene* the theme that Marie Axton finds in Robert Chester's and Shakespeare's allegorizations of the queen's two bodies through the phoenix and turtle: perpetuity in the body politic depends upon the bonding of monarch and subject by true love.[4]

And, finally, all through Spenser's life, the English perceived themselves to be threatened by the Rome-Madrid axis, a threat that manifested itself in invasion, in rebellion, and in subversion both from without and from within. I can well imagine a youthful and sensitive Spenser being affected by Tudor propaganda in the same way as sensitive American youths were affected by the anti-Communist propaganda of the late 1940s and 1950s. From "An Homilie against disobedience and wilfull rebellion":

> Or is it not most euident that the Bishop of Rome hath of late attempted by his Irish Patriarkes and Bishops, sent from Rome with his Bulles, (whereof some were apprehended) to breake down the barres and hedges of the publique peace in Ireland, onely vpon confidence easily to abuse the ignorance of the wilde Irish men? Or who seeth not that vpon like confidence, yet more lately hee hath likewise procured the breach of the publique peace in England, (with the long and blessed continuance whereoff hee is fore grieued) by the ministery of his disguised Chaplaynes, creeping in Lay mens apparell into the houses, and whispering in the eares of certaine Northern borderers, being then most ignorant of their duetie to GOD and to their Prince of all people of the Realme, whom therefore as most meete and ready to execute his intended purpose, hee hath by the said ignorant Base priests, as blinde guides leading the blinde, brought those seely blinde subiects into the deepe ditch of rebellion. . . .

I doubt that most of Spenser's contemporaries pursued their daily activities fearful of social dissolution. Shakespeare *uses* the mind-set I describe to create a Ulysses who *voices* those fears to some extent at least for reasons having to do with their rhetorical effect. But Spenser's continuing concern with mutability, or instability, both natural and social, indicates that he had internalized those fears. For Spenser, constancy is the cardinal virtue in the mutable social world as well as in the mutable natural world. And constancy in the social world is, as it is in the natural world, the product of a subordination that produces a complementarity of disparate elements.

Sir Thomas Elyot's view that even an understanding of justice is a product of proper thoughts expressed in proper living provides the entrée to characterization and quest in Book V:

> Verely the knowlege of Justyce is nat so difficile or harde to be attayned unto by man as it is communely supposed, if he wolde nat willingly abandone the excellencie of his propre nature, and folisshely applicate him selfe to the nature of creatures unreasonable, in the stede of reason embrasinge sensualitie, and for societie and beneuolence folowinge wilfulnesse and malice . . . (*The Boke Named the Gouernour*, 2:201)

The "nature of creatures unreasonable," "sensuality," and "wilfulnesse and malice," all say the same thing as do, on the other hand, "reason," "society," and "beneuolence." Proper subordination entails love and order and goodness and rationality, and the refusal to subordinate oneself entails malice and chaos and evil and insanity. The idea that underlies all the characterizations and all the relationships among characters in the middle books is that God's love operates *in* the virtuous, always imperfectly and sometimes belatedly, enabling them to subordinate themselves to the greater social good; and God's love, through the power of the prince, operates *on* the vicious, either compelling them to subordinate themselves or, more usually, by destroying them. The image of the elements in chaos, which had "lyen confused euer" and "with contrary forces to conspyre / Each against other . . . Threatning their owne confusion and decay" (*An Hymne in Honovr of Love*, 77–82), is especially relevant to the characterization of the vicious, because although initially seeming to possess great power, they lack the true integrating principle. They are comprised of inherently unstable forces that more or less explode when confronted with true power. Evil in Book V is insanity, an inability to achieve an internal order and consequently an inability to accommodate oneself to proper external order. The conflict in Book V is, finally, between sanity and insanity.

We do not know how Spenser's contemporaries reacted to the middle books of *The Faerie Queene*. Modern scholars have separated out Book V from the larger allegory of love and have reserved for it the distaste we have for that subordination of the self to the state which is at the heart of Spenser's program. Greenblatt rightly declares that *The Faerie Queene* is "wholly wedded to the autocratic ruler of the English state"; however, what Greenblatt calls Spenser's "repellent political ideology" is more than a "passionate worship of imperialism," and it is expressed in ways more fundamental than the "virtuous violence" with which a *Faerie Queene* hero defeats the demonic object of a quest.[5] It is an identification of the good of the individual with the good of the state and the good of the state with the subordination of individual to the state. The desperate need for civility that pervades the middle books manifests itself not so much in the defeat and mastery of alien cultures such as the American Indian or the Irish or even the rejection within the culture of such "alien" influences as Catholicism, but in the mastery of that truly pervasive enemy of civility, the unsubordinated self-love that causes native English, whether Protestant or Catholic, to be enemies of the state. Such is the commonplace *view* of society and the perhaps less than commonplace *feeling* about social stability that provide the entrée to the combination of Britomart's and Artegall's quests into a *Legend of . . . Iustice*.

In the prologue to Book V, Spenser sets the scene in the "stonie" age and describes the operation of justice in this present world, not necessarily Spenser's contemporary England but the fallen world where God must lend his power to princes, his vice-regents on earth, so that they can yoke fallen creatures, good and bad, into a proper, hierarchical social structure (5.proem.10). In the last stanza of the proem, the "magnificke might and wondrous wit" that Elizabeth uses to "aread" "righteous doome" to her people are equated with those same qualities that her "instrument," Artegall, finds necessary for his administration of justice in Faeryland. Spenser's equation of Artegall with the earlier champions of justice, Bacchus and Hercules, indicates that the justice that Artegall embodies is not the product of any evolutionary process that may have taken place since the destruction of the golden age.[6]

In fact, Spenser would seem to short-circuit any sense of development through time in this legend by having Artegall straddle the golden and the "stonie" ages, for it was before Astraea left earth, before the seeds of vice took root, that she found Artegall and brought him to Faeryland to rear as a champion of justice. And at the same time he has a place in history much later than the end of the golden age, for he is to be the husband of Britomart and the progenitor of the line that culminates in Elizabeth. The clear point made at the beginning of Book V is that in an age of vice, whether in Faeryland or Elizabethan England or in the world even shortly after the golden age, princely power is necessary to effect justice among fallen creatures, creatures governed by self-love. Spenser's practical plan in the *Vewe* for the destruction of the Irish culture, which was to begin

with the sword so that the "Royall power of the Prince" could thereafter "stretche
it selfe forthe in her Chiefe strengthe," was the necessary prolegomenon to a
moral reformation of "a people alltogeather stubborne and/vntamed," to "bringe
them from their delighte of licentious barbarisme," from "their libertye and
naturall fredome which in theire *madnes* they affecte" "vnto the loue of goodnes
and Civilitye" (emphasis added).[7] Britomart, Arthur, and Artegall function in
Book V largely as instruments of that power; and the "merciful" Mercilla functions largely as the focus of that power. The relationships between those "instruments" and Mercilla, as well as the relationship between Mercilla and her true
subjects depicted in her castle, constitute the positive image of justice.

II

I follow the traditional division of Book V into thirds: Artegall's initial adventures, the continuation of Britomart's quest, and the Mercilla episodes, which,
in this study, include Artegall's rescue of Irena. My final and essential task is to
work out the relationship between the continuation of Britomart's quest and
those quests of Artegall and Arthur which relate more clearly to foreign than to
domestic policy. Artegall's initial adventures illustrate the subordination of self-
love necessary for a healthy society, as does, in a different way, the continuation
of Britomart's quest into Book V and the episode at Mercilla's Castle. The problem is to understand Arthur's rescue of Belge and Artegall's rescue of Burbon
and Irena—adventures that take place outside Mercilla's realm—as expressions
of the same theme.

At the beginning of the book, Artegall has a series of three encounters with
those who, through false pride or unsubordinated self-love, do not properly subordinate themselves. The first is the knight, Sangliere, who had appropriated a
young squire's lady and then had beheaded his own lady when she pleaded with
him not to leave her. Sangliere's characterization consists exclusively of manifestations of false pride. The squire describes him to Artegall as "with pride
vpblowne," he is twice described as scornful, he answers Artegall's queries with
"sterne countenance and indignant pride," and, after the judgment, will not take
up the head of his dead lady until Talus has "his pride represt" (5.1.13–29).
More revealing is the psychotic impulsiveness of his beheading of his lady. Sangliere
is only the first of the villains in *The Legend of . . . Iustice* who is, in Elyot's words,
"in the stede of reason [following] sensualitie, and for societie and beneuolence
folowinge wilfulnesse and malice. . . ." Sangliere demonstrates instability either
by perceiving the squire's lady to be fairer than his own or by having wearied of

his own; and his instability becomes evidently psychotic when he simply throws his lady from his horse, grabs the squire's, and then in a fit of wrath beheads his lady when she pleads for death rather than rejection. Sangliere is Blandamour taken to the extreme.

The episode has been criticized for lacking verisimilitude—why, one may very well ask, was Sangliere not tried for murder? But the point, whether we like it or not, is that through his judicious application of Solomon's gambit, Artegall brings justice to a difficult situation in which a superior has wronged an inferior by appropriating the inferior's lady without cause. Artegall preserves the social structure by effecting justice without any action by the inferior against his superior, or even any questioning of his superior. As the homilies on obedience make clear, the correlative of the doctrine of the divine right of authority is the doctrine of nonresistance and passive obedience. The difficulties, from the point of view of the knight of justice, arise from the inapplicability of the judicial procedures of customary knightly romance: trial by oath would not work because Sangliere had, to Artegall's satisfaction, already proved himself a liar; trial by combat between a knight and a squire is clearly inappropriate; and trial by ordeal is designed to uncover hidden crimes. The squire has been called weak for choosing to yield rather than to fight, but his submissiveness is the appropriate response of an inferior to wrongs done to him by a superior. Pointedly, even after his judgment that Sangliere is to carry the head of the dead lady for a year, Artegall preserves the proprieties by addressing his inferior, the squire, as "thou" and his equal, the knight, as "you" (28). A similar submission to authority marks Artegall's quietly heroic response to the villainy perpetrated on him by Envy, Detraction, and the Blatant Beast in the final stanzas of Book V. The book of justice begins and ends on the same fundamental note: the hierarchical social structure must be maintained if civility is to survive.

Artegall's next encounter with Pollente and his daughter, Munera, is another variation on the correction of the misuse of power and authority. Pollente, a usurper on a larger scale than Sangliere but on a smaller scale than the tyrants in the later episodes, has risen to power wrongfully, "Hauing great Lordships got and goodly farmes / Through strong oppression of his powre extort" (5.2.5), and, having gotten power wrongfully, necessarily misuses it. Inevitably in *The Faerie Queene* those who exercise power wrongly are those who have acquired that power wrongly. It is as if for Spenser the valid acquisition of power precludes the misuse of power and the usurpation of power inevitably results in the misuse of power. This notion makes Spenser an even more doctrinaire supporter of rightfully established order than an ordinary upholder of the status quo such as Robert Crowley, who urges beggars to accept their lot, to avoid "wycked ambition" and content themselves "with that degree . . . and walke therein upryte." Crowley, however, inveighs against the misuse of power generally—against the poor who should quiet themselves rather than raise an uproar, and against the rich, as a group, not just those who acquired riches wrongfully.[8] For Spenser, properly acquired power does not corrupt, and absolute power is absolutely necessary in a properly operating society. Those in the Faery Court who, moved by envy, recall Artegall before he can effect reform in Irena's realm are morally corrupt because they have acquired power wrongfully. Like the false courtier in *Colin Clout*, each seeks "with malice and with strife, / To thrust downe other into foule disgrace, / Himself to raise" (690–92). However, because the power to so recall comes ultimately from the Faery Queen, it must be obeyed and obeyed without question.

Pollente's specific offense is either the mere fact of the levy of a toll on the goods that pass over his bridge on the way to the market, or, perhaps, that he violates the principle of equity by making poor and rich alike pay the same "passage-penny" to get across the bridge. The emphasis, however, is not on a specific crime but on the wrongful acquisition of power and on the pride resulting from that acquisition. Munera, having so filled the coffers of her "wicked threasury" with Pollente's ill-gotten gains that "many Princes she in wealth exceeds," despises the many lords who desire her for a wife. And the falsity and instability of Pollente's ill-gotten power on which Munera's pride is based are briefly indicated in the behavior of his cut-off head, which "bit the earth for very fell despight, / And gnashed with his teeth, as if he band / High God, whose goodnesse he despaired quight" (18). Although in his summary the narrator says Pollente's fate should be a lesson for *all* mighty men, "In whose right hands great power is contayned, / That none of them the feeble ouerren, / But alwaies doe their powere within iust compasse pen" (19), the message here as in the rest of Book V is that "mighty men" who acquire power properly do not abuse it. Those who acquire it wrongly necessarily must abuse it, because they lack the stability and rationality that are the products of proper subordination.

The Leveler Giant is motivated by a pride more intellectual than that of the other villains in Book V and consequently he makes a more theoretical attack on justice as order. The episode is interesting primarily in its insistence on the fraudulence of the attack, even to the point that Spenser initially begs the question in several ways: he describes the giant as having "weighed vanity" and being "admired much of fooles, women, and boys" (5.2.30); he points out in different ways that the giant is attempting to soar far above his "forces"; and he discredits the giant's motives—it was "not the right, which he did seeke; / But rather stroue extremities to way" (49). Spenser also has the giant contradict himself— the giant says that his intentions are "that wrong were then surceast, / And from he most, that *some* were giuen to the least" and then immediately after declares hat in the new order "*all* the wealth of rich men to the poore will draw" (37, 38; emphasis added). The unreliability of the giant's thought processes do, however, remind us that "injustice" results when one, in Elyot's words, chooses "willingly to] abandone the excellence of his propre nature, and folisshely applicate himself to the nature of creatures unreasonable." The point of the episode is that Spenser has the giant make the worst possible argument for the redistribution of power and wealth in the society. He has the giant deny the principles that were believed to govern the cosmic hierarchy and then infer that a social hierarchy hat is patterned on those beliefs is thereby defective.

Artegall not surprisingly defeats the giant's argument by demonstrating that he universe is indeed properly ordered and then asserting the propriety of a social hierarchy that reflects the proper order of the cosmos. Artegall gives the appropriate answers to the giant's arguments that the sea has encroached on the and and that death has augmented the earth and then moves logically to tie the social organization to the natural organization: "He maketh Kings to sit in souerainty; / He maketh subiects to their powre obay" (41), and so on. When he giant is unable to weigh concepts such as truth and falsehood and turns, in a temperamental fit, against his balance, Artegall points out that the scales are not he problem, that "in the mind the doome of right must bee" (47). And a rightly ordered mind is one that can see the comparability of God's making hills that do not disdain the dales and dales that do not envy the hills, with his making "Kings to sit in souerainty" and "subiects to their powre obay." Unlike those creatures, animate and inanimate, who instinctively move to their places in the scheme of hings, humankind must choose either order and rationality or disorder and insanity. And *our* instincts lead us to the latter. Justice in *The Faerie Queene* is as much a moral as an intellectual concept.

The final discrediting of the giant comes at the end, when the narrator returns to the giant's willful wrongheadedness by reminding us that he did not seek ight, "But rather stroue extremities to way" (49) and Talus throws him over the rock into the sea, where he bursts apart: "So was the high aspyring with huge ruine humbled" (50). The giant is the clearest example so far of a seemingly powerful figure who, when confronted with true power, comes apart because he is comprised of forces that are integrated not by love but by hate. The giant is, however, different from all the others who attack established authority in Book V, because he attacks not just those who rightfully exercise authority but the theory of society and the universe itself. He is, consequently, not only to be presented as evil; Spenser apparently also felt compelled to make him look foolish so as to guarantee that his ideas would look absurd.

III

The narrative action as well as the mythology in the initial Book V episodes and in the later Souldan episode presents justice as a masculine endeavor. In the Mercilla episodes at the end of the book, love and justice and order are embodied in a female monarch, and Artegall and Arthur function as the male agents of that female monarch. Strictly speaking, of course, Artegall is an agent of Gloriana, but Gloriana doesn't appear in the poem. Mercilla-Elizabeth is the closest we come to a fictionalization of the Elizabeth in her Body politic, and Artegall's rescue of Irena and Arthur's rescue of Belge allegorize Spenser's views on English foreign policy. At Isis Church, however, Britomart and Artegall are depicted as partners in justice both in the mythological images of Britomart's dream and in the prophecy of a fiction in which she accompanies Artegall back to Britain and the two together bring justice (i.e., order and proper rulership) to Britain by defeating the Saxons.

The continuation of Britomart's quest in the middle of the book of justice—a quest in which she first destroys and then reforms Radigund's Amazonian society into a proper patriarchal order—reintroduces the necessary complementarity of male and female and masculine and feminine into Spenser's allegory of love. The episodes present the final ideological recuperation of Britomart's masculinity and consequently, allegorically, the ideological recuperation generally of the female's capacity for masculinity, i.e., physical and psychic strength. Britomart not only acknowledges and reestablishes patriarchy after she defeats Radigund but is openly and visibly appalled by the rule of women. The place for female capacities and powers, both feminine and masculine, Britomart's action says, is provided by the female's subordination of herself to the male and to patriarchal order. It is Britomart's final and, at least from the perspective of this study, one of her more meaningful acts.

The recuperation of Britomart's masculinity had actually begun in her Book IV meeting with Artegall. When Britomart and Artegall meet in combat, the knightly Britomart is Artegall's equal until she recognizes him as Artegall. Then, although she tries to keep her knightly, masculine capabilities at the fore, her "wrathfull courage gan appall" (4.6.26); and she is reduced to using a female weapon, her tongue—and even that does not obey her will. The tone of affectionate condescension here, as in Britomart's falling in love, is as revealing of Spenser's feelings about the proper relationship of male and female as any of the more serious moments in the poem. Britomart's female sexual response to Artegall overpowers the masculine and even the aggressively feminine in her characterization; and, becoming feminine, she remains feminine thereafter in that relationship. After Britomart is won and wooed by Artegall, she yields "her consent / To be his loue, and take him for her Lord" (41); and when he has to leave, she is a dependent female who devises little strategies to delay her lord's departure (45–46). Britomart's characterization is better understood not as an amalgamation of masculine and feminine, not as androgynous, but as comprising a polarity of masculine and feminine, each of which is expressed in situations appropriate to it: "Faire Lady she him [to Redcrosse] seemd, like Lady drest, / But fairest knight aliue, when armed was her brest" (3.2.4). These polarities become complementarities when she takes Artegall as her lord.

Artegall undergoes a different kind of transformation at that meeting. He had been governed by a narrow and self-enclosing masculinity, having previously despised women; and now he must subordinate himself, not to Britomart (except during the wooing) but to love. Glauce describes the required change:

> And you, Sir *Artegall*, the saluage knight,
>> Henceforth may not disdaine, that womans hand
>> Hath conquered you anew in second fight:
>> For whylome they haue conquerd sea and land,
>> And heauen it selfe, that nought may them withstand.
>> Ne henceforth be rebellious vnto loue,
>> That is the crowne of knighthood, and the band
>> Of noble minds deriued from aboue,
> Which being knit with vertue, neuer will remoue.
>
>> (4.6.31)

Artegall as "saluage knight" expresses a free masculinity, an uncivilized masculinity, which must be subordinated if there is to be civility. Spenser does not champion freedom. Malecasta, Hellenore, Paridell, Ate, Duessa, and the rest of the villains are free agents. Scudamour has been accused of embracing a masculinity comparable to that of Artegall, but from the beginning Scudamour loves Amoret and so is bound, is civilized, in a way Artegall is not until Artegall falls in love.

In *An Hymne in Honovr of Love*, Cupid simply compelled the elements "To keepe themselues within their sundrie raines" (87) and caused all creatures, except human beings, to increase themselves, "without further care," moved by a desire purely and simply physical (101). For "man," however, because there are "yet in his deducted spright, / Some sparks remaining of that heauenly fyre" (106–7), Cupid tipped his arrows with a beauty that, being both earthly and heavenly (Britomart is the "peerelesse paterne of Dame natures pride" *and* the "heauenly image of perfection"), arouses those remaining sparks of heavenly fire at the same time as it arouses sexual desire. The Neoplatonic implications serve to validate the love of Britomart and Artegall as it partakes of cosmic manifestations of love. My focus, however, is on the relationship between sexual desire and love and heroic deeds, on Spenser's allegorization of the roles of males and females in society, rather than on the relationship of the mundane to the spiritual. So viewed, there is, in effect, no difference between virtuous beauty and heavenly beauty, between virtuous passion and sparks of heavenly fire. Britomart's beauty arouses Artegall's passions and at the same time creates in his psyche a proper imagination of love:

> Besides her modest countenance he saw
> So goodly graue, and full of princely aw,
> That it his ranging fancie did refraine,
> And looser thoughts to lawfull bounds withdraw;
> Whereby the passion grew more fierce and faine,
> Like to a stubborne steede whom strong hand would restraine.
>
> (4.6.33)

I have already used this passage as part of a demonstration that Spenser's love psychology bypassed the traditional Renaissance formula of rational suppression and made the imagination the key faculty in true love. The effect of Britomart's image on Artegall's imagination is to shape Artegall's love for Britomart, just as Artegall's image in the magic mirror had shaped Britomart's love for Artegall. The beauty and virtue of Britomart's image serve to discipline Artegall's psyche by permanently binding his sexual passions to that image, and the binding serves to strengthen those passions. Sexual desire bound by true beauty to the image of one other virtuous individual is the source of the energy of life; and this energy, because it is properly directed, is the source of all noble deeds and, in more general terms, the source of morality. In *An Hymne in Honovr of Love*, once the virtuous male falls in love,

> Then forth he casts in his vnquiet thought,
> What he may do, her fauour to obtaine;
> What braue exploit, what peril hardly wrought,
> What puissant conquest, what aduenturous paine,
> May please her best, and grace vnto him gaine:
>
> (218–22)

The "rugged forhead's" objection that Spenser's love stories appeal to the fancy and thus lead to "follie" those who were better "in vertues discipled" is based on the traditional application of faculty psychology. But because those like the "rugged forhead" cannot love, they cannot judge of love, they cannot understand that "naturall affection," sexual desire, is the "roote" "of honor and all vertue" and "brings forth glorious flowres of fame." The energies of life must be directed, not suppressed. That direction is effected in the stories of chaste love and true friendship by constancy of affection toward other individuals and in the justice episodes by conformity to the social structure. And this means subordination to one's role in society, whether the role be that of knight or commoner or monarch or male or female. The narrator says that it is not to such as the "rugged forhead" that he sings, but to that "sacred Saint my soueraigne Queene,"

> In whose chast breast all bountie naturall,
> And treasures of true loue enlocked beene,
> Boue all her sexe that euer yet was seene;
> To her I sing of loue, that loueth best,
> And best is lou'd of all aliue I weene,
>
> (4.proem.4)

Spenser has in mind the inclusive love that orders the middle books, the love that unites lovers and friends, and he is also looking forward to Mercilla high on her throne, loving and being loved by all the right-minded people in her kingdom and so uniting the commonwealth. This complex of relationships, this complementarity, constitutes a healthy commonwealth and insures corporate perpetuity.

Artegall's encounter with Radigund reintroduces the relationships between male and female that were secondary in the friendship stories and were missing from Artegall's initial adventures in Book V. Radigund's desire to overturn the roles of male and female and thereby to overturn the proper order of society is a form of insanity that results in a sexual confusion within Radigund and a corresponding social confusion in her kingdom. Radigund is "halfe like a man" (5.4.36) from the beginning, when she practiced masculine strategies of pursuit rather than feminine strategies of reception and wooed Bellodant, and wooed him, as one might expect, in order to win him to her will (5.4.30). (Britomart and Florimell go on quests to find their loved ones, but they do not court their loved ones.) Radigund's rejection by Bellodont inspires her campaign to use her physical strength and knightly skills to punish men by forcing them into feminine roles, a campaign that sets into motion an oftentimes grim comedy that parodies Britomart's quest to find Artegall and bring him back to England in order to re-establish rightful order in that kingdom. With detail after detail Spenser emphasizes that Radigund and her minions have, through pride, forsaken their rightful place in nature and, consequently, their rightful place in society. They specifically have discarded their natural obligation "T'obay the heasts of mans well ruling hand" in order "To purchase a licentious libertie" that causes them to "withstand" not only "rule" but "reason." Virtuous women, on the other hand "wisely vnderstand, / That they were borne to base humilitie, / Vnlesse the heauens them lift to lawfull soueraintie" (5.5.25), an act that is a product of God's necessarily just and proper contravention of nature's and society's order.

Unfortunately, when Artegall has defeated Radigund and has her at his mercy, he responds to her physical beauty and is moved to pity: "No hand so cruell, nor hart so hard, / But ruth of beautie will it mollifie" (13). Spenser never underestimates the power of sexual attraction, whether in the virtuous or the vicious. Nevertheless, that Artegall is moved to pity one who has overturned a whole society by refusing to accept her proper place in that society implicates him in that crime. The story turns into a comedy when, having subjected Artegall, Radigund's fundamentally female nature asserts itself and we observe Spenser's version of the inevitability of a female's being female despite her efforts to function as a male. Radigund's masculinity is being recuperated, at least in part, by her own female nature. She cannot control her "liking" for Artegall, it "Being fast fixed in her wounded spright," "Yet would she not thereto yeeld free accord, / To serue the lowly vassall of her might, / And of her seruant make her souerayne Lord: / So great her pride, that she such baseness much abhord" (27). She wants him unbound so as to get his goodwill, "Yet so, as bound to me he may continue still" (32). All of this is, of course, a parody of Britomart's falling in love, in which the chaos of masculine and feminine in Radigund's characterization is opposed to the complementarity of masculine and feminine in Britomart's. And the comedy broadens when Clarin, Radigund's erstwhile loyal servant, also falls for Artegall, causing her elementally female desires to obliterate her loyalty to Radigund. We must keep in mind that all through the comedy, neither Artegall's love for Britomart—he plays along with Clarin; but "Yet neuer meant he in his noble mind, / To his owne absent loue to be vntrew" (56)—nor his masculinity is essentially compromised. His "bigge hart," for example, "loth'd so vncomely vew" of men doing women's work (22); and Spenser, in clear psychological terminology, describes Artegall's constant love for Britomart: her "character [image] in th'Adamantine mould / Of his true hart so firmely was engraued, / That no new loues impression euer could / Bereaue it thence" (5.6.2). Artegall has merely gotten himself into a fix because a manly foolishness moved him to pity beauty. Artegall has merely suffered a lapse in his moral commitment, a lapse that makes him a typical *Faerie Queene* hero. Like the others, Artegall is not a paragon of virtue; his manly strength and his commitment to proper order make him a worthy defender of justice.

When we return to Britomart, she is as we left her in Book IV, a lovesick girl; and not having heard from Artegall in the appointed time, "She gan to cast in her misdoubtfull mynde / A thousand feares, that loue-sicke fancies faine to fynde." Her thoughts are moved by varying passions: "Sometime she feared, least some hard mishap / Had him misfalne. . . . Sometime least his false foe did him entrap. . . . But most she did her troubled mynd molest, / And secretly afflict with iealous feare, / Least some new loue had him from her possest" (5.6.3–4). These perturbations, continuing for some five stanzas, are the focus of her character-ization here; and when Talus comes, her feminine impulsiveness and irratio-nality surge. When Talus says a woman tyrant has captured Artegall, she immedi-ately jumps to the conclusion that it is a sexual conquest: "badly doest thou hide / Thy maisters shame, in harlots bondage tide" and goes in rage to her chamber, where she enters into a new round of perturbations and wandering fancies (11–14). Spenser is not departing from his allegorical scheme in order to humanize Britomart; both her feminine and masculine qualities are essential to her alle-gorical function. When she understands that Artegall's predicament does not involve a betrayal of their love, the feminine aspects of her characterization are eclipsed by her masculine qualities, those needed to avenge "that womans pride, / Which had her Lord in her base prison pent, / And so great honour with so fowle reproch had blent" (18). The contrast between Britomart's appropriate exercise of those polarities, masculine and feminine, and their confusion in Radigund underlies the continuation of the Britomart quest into Book V.

In a practical, political sense, if the commonwealth is to prosper, a proper relationship between male and female must obtain, because sexual desire prop-erly expressed is the source of the energy necessary for achievement. And if there is to be a proper relationship between male and female, there must be a proper relationship between the masculine and feminine in male and female. At least that is the clear point about the masculine and feminine in Britomart and Radigund. How far gender distinctions are internalized in the other characters is difficult to say. Amoret and Florimell are clearly all feminine unless one wishes to include any and all kinds of strengths in the masculine. And Belphoebe has, through the denial of her female sexuality, also suppressed her softer, feminine qualities—unless, of course, we wish to see compassion for the unfortunate as feminine. The problem of reconciling masculine and feminine qualities, so de-fined, is reflected in the disagreements about Scudamour's progress through the

Temple of Venus. I have already argued that, among other reasons, his progress is to be perceived as a positive expression of masculinity, because it is contrasted favorably in that episode with male weakness—should we call it male femininity? Artegall is the character who exhibits an uncivil masculinity in his initial appearance in Book IV as a "saluage" knight with armor like "saluage weed, / With woody mosse bedight," and so forth. He is adorned with a motto, *Saluagesse sans finesse*" (4.4.39) and described as having previously despised women. The difference between Scudamour and Artegall is not that one is more masculine than the other but that Scudamour has subordinated himself to love and the uncivilized Artegall has not. Spenser does not idealize an independent, unsubordinated, *free* masculinity—he does not idealize an independent, unsubordinated, free *anything*. Complementarity, not freedom, is the goal.

Britomart's exercise of her masculine capabilities in her defeat of Radigund avenges Radigund's unseemly attempt to feminize Artegall and also makes possible the restoration of proper order in that Amazonian nation. Both Radigund and Britomart completely suppress their femininity and, in fact, go at each other with a ferocity at least equal to any of the male combatants. Not only are they fueled by "greedy rage," but "through great fury both their skill forgot, / And practicke vse in armes." They "hackt and hewd" those "dainty parts" that "nature had created / So faire and tender, without staine or spot, / For other vses" as if, in a suggestive phrase, "such vse they hated" (5.7.29). The difference between Britomart and Radigund is that when Britomart suppresses her femininity she does so to exercise her masculine faculties in support of justice, while Radigund has the opposite goal. We understand Spenser's basic purposes in *The Faerie Queene* when we focus on the contrast between the virtuous and the vicious rather than on imperfections in the virtuous. Britomart's energy here, both psychic and physical, is the same converted or sublimated sexual energy that fuels her quest. In the middle books, Spenser's virtuous characters were to be "ensamples" of true (which, among other things, meant subordinated) members of the body politic, not "ensamples" of ideal persons.

Armed by virtue and, unlike Artegall, immune to Radigund's feminine charms, Britomart makes short work of Radigund, knocking her out with a blow to her helmet. Britomart then

> Stayd not, till she [Radigund] came to her selfe again,
> But in reuenge both of her loues distresse,
> And her late vile reproach, though vaunted vaine,
> And also of her wound, which sore did paine,
> She with one stroke both head and helmet cleft.

(34)

No weakness from pity here. Radigund gets what she deserves and gets it with dispatch. After Britomart decapitates Radigund, however, her femininity reasserts itself. The sight of the "carkasses" "slaughtred" by Talus "did . . . almost riue" her heart and she, contrary to the practice of the masculine Artegall, willed Talus to stop his fury (36). And her own womanliness—her internalization of accepted notions of gender differences—appears to heighten her sense of outrage at the feminization of Radigund's male prisoners. Britomart functions as do the worst enemies of feminism, those females who are emotionally committed to patriarchy. When she sees the "lothly vncouth sight, / Of men disguiz'd in womanishe attire," her "heart gan grudge, for very deepe despight / Of so vnmanly maske, in misery misdight" (37); and when she sees Artegall, she turns her head aside "At sight thereof abasht with secrete shame" (38). Britomart's words to Artegall are a memorable description, by recollection, of Spenserian manliness:

> Ah my deare Lord, what sight is this (quoth she)
>   What May-game hath misfortune made of you?
>   Where is that dreadful manly looke? where be
>   Those mighty palmes, the which ye wont t'embrew
>   In bloud of Kings, and great hoastes to subdew?
>   Could ought on earth so wondrous change haue wrought,
>   As to haue robde you of that manly hew?
>   Could so great courage stouped haue to ought?
> Then farewell fleshly force; I see thy pride is nought.
>
> (40)

Britomart reigns in Amazon land as "Princess"—any position other than one to which she was born would have been improper—and sets things straight again. She "The liberty of women did repeale, / Which they had long vsurpt; and them restoring / To mens subiection, did true Iustice deale" (42); and she makes magistrates of all of the knights—as men they can take nonhereditary roles of authority. She is sad to see Artegall go on his mission, but she "wisely moderated her owne smart" because she saw that his honor consisted much in that adventure and so "womanish complaints she did represse, / And tempred for the time her present heauinesse" (44). Once again, as she relates to Artegall, Britomart is the dependent feminine female who subordinates herself to her lord.

That the "sterne" Artegall, unlike Samson, Hercules, and Anthony, would not allow "beauties louely baite" to keep him from his manly duties and so leaves Britomart—"And rode him selfe vppon his first intent" (5.7.1–3)—strikes an appropriate note thematically. True love between a man and a woman is not to be contained within a private relationship between the two. It is to provide the

energy necessary for heroic deeds. Had his love for Britomart prevented him
from continuing his quest, he would not have been an "ensample" of justice.
That he is said to leave her "albe her strong request . . . in languor and vnrest"
(3), however, is inappropriate to the fictional situation. In the first place, Britomart
had, just four stanzas before, suppressed her desires to keep Artegall with her.
The observations also violate the sense of the just completed episode in which
Radigund's female beauty had triumphed over Artegall's manly strength. My study
does not bear significantly on the evolution of the poem, but one cannot follow
story in *The Faerie Queene* without noticing what Josephine Bennett called "shifting aims and plans" or, here perhaps, even a "scissors-and-paste technique."[9]
These comments would not have violated story had they appeared following
Artegall's taking leave of Britomart after he had won her love in Book IV. Artegall
was described there also as being "bound / Vpon an hard aduenture," but there
Britomart was "sore displeased . . . to leaue her late betrothed make" and had
"sundry purpose found / Of this or that, the time [of Artegall's departure] for to
delay" (4.6.42, 45). Nevertheless, to deal with the poem as it is, these comments, however provisional, signal the shift from the continuation of Britomart's
quest to Artegall's and Arthur's masculine endeavors in service of Mercilla. They
reflect on Artegall's part a commitment to the nation that properly eclipses a
commitment to a woman. Immediately after the narrator has his say, Artegall
meets Arthur—and Britomart, having established the proper role of the female
and the masculine and the feminine in the female, disappears from the poem.

   But we have as yet to examine Britomart's appearance at Isis Church, the
episode that significant studies understand as the central, defining episode in
Book V. For Jane Aptekar it is Spenser's "fullest definition of justice"; and the
icon of Isis and the crocodile is determinative, embodying the "whole significance of the Legend of Justice," the "proper submitting . . . of rigor to clemency,
and of law to equity."[10] For one who looks to the "allegorical cores" and the
icons therein for enrichment of rather than for the determination of significance, the themes of equity and clemency are considerably less important. Here
in the temple, both equity and clemency appear largely in the form of statement.
Isis is declared to figure "That part of Iustice, which is Equity" (5.7.3), but how
she does that is neither pictorialized nor explained. And outside the temple,
equity, whether in the stricter sense of the application of natural justice in cases
where statute law does not apply or in its general sense of fairness, is important
only in the Amidas and Bracidas episode. Only there are things divided out according to a system of fairness. In the other episodes, a villain, having forsaken
his proper place in the scheme of things, attempts to appropriate something—
anything, from a lady to a kingdom—belonging to someone else; and Artegall or

Arthur or Britomart (in the case of Radigund) prevents the attempt and restores that something to its rightful owner(s). And although the priest explains that Osiris as crocodile sleeps under Isis's feet "To shew that clemence oft in things amis, / Restraines those sterne behests, and cruell doomes of his" (22), neither Isis and Osiris, nor Britomart and Artegall, express those roles elsewhere, within or without the temple. That Isis is depicted with one foot on the crocodile and the other on the ground to signify her capacity to suppress "both forged guile, / And open force" (7) is also puzzling. In neither Britomart's vision nor the priest's interpretation is forged guile suppressed and the crocodile never acts so as to embody forged guile. (The syntax in the placement of Isis's feet indicates the association of the crocodile with forged guile rather than open force.)

Whatever we are to make of other aspects of Britomart's appearance at Isis Church, the episode embodies the healthy sexuality that, in both male and female, provides the energy necessary for a healthy commonwealth. In Britomart's vision, when the tempest in the temple rises suddenly and begins to blow the embers from the holy fire, the crocodile wakes up, troubled by the "stormy stowre and, "gaping greedy wide, did streight deuoure / Both flames and tempest." Then grown great and "swolne with pride of his owne peerelesse powre," he "gan to threaten her likewise to eat." However, checked by Isis, his pride turned to "humblesse meeke" and he sought grace and love. Britomart accepts and "of his game [amorous sport or play] she soone enwombed grew." She gives birth to a lion son who brings order to the other beasts (15–16). The crocodile's attack on Britomart could be described as open force, but it is more reflective of a thinly disguised, unsubordinated masculinity, particularly since the devouring of the flames and the tempest is reminiscent of the Renaissance theory of erection, the efficient cause of which was "heate, spirites, and winde, which fill and distend . . . [the] hollow bodies [in the penis]" (Crooke, *Microcosmographia,* 248). This part of the vision either looks back at the initial meeting of Britomart and Artegall or, curiously, intimates that another courtship of Britomart is to occur after she brings him back to England. The priest's interpretation, however, ignores the suggestion of another courtship episode and focuses entirely on the vision as political prophecy, of the return of the pair to England, the defeat of Britomart's Saxon foes, and the birth of their son, which begins the line of descendants that will end with Elizabeth.

The Isis Church episode is crucial to my understanding of Books III, IV, and V as an allegory of love, because it brings the mythology of generation into *The Legend of . . . Iustice.* On one level, the mythology here is equivalent to that which augments and amplifies story in Books III and IV. There are clear references to the myth of Isis and Osiris in the impregnation of Chrysogonee, the mother of

Belphoebe and Amoret (3.6.9). As the Nile, Plutarch's Osiris represents seminal moisture and as the sun the first cause of generation; and Isis as the earth and/or moon is another Venus who represents that property of nature which is feminine and receptive. But the myth has political import, because it was Osiris who brought law to Egypt. And that we are to understand Osiris to embody a concept of justice comparable to that manifested in Artegall's adventures is made clear just prior to the Isis Church episode by the identification of justice with patriarchal control: in heaven, justice is "right" as practiced by "highest" Jove when he dispenses true justice to his "inferiour Gods" and "euermore / Therewith containes his heauenly Common-weale" (5.7.1). And since Jove reveals the skill of governance directly to "Princes hearts," it is clear why justice was deemed a god in the antique world and why a human king such as Osiris who exercised the heavenly faculty of justice would have been thought a god. The mythology of generation here is comparable to that in III and IV, but the continuing focus on the *control* of natural energy differentiates Isis's temple from mythological centers in Books III and IV, the Marriage of the Medway and the Thames, the Garden of Adonis, and the Temple of Venus, where the emphasis is on the *expression* of natural energy. Isis's priests have taken vows of celibacy. They "bake" [harden] their sides on the stone floor to inure themselves to "sufferaunce" and "proud rebellious flesh to mortify" (9). They sleep on Mother Earth but they abstain both from meat, that which contains actual blood, and wine, the blood of the giants, by which Mother Earth attempts to revenge herself against the gods by stirring up rebellious thought in men (11). Besides the abstinent life of her priests, Spenser's Isis, unlike his Venus in the Temple of Venus (who merely smiles at Scudamour's taking of Amoret), prevents the sexually aggressive moves of Artegall-as-crocodile in Britomart's vision until he woos her properly and sues for grace—until he, as this image reflects back to the Book IV meeting, subordinates himself to love.

Although the episode at Isis Church, like the other highly symbolic episodes, is shifty ground on which to base interpretation of the quests, it, like the other "allegorical cores," provides the means for incorporating cosmic principles into the quests. The initial associations of Osiris with the sun and Isis with the moon are, like the initial observations on justice, hierarchical and patriarchal. They are also sexed and gendered: the Isis priests wear "rich Mitres shaped like the Moone, / To shew that *Isis* doth the Moone portend; / Like as *Osyris* signifies the Sunne" (4) and thus bring in all of the associations of the sun with Jove, God, the king, maleness, and the associations of the moon with the corresponding female powers and qualities. Just as male and female and masculine and feminine are, when properly subordinated, complementary, so are the sun and the moon and Isis and Osiris: "For that they both like race in equall iustice runne" (4). Throughout

Plutarch's essay on Isis and Osiris, whether Isis is identified with the moon or earth or the feminine, receptive principles, and Osiris with the sun or the Nile or the impregnating principles, and whatever names are brought up—Plutarch reports Isis as the goddess with a thousand names—the common denominator is the necessary complementarity of the two. Osiris represents the necessary first cause and Isis the necessary faculty of reception. Our primary understanding of the way these principles are to function in society is to be found, however, not in an analysis of Isis Church but in the behavior of the characters, in the adventures of Britomart and Artegall. The Isis and Osiris myth gives resonance to those adventures. The association of the Book V adventures of Britomart and Artegall with the mythology of generation in Books III and IV clarifies and enriches the roles that sex and gender play in the legend of justice and consequently in the commonwealth.

Lewis advised those who had lost their way in the complex of stories in III and IV "to look for the allegorical centres."[11] I suggest that when we sense we are losing our way in the "allegorical centres" of III, IV, and V we should look to the story.

IV

The defeat of the Souldan that occurs immediately after Britomart rescues Artegall from Radigund is a culmination of the previous episodes in Artegall's quest in that the Souldan and Adicia combine in themselves the insanity of Pangliere, the greed of Pollente, and the attacks on the commonwealth represented by the Leveler Giant and Radigund. Jane Aptekar's characterization of the Souldan as a Phaeton, a false sun, and consequently a parody of Philip II of Spain, who envisioned himself as an Apollo, a true sun, locates the iconography correctly within a context of dramatic action. Aptekar's insight expands the traditional identification of the Souldan and his chariot with the Spanish Armada and his defeat by Arthur as the providential defeat of the Armada by the English.[12] It is instructive, however, to consider the ways in which the Souldan is *not* Philip. The Souldan is only a "mighty man" whose efforts are to "subuert" Mercilla's crown (5.8.18) rather than a monarch who is attempting, like Geryeono and Grantorto, to usurp a kingdom. There is also in this episode a sense of location within rather than without Mercilla's realm, and there is no sense of an invasion of that realm. The episode begins when Arthur, Artegall, and Samient come together where they are, according to Samient, close both to Mercilla's palace and the Souldan (5.8.16, 18). At the end of the episode, when Artegall

and Arthur put things right in Souldan's "place"—it is never called a kingdom—
they do so by putting the "place" and all its wealth under the rule of Mercilla.

I think the most workable identification is that of the Souldan with powerfu
Catholic lords, whose threat to Elizabeth explains both the sense of locatio
within Mercilla's kingdom and also the infidel title. That identification also ex
plains the presence of Malengin close by. Malengin has, on the basis of his ap
pearance, been identified with the wild Irish rebels, but Malengin is a deceiver,
preacher of false, seductive doctrine, a fisher of men on dry land, a fisher for th
fools who would listen to him (5.9.11). And his cave goes down to hell (6). Lik
Josephine Bennett and others, I understand him as being more like one of thos
"disguised Chaplaynes, creeping in Lay mens apparell into the houses, and whis
pering in the eares of certaine Northern borderers," who are warned against i
"An Homilie Against disobedience and wilfull rebellion." He is like one of thos
"ignorant Base priests, as blinde guides leading the blinde," who brought "thos
seely blinde subiects into the deepe ditch of rebellion."[13] The suggestions tha
the Souldan is a Catholic lord do not work against his identification with Philip
they help to include that allusion into the larger issue of the Catholic threat t
order in the commonwealth.

Possibly to the initiated among Spenser's contemporaries there was a refer
ence to one particular Catholic lord in the curious statement that the Souldan'
wife, Adicia, surpassed tigers in cruelty and outrage "To proue her surname true
that she imposed has" (5.8.49). Her "imposed" "surname" is clearly not "Adicia
and thus is likely the family name of her husband. The characterization of Adici
makes the necessary point that all opposition to established order is an expres
sion of an alien madness. First of all, as almost a definition of "Adicia" (injus
tice), she urges the Souldan, through "might, / To breake all bonds of law, an
rules of right" and she does so out of a professed antipathy to "Iustice" or orde
(20). She is, in her response to the Souldan's defeat and death, compared t
several mythological figures, all of whom went mad: Ino, Medea, and that "mad
ding mother" who accompanied the Maenads (47). But the radical disorder i
her psyche is made apparent by the comparisons to beasts. She is like an "en
raged cow" robbed of its calf, "All flaming with reuenge and furious despight
(46) and "a mad bytch, when as the franticke fit / Her burning tongue with rag
inflamed hath, / Doth runne at randon" (49) and, finally, in a complete stanza

> What Tygre, or what other saluage wight
> Is so exceeding furious and fell,
> As wrong, when it hath arm'd itselfe with might?
> Not fit mongst men, that doe with reason mell,

> But mongst wyld beasts and saluage woods to dwell;
> Where still the stronger doth the weake deuoure,
> And they that most in boldnesse doe excell,
> Are dreadded most, and feared for their power:
> Fit for *Adicia*, there to build her wicked bowre.
>
> (5.9.1)

Here again is Elyot's equation of rationality with accordance to—which means subordination to—the structures of society. Adicia is not fit to live among men "what doe with reason mell." In the *Vewe*, the "naturall fredome" that Spenser would have the Irish, in "theire madnes . . . affecte," is the freedom of nature in the sense of the freedom of animals. Subordination, especially for those who exercise power, is necessary for civility. Some dislocation of civility results when those lower down merely refuse to do their duty, but when wrong "hath arm'd itselfe with might" serious dislocations result, accounting for, again as with Elyot, the equation of bestiality with the refusal to adhere to the mores of society, and, on a somewhat stronger note than that in Elyot, the chaos of forces that is unleashed by incivility. There is here, especially in the phrase, "Where still the stronger doth the weake deuoure," the anxiety about unyoked, brute power that energizes Ulysses' speech on degree (*Troilus and Cressida*, I.iii.75–137).

The Souldan himself embodies the same false pride that we have observed on a smaller scale in Sangliere, Pollente, and the giant. Phaeton had always been a favorite example of the pride that leads mortal men to attempt that which is above them and the inevitable destruction that awaits the victims of false pride when they finally confront reality. The forces of the Souldan's meat-eating horses and his apparently irresistible war chariot are dangerous and threatening, but they are not energized by true power. True power is force expressed through proper order. The Souldan's forces are merely held in check by false principles comparable to those which temporarily hold the false friends together. Consequently, when confronted by true force in Arthur's shield, the false principles dissipate and the forces erupt: "Soone as the infants sunlike shield they [the Souldan's horses] saw, / That all obedience both to words and deeds / They quite forgot, and scornd all former law . . . And tost the Paynim, without feare or awe" (5.8.41). The Souldan was then torn to pieces by his own chariot. In a way most welcome after his nondescript appearance in Book IV, Arthur and his shield have again taken on the providential power with which they were invested in Book I. They represent the answer to the plea that the heavens defend Mercilla against this "miscreant" "That neither hath religion nor fay, / But makes his God of his vngodly pelfe, / And Idols serues" (19).

Arthur and Artegall are no more than admiring observers at Duessa's trial, but with their quests to rescue Belge and Irena they become the "limbs" that extend the power and influence of Gloriana-Mercilla-Elizabeth's "bodified" state beyond the borders of England. Mercilla's court becomes the Book V equivalent of Gloriana's Faery Court when Belge seeks assistance and Mercilla sends Arthur to the rescue. And although Artegall's mission began in Gloriana's court and he is recalled to that court at the end of Book V, it must remain a mystery how his quest was to relate to the Faery Queen or how Mercilla and Gloriana would have differed in their representation of Elizabeth in her Body politic had Spenser achieved more of his grand scheme. As they appear in Book V, both courts are thinly disguised representations of Elizabeth's; and, whatever the plans Spenser may have had for his Faery Queen in his "generall intention," it is Mercilla's rather than Gloriana's court that in Book V represents the ideal. As it appears in Book V, Gloriana's court is governed by Envy and Detraction and is clearly something apart from the Faery Court of the Letter.

One way to understand how these final episodes are to function in an allegory of love intended to fashion its readers into proper members of the commonwealth would be to posit a chauvinistic Spenser who, despite the failures of the actual English campaigns that underlie the fiction, insisted upon presenting them as models of English achievement to be admired and emulated. Such an understanding accounts in part for the tendency to dismiss the final episodes as unimportant to Spenser's concept of justice. A better understanding of Arthur's rescue of Belge and Artegall's rescue of Burbon is to be found in the contrast between the fiction and the actual events alluded to in the fiction. So read, these episodes contain the same message as does the final failure of Artegall's attempt to pacify Irena's kingdom. Had Elizabeth's court been like that of Mercilla's, had Elizabeth's citizenry and Elizabeth herself subordinated themselves to the welfare of England the way Mercilla, Artegall, and Arthur subordinate themselves to their assigned tasks, then Leicester's foray on the Continent *could have been* comparable to Arthur's rescue of Belge, Essex's attempt to aid Henry IV *could have been* comparable to Artegall's rescue of Burbon, and Lord Grey would not have been recalled to England before he brought civility to Ireland. Further, if England became a nation as envisioned in the middle books of *The Faerie Queene*, a nation in which the citizenry, including the queen, was fashioned in the "vertuous and gentle discipline" advocated in these middle books, then the extension of English power and influence outside its borders would be more like Arthur's rescue of Belge, Artegall's rescue of Burbon, and, before he was recalled, Artegall's rescue of Irena. These episodes should be read as interrogating the policies of Queen Elizabeth, but not Tudor doctrine.

These concluding cantos to Spenser's allegory of love should be read both as a rather pessimistic appraisal of the moral condition of those responsible for English polity and, at the same time, more optimistically, as an assessment of the work to be done by the poem. The final three cantos of Book V have the same purpose as the rest of Spenser's allegory of love: to relate individual morality to the political health of the commonwealth. The purpose is to promote the ideal that William Starkey had Cardinal Pole articulate: "[I]n a cuntrey, cyty, or towne, ther ys perfayt cyuylyte, ther ys the true commyn wele, where as al the partys, as membrys of one body, be knyt togyddur in perfayt loue and vnyte." The reality with which the middle books end, the attack of Detraction, Enuie, and the Blatant beast on Artegall, is described by "Lupset": "For me semyth playnly wyth vs euery man, vnder the pretens[e and] colour of the commyn wele, regardyth the syngular, by the reson whereof our cuntrey lyth rude, no thyng brough[t] to such cyuylyte as hyt myght be by gud pollycy."

As story, these concluding adventures, like the stories of concord in Book V, fail to engage the imaginations of modern readers. But they are, like the concord stories, important to Spenser's allegory and must be examined as story. Although theme remains the same, the shift in locale to non-English areas of Faeryland is accompanied by a shift in the tone and substance of the narrative. Until the Belge episode, the direct threat to order and authority is found in the self-love that prevents proper subordination of the members of the English commonwealth even when, as with the Souldan, the impetus for insubordination comes indirectly from a foreign source. Now, however, because a political allegory specific to the Spanish-Catholic threat occupies the foreground, the source of the villainy is no longer a more or less particularized inner self-love but the generalized villainy of the foreigner. Consequently the political import of the episodes does not, as it did in the earlier episodes, arise specifically and directly from the moral condition of those who threaten the commonwealth.

The characterizations of the latter villains do not lack the psychological components necessary for the political allegory to arise from moral allegory, but the psychologizing does not account for the villainy that the villains represent. When Geryoneo, the giant who has usurped Belge's crown, hears of the defeat of his seneschall and the knights, his response is as complex internally as that of the earlier villains. He is described as burning in rage and freezing in fear and, reminiscent of the internal weakness of the Souldan, "Doubting sad end of principle vnsound" (5.11.2). Geryoneo also exhibits a debilitating pride—his laughing with teeth "enraung'd disorderly, / Like to a rancke of piles, that pitched are awry" (9) is perhaps to be read as an icon of disorder. His internal state causes him, after Arthur manages to hack off a few arms, to grow "all mad and furious"

like "a fell mastiffe" and not to care "which way he strooke," a state of mind tha
makes him vulnerable to the careful and calculating Arthur, who, when Geryonec
had "in his rage him ouerstrooke," is able to strike the death blow (13). The
combat focuses on the techniques Arthur uses to deal with this six-armed foe
who can shift his weapon from hand to hand and has double strength in each
hand. By waiting carefully for an advantage, Arthur gets an opportunity to strike
the blow necessary to cut through all three of the bodies—otherwise, as I read it
in order to prevail he would have had to slay each body individually and at the
same time. The significant aspect of Geryoneo's makeup, his threefold body, is
unrelated to his psychology; if it has any significance, it would, I suppose, have to
allegorize the multifacetedness of the Spanish-Catholic threat.

Arthur's next conquest, the monster who lives under the idol in the Catholic
temple, is much more representative of the specific evils perpetrated by the Spanish
Catholics on the Low Countries than it is of any generalized concept of error or
evil—despite the superficial resemblances to Errour in Book I. The inquisition
instituted by the Duke of Alva is the focus; at the center of the allegory are the
specifics of the sacrifice of Belge's children to the idol and the specifics of the
falsity of the Catholic teachings. The primary point of Arthur's quest to rescue
Belge is to make clear the villainous threat of Spain as a foreign, Catholic power
and to also make clear that the only way to counter that threat is by means of a
healthy England, symbolized by the relationship developed between Mercilla and
Arthur, a relationship that is clearly differentiated from the relationship of En
gland and Elizabeth and Leicester.

Inasmuch as the Burbon episode refers to historic events, Artegall's defeat
of the "pesants" sent by Grantorto (Spain, Philip, Charles V, the Pope, and so
forth.) to attack Burbon reminds us of the Essex expedition to aid Henry IV
against the Catholic League. In that way, the relationship of the fiction to the
political allegory is comparable to that of Arthur's rescue of Belge. Had English
domestic polity been what it should be, then Essex's expedition could have been
as successful in routing the Catholic League as Artegall and Sergis and Talus were
in routing the mob that had captured Flourdelis. The central issue of the epi
sode, the loss of proper order within Burbon's kingdom, reminds the reader, by
way of contrast, that proper order at Mercilla's Castle includes a harmony of th
divine and the political. In Burbon's kingdom, on the other hand, order has been
upset not only by Grantorto's invasion but also by Burbon's throwing away his
shield, the shield given to him by Redcrosse, the shield with which Burbon did
"appall" Grandtorto "And made him oftentimes in field before [Burbon] fall"
(5.11.53). Since Burbon has lost his moral authority, proper order cannot be

restored simply through the defeat of the "army" that Grandtorto has sent to wage war against Burbon.

And even that "army," a "rude rout" sent by Grantorto and therefore allegorical of the Catholic League, is as allegorical of domestic discord, rebellion, and sedition as it is of a foreign army. It is a mixture of an army (it has "captains" whom Artegall and Sergis fight) and a mob—Talus subdues the "raskall manie" (59) earlier compared to a swarm of flies (58), a mob much like the "rascall crew" that follows the Leveler Giant. The ambiguity shades into confusion in the central issue of the episode, Burbon's discarding of his shield. In the action of the episode, the "crew" so attacked Burbon that "they his shield in peeces battred haue, / And forced him to throw it quite away" (46). However, Burbon later describes a domestic attack prompted by envy: "But for that many did that shield enuie . . . , That bloudie scutchin being battered sore, / I layd aside, and haue of late forbore, / Hoping thereby to haue my loue obtaynde" (54). In the latter account, Burbon has, in effect, swerved from the truth and given in to Envy and Detraction in order to get along. He, in effect, has done voluntarily what Artegall-Lord Grey is forced to do at the end of Book V. But those envious courtiers to whom Artegall submits are authorized representatives of the queen, not a mob. And insofar as Burbon's enemy is a mob, it exists, like all mobs, because authority has broken down. That internal, domestic difficulties are the focus of the episode is also reflected in Burbon's later explanation that Grantorto had with "golden giftes and many a guilefull word / Entyced her [Flourdelis], to him for to accord" and since then she "hath me euer since abhord, / And to my foe hath guilefully consented" (50). As is usual with Spenser, the populace is mindless and purposeless on its own, and it resents and resists lawful authority only when stirred up by an evil figure.

Flourdelis is restored to Burbon, but because he is not a true source of authority he cannot command her respect and obedience. Earlier, immediately after Sergis and Artegall had rescued him, Burbon had admitted that he did not know whether Flourdelis was being "withheld from [him] by wrongfull might, / Or with her owne good will" (49). And that Flourdelis had been "entyced" away from her true love, that she is presented in terms of feminine frailty, is another indication that nothing happens in *The Faerie Queene* unless a power figure initiates the action. The initial situation in which Burbon is in "daungerous distresse" from a "rude rout" that "sought with lawlesse powre him to oppresse, / And bring in bondage of their brutishness" (44) is, given Burbon's identification with Henry IV, a clear example of a nation that is out of control, a society in which degree is no longer maintained. Nevertheless, as this episode represents English foreign policy, the lesson is the same as that of Arthur's rescue of Belge: had Elizabeth's court functioned as does Mercilla's, Essex could have rescued Henry.

Artegall's defeat of Grantorto is also of little interest. The emphasis throughout the combat is on technique; and opportunities for allegorical significance are slighted. The representation of Grantorto as villain, for example, is dependent upon a phrase or two, such as "proud presumptuous" (5.12.14). The beginning stage of the restoration of Irena's kingdom that Artegall is permitted to effect, the ruthless cutting off of those unwilling to subordinate themselves, is more interesting. It is an abbreviated version of the initial phase of Spenser's plans in the *Vewe* in which reformation of Ireland is not by laws but by the sword (147–48). In this initial stage the focus is, in the language of the *Vewe*, on the "foule mosse" that must be "clensed and scraped away before the tree cane bringe forth anye good fruite" (148). In the *Vewe*, those in whom self-love has become ungovernable are to be cut off forthwith: "stoute and obstinate Rebells . . . havinge once tasted that licentious liffe . . . will euer after be readye for the like occacions so . . . theare is no hope of theire amendment or recouerye and therefore [are] nedefull to be cutt of" (157). And after the bulk of the population is "tithed and ordered and euerie one bounde to some honest trade of liffe," the residue of incorrigibles are to be similarly dealt with. Spenser would allow provost marshals to use whatever punishment they wish—whips, rods, etc.—against "straglers and Rvnagates which will not of themselues come in and yealde themselues to this order" (219). This emphasis on the strict subordination of the individual and the use of force to achieve that subordination appears in the poem as the destruction of those who took Grantorto's part "with close or open ayde": Artegall "sorely punished [them] with heauie payne . . . Not one was left, that durst her [Irena] once haue disobayd" (25).

V

Mercilla's Castle, the symbolic center for the social vision in the middle books, is informed by the same strict subordination of the individual. Mercilla embodies the love, or order, that created and sustains the civility that makes possible, and is made possible by, the fruitful sexual relationships toward which the quests of Florimell, Scudamour, and Britomart are leading. The episode at Mercilla's Castle is the fictional fulfillment of the definitions of earthly justice earlier in Book V as partaking of, not merely reflecting, the divine. At the beginning of Book V, justice is defined as a "Most sacred vertue . . . Resembling God in his imperiall might," power that God "doth to Princes lend, / And makes them like himselfe in glorious sight" (5.proem.10). And just prior to the Isis Church episode, the definition is reiterated as "this same vertue, that doth right define: / For th'heuens themselues . . . are rul'd by righteous lore / Of highest Ioue, who doth true iustice deal / To his inferior Gods, and euermore / Therewith contains his heauenly Common-weale" (5.7.1). We cannot, as Tillyard observed, remove English Renaissance "man" from "his" cosmic setting, at least as "man" is represented in the middle books of *The Faerie Queene*.[14]

The introductory description of the architecture of Mercilla's Castle, with its "many towres, and tarras mounted hye" and "all their tops bright glistering with gold, / That seemed to outshine the dimmed skye" (5.9.21), makes the initial connection of the Castle with the upper reaches of the cosmic hierarchy. And the justice administered therein is consonant with the justice that the Christian Father-God administers to human beings: approval and favor to those who subordinate themselves to him and condemnation and punishment to those who do not. The Castle "Stood open wyde to all men day and night" but is guarded by the giantlike Awe, who keeps out the undeserving. Within the Castle, the introductory aspects of justice, conducted under the auspices of Order, constitute an idealized justice or order or right appropriate to the architecture. Mercilla's throne is surrounded by Litae, daughters of Jove, who appease their father's wrath and "cruell vengeance" and who also, by their father's divine permission, wait on the thrones to entreat for "pardon and remission" for those who offend through "frayltie" (31–32). The undeserving who are prohibited entrance or are there to be tried and punished have offended willfully through "guyle," "malice," and "despight" (22).

Neither the Litae nor anyone else entreats for Malfont, who, led by willfulness, did falsely "reuyle" and "foule blaspheme" Mercilla and now has his tongue nailed to a post (25). The symbolic value of this emblematic figure is clear: one's tongue is to be used to support, not to oppose, divinely sanctioned authority. But to dismiss the brutality of the emblem, to say that Malfont is not a character capable of eliciting sympathy, is to miss a large point. Malfont should remind us not only of the actual poet, John Stubbes, who had his right hand removed for comments about the prospective marriage of Elizabeth to Alençon, but also of that part of Spenser's program in the *Vewe* in which the magistrates are to be given a free hand to deal with Irish vagabonds, i.e., those who willfully refuse to subordinate themselves to the economic and social order designed by Spenser to uproot the Irish way of life and replace it with the English. The brutality resulting from that, as well as other such policies, is a necessary first step in Spenser's program to bring the "stubborne nacion of the Irishe . . . from theire delighte of licentious barbarisme vnto the loue of goodnes and Civilitye" (*Vewe*, 54). Elyot's view of those who have no understanding of justice, or, to say the same thing, those who alienate themselves from society, "in the stede of reason embrasinge sensualitie, and for societie and beneuolence folowinge wilfulnesse and malice," comes to mind again. Justice is a psychological state and therefore, in Renaissance psychology, a moral state. The message in Malfont is that those English as well as Irish who cannot suppress eccentric behavior must be brought under control by external means. The final tone of Spenser's vision of and for his nation is determined by its perception of, and answer to, threat.

Mercilla herself, both as icon and as fictional personage, is the focal point, the connecting link between earthly and cosmic love. The cloth of state above her throne, like a cloud with "spreading wings" and skirts "bordred with bright sunny beams" through which "litle Angels" creep, continues the iconology begun with the initial description of the Castle (28). Other angels uphold the cloth while a thousand angels sing "Hymnes to high God" and carol "heauenly things"; and Mercilla herself is the "Angel-like . . . heyre of ancient kings" (29) surrounded by the Litae. The downward thrust of Mercilla's majesty is symbolized by the rusted sword (at the ready for use against foes or for friends seeking aid) and, more interestingly, by the huge lion "like captived thrall, / With a strong yron chaine and coller bound, / That once [under any circumstances] he could not moue, nor quich at all; / Yet did he murmure with rebellions sound, / And softly royne, when saluage choler gan redound" (33). Jane Aptekar found only one chained lion in the emblem books, and it signified the subjection of power and nobility to fortune.[15] This particular lion in this particular context, however, signifies most clearly that self-love, the energy and force peculiar to individuals and collectively to the commonwealth (the lion of England), although essential to society, is inherently rebellious until it is bound to the larger order. Spenser uses another form of "quich" in the *Vewe* to describe the control he would effect over the Irish: "no parte of all that realme shal be able or dare to quinche" (198). The chained lion, like the crocodile under Isis's feet, is an icon of energy under control—the control of English mobs, as Aptekar suggests, and also the control of the tendencies toward eccentricity that are found even in the virtuous. However, to those who live within bonds of submission and control, Mercilla, "sitting high in dreaded souerayntie" (34), is open and available. She is, when Arthur and Artegall make their appearance, dealing justice "with indifferent grace, / And hearing pleas of people meane and base" (36)—not, however, hearing the pleas of those excluded from the Castle or whatever pleas Malfont might be able to noise.

The trial of Duessa justifies the beheading of Mary Stuart, but more to the point of this study, it completes the Book IV representation of Duessa, now

Duessa-Mary Stuart and her handmaiden, Ate, as elemental disorder and brings those icons of disorder under the control of Mercilla, the figure who embodies the ultimate ordering principle of the middle books. Ate and Duessa were not, it must be remembered, brought under control in Book IV. The trial is another important episode designed to move a "gentleman or noble person" toward identification with Elizabeth as the "bodified" state. First of all, its providential framework, the discovery of Duessa's plot having been effected through "high heauens grace, which fauour not / The wicked driftes of trayterous desynes, / Gainst loiall Princes" (42), reinforces the essential rightness of proper authority generally and the Tudor regime particularly. The trial proper consists of a debate before Mercilla as judge, but unlike the debate or strife, "Amongst fraile men," of which Ate is the mother in Book IV (4.1.19), the debaters here, especially those on the side of the state, are authorized personnel: Kingdomes care, Authority, law of Nations, Religion, the Peoples cry, Commons sute, and lastly Justice. On the other side, except for the appeal to Nobility of Birth, are appeals to emotion rather than to order and justice. Not Mercilla alone but Mercilla acting in concert with her loyal subjects, here Mercilla-in-council, constitutes the Body politic. Significantly, in a politically oriented poem written when an accommodation of Parliament and the monarch was beginning to be worked out, the House of Commons is mentioned only once, and then only obliquely and as it subordinates itself in a petition to the queen. Spenser's vision of and for his nation looks forward to the Stuarts and the exercise of divine right, not to what turned out to be the English genius for government by evolution and compromise. Such details as these continue to undermine the efforts of those to understand Spenser as sympathetic to forces of change that we, looking back, see at work in Elizabeth's England.

Artegall's constant stand against Duessa throughout the emotional appeals could provide evidence for character development subsequent to his unfortunate emotional response to Radigund, but it more likely is intended to contrast with the more complex and interesting response in which Arthur is moved, not in understanding but in sympathy, by the "wretched ruine of so high estate" exemplified by Duessa-Mary, so that "for great ruth his courage gan relent" (46). It is an emotional response comparable to Artegall's response to the wounded Radigund. Apparently in order to counteract such responses, Zele brings in Ate, the principle of chaos, whose association with Duessa makes clear that Duessa's treason is motivated by a desire for chaos and misrule, that her sins are willful, not the product of frailty. Zele then brings in "Abhorred *Murder* . . . with bloudie knyfe"; "*Sedition*, breeding stryfe / in troublous wits and mutinous vprore"; "*Incontinence* of lyfe"; "foule *Adulterie*"; and "lewd *Impietie*" (48). This catalog of crimes and sins reminds the reader of that most sustained effort to fashion all members of the commonwealth, gentle and common, in a "vertuous and gentle discipline," the homilies on obedience. As it says in "An Homilie against disobedience and wilfull rebellion,"

> For he that nameth rebellion, nameth not a singular or one onely sinne, as theft, robbery, murder, and such like, but he nameth the whole puddle and sinke of all sinnes against GOD and man, against his Prince, his country, his countrymen, his parents, his children, his kins folkes, his friends, and against all men uniuersally, all sinnes I say against GOD and all men heaped together nameth he, that nameth rebellion.

Within the fictional situation, the latter images brought out by Zele work on Arthur's imagination so as to move his passions against Duessa-Mary. Arthur's imagination of her had been determined by the effect of ameliorating images— Pittie, Regard of womanhood, Griefe—so as to overvalue Nobilitie of birth in this particular case; and he was consequently moved so as to see evil, in Milton's words, as "fair appearing good" (PL 9.354-55). Arthur, now moved by "Abhorred *Murder* . . . with bloudie knyfe," and so forth, "His former fancies ruth . . . gan repent, / And from her partie eftsoones was drawn cleene" (49). He comes to identify with Mercilla, with the "bodified" English state. Within the fiction the episode effects in Arthur the loyalty in mind and heart that Artegall maintains throughout the trial: "But *Artegall* with constant firme intent, / For zeale of Iustice was against her bent" (49). Arthur's psychological experience is, of course, the same that a reading of Spenser's allegory of love was to have effected in its readers.

I gave appropriately cursory treatment to the foreign policy stories that constitute the fiction of the latter part of Book V. When one pays serious attention to storytelling in *The Faerie Queene* rather than, as has been the practice in the several decades since Josephine Bennett's book, denying or dismissing story or understanding story to be the servant of myth or icon, one is reminded that *The Faerie Queene* is not only an unfinished but an uneven work. However, the ending of Book V, the attack of Envy and Detraction as Artegall wends his way back to the Faery Court, requires closer attention. The encounter brings us back to the central concern of Spenser's allegory of love: the management of self-love in a basically ordered society. Its mismanagement in the Faery Court had caused Artegall to be recalled from his attempt to return order to the disordered society in Irena's land. The central point of these final stanzas of Spenser's allegory of love can be approached through the reason given for Artegall's recall to the Faery

Court and consequently Lord Grey's recall to England: "enuies cloud still dimmeth vertues ray" (5.12.27).

The details of Spenser's description of Envy and Detraction come from the iconographical tradition, but the basic concepts that these figures clothe are psychological commonplaces. Envy corrupts the proper expression of self-love, that "inclination, faculty, or power" by which Thomas Wright says every "creature," animate or inanimate conserves itself (*Passions of the Minde*, 12), the self-love that God imparted to human beings "that we might thereby be stirred vp to attempt those actions which were necessary for vs, or flie those inconueniences or harmes which might annoy vs" (13). In fallen creatures, however, self-love must be subordinated to purposes larger than and outside of individual proclivities if there is to be civility, and envy militates powerfully against proper subordination. When we are not satisfied with our lot and begin to compare ourselves unfavorably with others, we begin to envy, to resent their successes and to rejoice in their failures; and so we become psychologically dislocated from engaging ourselves in the functions proper to our own state of being. The ideal solution within a supernaturally sanctioned hierarchical society is not merely to content ourselves with what we are rather than attempt what we would like to be, but to engage ourselves positively in the lives that have been ordained for us. Robert Crowley's advice to beggars in "The Beggars Lesson," while to modern sensibilities calloused to the point of ridiculousness, makes the point:

> If God haue layede hys hande on the,
> And made the lowe in al mens syght,
> Content thiselfe with that degre,
> And se thou walke theirin upryght.

The details of the figures of Envy and Detraction flesh out these generalizations. Envy is the elder because Envy is the psychological source of Detraction in the way that *Fancy* is the sire of "amorous *Desyre*" in the Maske of Cupid. Envy is the state of mind: she slavers as she speaks "Yet spake she seldom, but thought more, the lesse she sed" (29). Detraction is Envy in action. Whatever Envy concealed, Detraction "spred abroad . . . mens good name to haue bereaued" (33). Detraction excels Envy in mischief because Envy "her selfe she onely vext"; but Detraction "both her selfe, and others eke perplext" (35). Envy grieves about, grudges at, and is vexed by things done "prays-worthily" and then eats her gall— all internal actions. And if she has no external "food" she "feedes on her owne maw vnnaturall" and "of her owne foule entrayles makes her meat" (31). Envy always stems from a basic dissatisfaction with self or a dissatisfaction with the way self is perceived by others. It stems from an inability to "walke . . . upryght" in the conditions created by lives as they have been lived. If Envy heard of any good, she "inly" fretted and tore her flesh, which she "inward hid" (32). Envy personifies the internal operation of self-love gone awry; Detraction personifies the outward expressions of self-love gone awry. The ugliness of these creatures "Most foule and filthie" (28) embodies the cacophony within individuals produced by self-love gone awry.

Attempts to find criticism of Lord Grey in these stanzas focus on the tangential and the peripheral. Jane Aptekar, for example, believes the image of Artegall as "rauenous Wolfe amongst the scattered flockes," at whom Envy and Detraction bark as would "shepheards curres," gives some credence to the accusations of the pair.[16] However, in her primary accusation, Detraction couples her complaints that Artegall had stained the sword of justice with "reprochfull crueltie, / In guiltless blood of many an innocent" with another complaint that is patently false—that Artegall had used treachery against Grantorto. And that Detraction would say one thing that is clearly false tends to negate the other accusation, cruelty to the innocent. Also, these accusations are directly refuted: the "bitter wordes" of Envy and Detraction are declared to be "Most shamefull, most vnrighteous, most vntrew" (42). The accusations of Envy and Detraction run afoul not only of direct statement but also of the signification of the figures. The two now "had themselues combynd in one, / And linckt together gainst Sir *Artegall*" and their motive for the attack is that he had freed Irena from their snares (37). That Enuie grieves at all that is "doen prays-worthily" is another indication that Artegall-Grey is to be seen as virtuous. Perhaps more applicable specifically to Grey, Detraction would "turne to ill the thing, that well was ment" (34) and if she heard of any ill she would make it worse by her telling of it (35).

And, finally, that Artegall-Grey simply submits to the attacks of Envy, Detraction, and the Blatant Beast makes the same point as was made at the beginning of Book V by the Squire's refusal to defend himself against Sangliere. It is the point made by Timias's submission to Belphoebe despite his belief that he had been "misdeemed." Had Artegall attempted even to defend himself, he would have been opposing the authority of the queen as that authority is expressed through officials authorized by the queen to recall him. Whether the attacks were justified or not, resistance to authority expressed through the proper mechanism is not allowed. To do otherwise would be to overturn proper authority, to sacrifice proper authority on the altar of self-love. Whether with justice, friendship, or chaste love, we are not to devote our lives to our selves; we are to subordinate those selves to a greater good. That is the continuing signification of Spenser's allegory of love.

Notes

Introduction

1. Treating Books III, IV, and V as a unit is not totally without warrant from previous Spenser scholarship. H. Clement Notcutt commented that the three books form a thematic unit in which woman is dominant in Book III, man in Book V, and Book IV represents the common ground of friendship. Notcutt understands Spenser to link chastity, friendship, and justice by bringing Britomart and Artegall into friendly relations in the middle of Book IV. Building upon C. S. Lewis's seminal thesis that Books III and IV are in theme a single book of love, Leicester Bradner observed that the continuation of the Britomart quest into Book V links three manifestations of the medieval and Renaissance concept of earthly love: in Book III the love that unites individuals of different sex (chastity), in Book IV the love that unites pairs and groups of individuals regardless of sex (friendship), and in Book V the love that unites the members of a commonwealth (justice). Although touching on a basic Renaissance theme and revealing a structural principle for a major portion of the poem, Bradner's perception did not produce an analysis and has been ignored in subsequent studies. Occasionally one runs into other comments that imply that III, IV, and V should be read together. Kathleen Williams observed that "In a sense not only she [Britomart], but the whole tissue of events she has contributed to in the third and fourth books, moves inevitably towards the themes of Book Five"; but no one has come up with the means by which one can do a sustained reading of the three books as an integrated vision. Notcutt, "The *Faerie Queene* and its Critics," 69; Bradner, *Edmund Spenser and The Faerie Queene*, 91; Williams, *Spenser's World of Glass*, 167.

2. "A Letter of the Authors," appended to Book I of *The Faerie Queene*. Spenser, *The Works of Edmund Spenser: A Variorum Edition*, ed. Greenlaw et al., 1:167. Citations to the poem, hereinafter parenthetical, are from this edition.

3. Alpers, "Review Article: How to Read *The Faerie Queene*," 434.
   C. S. Lewis's objection to treating Spenser's characters as selves, as fictional personages, has been most influential: "Occasionally, of course, . . . [Spenser] makes a very brief approach to the kind of fiction now valued in the novel: the conversation between the lovesick Britomart and her nurse, for example. . . . We should never concentrate, however, on passages such as these. . . . The novel calls for characters with insides; but there are other kinds of narrative that do not" (*Spenser's Images of Life*, 113). Subsequent objections to treating Spenser's creations as fictional personages are, like Lewis's, objections to treating them as characters in modern psychological novels. Modern systems of psychology, at least those in the service of bourgeois humanism, lead us to understand thought and the consequent interior life as idiosyncratic and to undergo continuous modification;

and so convincing characters in fiction written according to such a psychology are those who possess an organic, dynamic individuality. Renaissance psychologists also understood the vagaries of the psyche, but for them, it was the control of an interior state, not the interior state itself, which makes us truly human.

Despite my differences with Lewis, my debt to his seminal thesis that Books III and IV form a single book of love and to his understanding of the poem's embodiment of the forces of life and death, good and evil, and health and sickness is such that I felt justified in appropriating his title. Had Lewis been able to respond to, rather than shy away from, Britomart's sexuality, my task might have been different (*The Allegory of Love*, 338–47 and *Images of Life*, 64–97).

Thomas Roche follows Lewis's notions about character in *The Kindly Flame* (6), but a more recent statement is his most useful variation on Lewis: "We have as yet to find a way to describe with any accuracy Spenser's method of depicting character, or defining what 'character' is. For a beginning it is a misnomer, for no figure in Spenser has an interior life that lets us ascribe our judgments to that figure's actions in the poem" ("Britomart at Busyrane's Again," 140). There is, however, a swirl of impulses and appetites in the vicious characters that does have a direction of its own and we do ascribe our judgments of those characters to actions that are a product of an interior state set free. Except for their greater strength, the impulses and appetites in the virtuous are not in themselves different from those in the vicious. Let free, the swirl would determine the actions of the virtuous; but it is disciplined, although often inadequately and sometimes belatedly. We finally judge the virtuous not according to the impulses and appetites but according to the control exercised over those impulses and appetites and consequently according to the virtuous deeds that are the product of impulses and appetites under control.

4. Miller, *The Poem's Two Bodies*, 4–8.

5. Wright, *The Passions of the Minde in Generall* (1621), 11–12.

6. Renaissance psychology, which includes both psychology and physiology, has not figured seriously in analyses of Renaissance characters since the ill-fated attempts earlier in the century to apply it to Renaissance drama (see Forest, "A Caveat for Critics Against Invoking Elizabethan Psychology," 651–72). As part of his justification for the use of Jungian psychology in studies of *The Faerie Queene*, Lockerd points out that the use of faculty psychology has led to overly schematic interpretations of *The Faerie Queene*, that in "place of a fixed, one-dimensional allegory" of Holiness, etc., we get "a comparably flat allegory of Rational, Irascible, and Concupiscible Faculties" (*The Sacred Marriage*, 16). Lockerd has reference to Reid, "Spenserian Psychology and the Structure of Allegory in Books 1 and 2 of *The Faerie Queene*," 359–75; Hughes, "Psychological Allegory in *The Faerie Queene* III.xi–xii," 129–46; and Hankins, *Source and Meaning in Spenser's Allegory*, 28. Such studies, however, do not examine Spenser's use of faculty psychology in the creation of fictional personages, in the creation of characters as selves. My contention is that Spenser's characters, simpler and much more didactically conceived fictional personages than are the characters in the drama, are especially amenable to Renaissance psychophysiological analysis. More recently, scholars such as Thomas Laqueur (*Making Sex: Body and Gender from the Greeks to Freud*) and Gail Kern Paster (*The Body Embarrassed: Drama and the Disciplines of Shame in Early Modern England*) have used Galenic physiology to get at the social construction of sexual difference in the Renaissance. I became acquainted with their work too late to profit much from it, but I am pleased that, governed by different critical practices and focused on a different aspect of Galenic humoralism, namely seed theory, I have found concerns similar to theirs embedded in the middle books of *The Faerie Queene*.

Renaissance physiology is as important to my study as is Renaissance psychology. John

Hankins's examination of the physical allegory of the Garden of Adonis prompted me to look into Renaissance physiology of love. Hankins's interest in the physical allegory, however, is limited to its providing a basis for a Neoplatonic interpretation of the Garden; and he also, inadvisably in my opinion, uses Aristotle on generation rather than the au courant Galen (*Source and Meaning*, 230). James Nohrnberg's inquiry into the physical allegory of the Garden does not include explicitly physiological treatises; and consequently the closest he gets to the "physical side" of the tradition of seeds is a statement by Plotinus that "men generate due to the activity within them of the seminal reasons." Nohrnberg, like previous scholars, is truly interested only in the "metaphysical side" not only of the tradition of seeds but of the Garden of Adonis (*Analogy*, 538). David Lee Miller's examination of the Garden is also done within a Neoplatonic framework: "Book III reverses [the emphasis of Books I and II on 'motives of ascent'], borrowing the structures of Neoplatonic symbology to focus on the erotic motives of the spirit's descent and unfolding in the forms of natural being" and "The most comprehensive image of this cycle ['descent,' 'conversion,' and 'reascent'] in Book III is the Garden of Adonis, but the surrounding narrative is also filled with images of descent into multiplicity" (*The Poem's Two Bodies*, 221–23). Miller also, following Hankins, uses Aristotle on generation rather than Galen (see the discussion of the birth of Amoret and Belphoebe in my chapter 3).

7. The irrepressible appeal of the Neoplatonic approach is that it provides, ready made, a term complementary to earthly love and has thus enabled allegorical readings of III and IV, which have been, after Lewis, considered to be Spenser's books of love. I have in mind Janet Spens's *Spenser's Faerie Queene*, which introduced Neoplatonism to *Faerie Queene* studies, and William Nelson's more formidable *Poetry of Edmund Spenser*. Both lean heavily on the Letter to Raleigh, especially the Letter's description of Arthur's role in the poem. But the Letter, designed for Raleigh's "better light in reading" the 1590 installment of the poem, is of questionable help with such matters in the middle books, because it presents a distorted account of the interwoven structure of quests that have only their initial episodes in that installment. Three of the "accidents" (as opposed to "intendments") mentioned in the Letter—"the loue of Britomart," "the misery of Florimell," and "the vertuousness of Belphoebe"—actually refer to three of those quests: Britomart's quest for the love of Artegall, Florimell's quest for the love of Marinell, and Timias's quest for the love of Belphoebe. The Letter would have the other major quest, Scudamour's for the love of Amoret, originate in the Faery Court, but not a word in either Book III or Book IV reminds us of such a quest. Nor is the Letter of help with narrative in Book V. Although Artegall's quest to rescue Irena is described as having originated at the Faery Court (5.1.3–4), the Faery Court to which Artegall is recalled at the end of Book V, instead of evoking notions associated with the Gloriana of the Letter, is rife with envy and detraction. Artegall's quest to rescue Irena appears in the text as comparable to Arthur's quest to rescue Belge; and the "allegorical core" for both quests, I shall argue, is better understood as Mercilla's rather than Gloriana's court. Arthur's other appearances in these books are also unrelated to his quest as described in the Letter. Given these disparities, I suggest that the structure of interwoven quests that comprises Books III, IV, and V should be approached within the larger confines of didactic purpose and method as outlined in the Letter but not as determined by the grand scheme of twelve books organized by the feast at Gloriana's court and/or by Arthur's pursuit of Gloriana, Neoplatonic interpretations of which have authorized Neoplatonic interpretations of the love that moves the heroes and heroines on their quests.

The quasi-Neoplatonic, mythologically oriented studies of A. C. Hamilton, Thomas P. Roche, and Kathleen Williams are not so dependent on the Letter. In the latter, the characters, perceived loosely as types of mythical figures, are meaningful primarily as they reflect the cosmic significances associated with those figures (Hamilton, *Structure of Allegory*; Roche, *The Kindly Flame*; and Williams, *Spenser's World of Glass*). Rather than relationships between earthly and celestial or supercelestial love, I propose to examine allegorical relationships between the forms of earthly love that appear in the literal level, on the surface the poem: the love that unites individuals of different sex, the love that unites individuals regardless of sex, and the love that unites inhabitants into a commonwealth.

The centrifugal thrust of the middle books of *The Faerie Queene*—that which causes the reader's sense of being drawn away from, if not necessarily up from, narrative action—has been explored through Neoplatonic interpetation and also through what Norhnberg calls the poem's "resourcefulness" (*Analogy*, ix) and what later critics refer to as "intertextuality" in its stricter sense of the way Spenser incorporated earlier works into his poem. My interests, however, lie in the centripetal rather than in the centrifugal—except in the way the hierarchy of quests suggests a social vision. Mine is a narrower than usual look at the *The Faerie Queene*, a look that is, I trust, compensated for by its more rigorous than usual discipline.

8. Strong, *The Cult of Elizabeth*, 43, 112. All of the pictures I discuss can be found in this book.

9. Working primarily from the Letter to Raleigh, S. K. Heninger develops the interesting hypothesis that although Spenser began *The Faerie Queene* with a Neoplatonist aesthetic in which the fiction exists simply to clothe a preexistent idea, he was influenced by Sidney to move toward a poetic art based upon Aristotelian imitation, an art that Spenser never mastered. The "richness and resiliency" of *The Faerie Queene*, Heninger says, can be explained by Spenser's change of plans, "by his refusal to remain a simple allegorist, and yet his inability to become wholeheartedly a poet historical as Sidney had prescribed" (*Sidney and Spenser*, 394–95). I have found no reasons to question Heninger's hypothesis about a change in plans, but I understand Spenser to have made an appropriate use of Aristotelian imitation in his allegorical poem.

10. Roche, *Kindly Flame*, 103; Williams, *World of Glass*, 91.

11. Kantorowicz, *The King's Two Bodies*. Plowden is cited on p. 9 and Blackstone on p. 5. Kantorowicz's phrase, "organological whole," is on p. 270 and the phrase, "politic capacity," Sir Edward Coke's, is cited on p. 15.

12. Tillyard, *The Elizabethan World Picture*, 102. A serious interest in the older scholarship may puzzle those who view anything done more than fifteen or so years ago as the quaint ruminations of olden, precritical days; but present-day Renaissance scholarship continues an evolutionary process. The difference between the Old and the New Historicisms, at least as the New Historicism is found in Stephen Greenblatt, is not in the acceptance or dismissal of the "Picture" but whether the "Picture" is the beginning or the ending point. Greenblatt says he has not ceased "to believe that Renaissance society was totalizing in intention"—i.e., that it posited "an occult network linking all human, natural, and cosmic powers" and claimed "on behalf of its ruling elite a privileged place in this network"—but that "Elizabethan and Jacobean visions of hidden unity seemed like anxious rhetorical attempts to conceal cracks, conflict, and disarray" (*Shakespearean Negotiations*, 2).

I also begin with Tillyard's "Picture." However, in the middle books of *The Faerie Queene*, hierarchy is not just the organizing principle for the cosmic background; it is central to the stabilization and direction of behavior in the social hierarchy. For Greenblatt, the "cracks, conflict, and disarray" in Elizabethan society are in part the product of what he understands as the *real* hierarchy, a secular hierarchy created by power relations, operating underneath or within and contrary to the ordained. My intention is not to argue that power, so understood, was missing from Elizabethan England; however, my subject is the middle books of *The Faerie Queene*, not

Elizabethan England. And as I read those books, such an exercise of power is neither legitimized nor, as in Greenblatt's reading of Harington's comment about Queen Elizabeth's exercise of power, to be understood and consequently accepted as a fact of life in the real world (*Renaissance Self-Fashioning*, 168–69).

If we are to do more than project our own consciousnesses back onto Spenser's poem, we must not discard or consciously modernize what was the central concept in the dominant social discourse of the day. Elizabethan versions of hierarchy provide keys to the structures of meaning in the middle books because in Elizabethan England hierarchy was *the* acceptable way of organizing social thought and the behavior consequent upon that thought. It provided the socially accepted means by which one thing was related to another, one act was related to another. To use fairly current jargon, hierarchy provided a Geertzian control mechanism, a set of instructions like those of a computer program, that governs behavior in the middle books of *The Faerie Queene* (Geertz, *The Interpretation of Cultures*, 44). An understanding of hierarchy as structuring, an understanding of self-love as the source of vital energy and consequently the source of potential discord, and an understanding of subordination as the means by which potential discord becomes concord are necessary to an adequate understanding of the middle books' expression of the *discordia concors* theme. Proper subordination is the means to a concord, a proper complementarity, of the heterogeneous elements of a society.

13. Sir John Davies, *Orchestra* (1596). Stanza 56.

14. I follow Angus Fletcher in understanding Spenser to belong to the "broader tradition [of prophecy], which is only partially predictive, a tradition that balances anticipation of the future with a concern for the past and, even more important, for the present." I see Spenser's prescience, however, as being limited to his looking forward to the absolutism of the Stuarts; and, unlike Fletcher and Fletcher's mentor on the subject, Harry Berger Jr., I find no reasons to think that Spenser both understood and sympathized with what we see as evolutionary forces at work in Elizabethan society. I read the middle books of *The Faerie Queene* as a conservative reaction against those forces (Fletcher, *The Prophetic Moment*, 4, 7, 45–46n).

15. Greenblatt, *Shakespearean Negotiations*, 4.

16. Abrams, *Doing Things with Texts*, 304.

17. Berger, "Narrative as Rhetoric in *The Faerie Queene*," 41, 47.

Chapter 1. Britomart's Initiation

1. Starkey, "A Dialogue Between Cardinal Pole and Thomas Lupset," 54–55, 67.

2. Wright, *Passions of the Minde*, 11–12.

3. Lewis, *Images of Life*, 67.

4. Coeffeteau, *A Table of Humane Passions*. Quoted in Herschel Baker, *The Image of Man*, 283. Baker's is still the best introduction to faculty psychology.

5. Williams's observation that one finds in Britomart a "completeness as woman and warrior, an armed figure like Minerva or Venus armata, in whom feminine and masculine qualities are balanced" is typical (*World of Glass*, 91).

6. Burton, *The Anatomy of Melancholy* 3:180.

7. Helkiah Crooke, Μικροκοσμογραφια. *A Description of the Body of Man. Together With The Controversies Thereto Belonging. Collected and Translated out of all the Best Authors of Anatomy, Especially out of Gasper Bauhinus and Andreas Laurentius* (1631), 284.

That I make extensive use of a work published after *The Faerie Queene* requires some explanation. When I say "Crooke" or refer to his book, I refer to the traditional physiological lore that Crooke published in 1615 and is reprinted in the widely accessible microfilmed 1631 edition.

The basic science found in Crooke is the science of Galen, Aristotle, and "Hippocrates"; and the controversies referred to in the title are essentially those between the followers of Galen and those of Aristotle. Nancy Siraisi notes that by the mid-thirteenth century, discussion of the differences between "the physicians and the philosophers" became commonplace in medical literature (*Medieval & Early Renaissance Medicine*, 80–81). For my purposes, the relevant quarrel between the physicians and the Peripatetics is whether or not women produced seed in the form of semen. Aristotle rejected the Hippocratic theory of two seeds and developed his own theory that the female provided the catamenia, the material for generation, material that required only the further source of movement and change provided by male semen. Galen, however, reverted to the two-seed theory, partly because the Alexandran anatomist, Herophilus, had discovered the ovaries, organs that Galen characterized as internal testicles and understood to generate seed similar to that generated by the external testicles of males.

The controversies in Crooke's fourth book, "Of the Naturall Parts belonging to generation, as well in Men as in Women," and in his fifth book, "Wherein the Historie of the Infant is accurately described . . . as neere as may be according to the Opinion of Hippocrates," fulfill the historical promise made in the title of the fifth book. A selection of Crooke's headings from the controversies of those books, "Of the vse of the Testicles"; "How the parts of generation in men and women differ"; "What seed is"; "Whether women yeeld seede"; "Whether it be necessary to Conception that the seed of both Sexes should issue together, and that with pleasure, and be presently mingled"; "Whether the wombe haue any operatiue or active power in the conformation of the Creature"; and "Whence it commeth that children are like their Parents," reflect the arguments about male and female sexual physiology that go back to the Hippocratic tradition (see: Preus, "Galen's Criticism of Aristotle's Conception Theory," 65) and were debated endlessly until the discovery of the ova and the sperm late in the seventeenth century provided the means by which present notions about generation evolved.

Ian Maclean does not refer to Crooke, but Crooke thoroughly discusses and references all of the questions about the Renaissance view of the nature of women that structure Maclean's chapter on medicine, anatomy, and physiology: "Is she a monstrous creation? Is she an imperfect version of the male? Does she produce semen, and is this fertile? How is sex determined? What physiological features are unique to woman, and what effects are these thought to have? What are the psychological differences between the sexes?" (*The Renaissance Notion of Woman*, 30).

Maclean's study has been most helpful in reinforcing the idea that the reproductive science which is found in Spenser and in Crooke is to be found all over. Maclean could have gotten all of his basic ideas from Crooke, but an acquaintance with Crooke was not necessary for Maclean's purposes. Howard Adelmann's *Marcello Malpighi and the Evolution of Embryology* serves the same purpose. In his discussion of sixteenth- and early-seventeenth-century embryology, including the "thoroughly reactionary and retrogressive disquisition of du Laurens" (from whom Crooke borrowed his controversies), Adelmann points out that

> By one or another in this group [Vesalius, Faloppio, Eustachio, Fernel, et al.] the usual questions are raised. What is the origin of semen? Do both sexes form it? . . . What determines the sex of the offspring and its resemblance to its parents? . . . They answer variously, some siding with one authority, some with another, and some now and then advancing interpretations of their own.

And, most important to this study, because previous attempts to understand Spenserian sexual physiology have been based on Aristotle, "To a man they agree with Hippocrates and Galen that semen is produced by both sexes" (*Marcello Malpighi,* 2:755).

I have found Crooke more congenial to my purposes than Galen himself because, as is indicated by Crooke's title and is made evident in his introductory chapter, "Of the Excellencie of Man," his understanding of the science of Aristotle, Galen, and the rest is organized by the same commonplace notions that organize the science of Spenser's time and consequently the science in Spenser's poem. For my purposes, the only useful idea that is found in Galen and not in Crooke is that the power that is distributed from the testicles to the rest of the body is not only the cause of strength and masculinity in males but in females is the cause of "their very femininity" (*On Semen,* 137). Abbreviated versions of Galenic reproductive science can be found in such popular sources as Thomas Vicary's *Profitable Treatise of the Anatomie of mans body,* 1577; John Huarte's *Examination of mens wits,* 1594; and Pierre de La Primaudaye's *The Second Part of the French Academie,* 1594; but the details in Crooke's 150 folio pages on Renaissance reproductive science are what have been essential to my project. Crooke's is the most appropriate, the most complete, and the most accessible source for an understanding of that science.

John E. Hankins prompted my interest in Spenser's use of Renaissance reproductive science, but Hankins depends upon Aristotle. In his examination of the physical allegory of the Garden of Adonis, Hankins draws upon identifications of Venus with the "seed of animals"— which Hankins apparently assumes refers only to male seed—by Natalis Comes and Cornutus and concludes that "even at this level, Venus is both literal and metaphorical. Literally she is the fluid emitted during coitus; metaphorically she is the desire caused in part by a superabundance of that fluid" (*Source and Meaning,* 245–46). Hankins moves to the cosmic implications of the myth, Adonis as sun and father of all forms and Venus as moon and mother of all forms—and then to a Neoplatonic interpretation of the Garden of Adonis. I am interested in Venus as seed as she functions within individual human beings, both male and female; and consequently Galen, not Aristotle, serves my purposes as, I believe, Galen served Spenser's purposes.

8. Ebreo, *The Philosophy of Love,* 151–52.

9. Nelson, *Poetry of Edmund Spenser,* 232–33; Williams, *World of Glass,* 93; Quilligan, "Words and Sex," 200.

10. Nohrnberg, *Analogy,* 437.

11. Alpers, *Poetry of The Faerie Queene.*

12. Ellrodt quotes this stanza as an example of Spenser's interests in the "moral and psychological aspects of the Renaissance philosophy of love." Ellrodt says that "the opening lines raise an expectation of the Neo-platonic contrast between love as a desire of contemplation kindled by intellectual beauty, and love as a desire of generation excited by earthly beauty [as in Ficino and Pico]. But from the closing lines it appears that the higher love is conceived as a spur to virtuous action on earth rather than an invitation to fly back to heaven." Ellrodt also comments that the love that moves Britomart on her quest is obviously not a desire of intellectual beauty, yet "that same love has been described as "ykindled first above," and contrasted with brutish love. The distinction therefore was not drawn on the metaphysical level, between the earthly and the heavenly Venus, but on the ethical—and Christian—level, between virtuous love and "filthy lust" (*Neoplatonism in the Poetry of Spenser,* 34, 35). I have not discovered any reasons to disagree with Ellrodt's notions about Spenser's Neoplatonism.

13. Nelson, *Poetry of Edmund Spenser,* 222.

14. Lewis, *Allegory of Love*, 331–32, 340; Roche, *Kindly Flame*, 68–70; Hamilton, *Structure of Allegory*, 142; Williams, *World of Glass*, 111–12; and Alpers, *Poetry of The Faerie Queene*, 374–80.

15. Lewis, *Allegory of Love*, 340.

16. Roche, *Kindly Flame*, 70.

17. Nohrnberg, *Analogy*, 445.

18. Axton, *The Queen's Two Bodies*, 69, 104.

19. Ferguson, *Clio Unbound*, 350–51.

20. Ibid.

21. For a contrary view, see Harry Berger Jr. and Angus Fletcher, both of whom understand Spenser to be aware of and sympathetic toward the evolutionary forces that we see at work in the Elizabethan society. Berger wrote a series of articles on Books III and IV, some of which—namely, "Archaism, Immortality, and the Muse in Spenser's Poetry"; "The Spenserian Dynamics"; "Spenser's Garden of Adonis"; "The Structure of Merlin's Chronicle"; and "Two Spenserian Retrospects"—incorporate his evolutionary views. Fletcher acknowledges Berger as his mentor on the subject of evolution in *The Faerie Queene* (*The Prophetic Moment*, 4, 7, 45–46). In the introduction to a reissue of Berger's essays, Louis Adrian Montrose points out that the essays mentioned above were "quarried" from a manuscript on Books III and IV that was never published (*Revisionary Play*, 4). Perhaps Berger never found a workable organizing principle.

22. Strong, *Cult of Elizabeth*, 111.

23. Bamborough, *The Little World of Man*, 127.

24. Greenlaw, "Spenser and British Imperialism," 20–21.

25. Bamborough, *The Little World of Man*, 128.

Chapter 2. Marinell's Quest for the Love of Florimell

1. The important attempts to understand Florimell have been the identifications with mythic figures and/or Neoplatonic notions of beauty. Frye's brief and general reference to Marinell and Florimell as reflections of vegetation myths is, in my opinion, at least as helpful as the more elaborate attempts to understand Florimell through reference to the mythic background. ("The Structure of Imagery in *The Faerie Queene*," 166). No myth or collection of myths serves, as Roche says the alternate Helen of Troy myth serves, "to control the adventures of Florimell and Marinell" (*Kindly Flame*, 152). Florimell and Marinell are, as I shall argue, more clearly reflective of the Medway-Thames "river myth" than they are of other myths with which they have been associated. But even this "myth" does not control the adventures or the attributes of the characters; it serves to broaden and to clarify the significance of the characters and their adventures.

The attempts to see Florimell as a reflection of Neoplatonic notions of beauty and love are comparably flawed. (Robert Ellrodt's examination of Spenser's use of Platonism is still, at least for my purposes, the most useful.) Florimell, Roche says, is "Spenser's figure of the spiritual beauty of the soul manifested through physical beauty" and Proteus's wooing of her is "the physical attempting to claim beauty for its own" (*Kindly Flame*, 161). If we are to assume, as Roche does, that beauty and love in *An Hymne in Honovr of Beavtie*, can be equated with beauty and love in Books III and IV of *The Faerie Queene*, then such an interpretation is likely. But are we to equate the two? If Proteus's unsuccessful wooing of Florimell is Spenser's way of "telling the reader that beauty and love are above the physical, mutable realm of Proteus" (*Kindly Flame*, 162), then what are we to say about Marinell's successful wooing of Florimell, or Artegall's of Britomart, or Scudamour's of Amoret? There are no words that indicate that these courtships are a way of approaching the spiritual through the physical. Still, Roche's argument for an identification of Florimell with Beauty is at least as substantial as the usual argument that everyone is attracted to her, because there is no indication in the text that her beauty has either a divine origin or a divine nature. Of course, if a Neoplatonic context for the story is assumed, then all beauty is a reflection of Beauty to those who are able to so perceive it. But no character in the poem so perceives the beauty of Florimell, and there are no substantial indications in the poem that the reader is to so perceive it. In fact, there is more evidence in the poem for an identification of Britomart with Beauty than there is for Florimell. When Britomart raises her visor at the Castle Ioyous, the imagery describing her beauty is celestial: "Such was the beautie and the shining ray, / With which faire *Britomart* gaue light vnto the day" (3.1.43) and, specifically, at Malbecco's Castle her effect on others has clear celestial or even supercelestial overtones:

> Yet note their hungry vew be satisfide,
>> But seeing still the more desir'd to see,
>> And euer firmely fixed did abide
>> In contemplation of diuinitie:

(3.9.24)

And Artegall's perception of her as a "heauenly image of perfection" (4.6.24) is, at least, loosely Platonic. No such imagery is used for Florimell, and the only reason scholars advance for the identification of Florimell with Beauty is that everyone chases after her. The description of Florimell most like Platonism is in the old witch's perception of her; but the point there is that the old witch's perceptions are limited, not that Florimell has a celestial nature (3.7.11). I am also convinced the reason Britomart has not been identified with Beauty is that there are clearly more important significances for her in the poem, and the reason Florimell has been identified with Beauty is the difficulty of finding such significances for her.

    2. Representative are Kathleen William's view of her plight on the fisherman's boat as "a pathetically convincing result of her helpless charm, her lack of judgment, her way of throwing herself on the wrong people's mercy" (*World of Glass*, 116) and Padelford's view that her "hysterical fear" is intended to contrast with the "steadfast courage and stout hardiment of Britomart" ("Allegory of Chastity," 371).

    3. Laqueur, *Making Sex: Body and Gender from the Greeks to Freud*, 8.

    4. Quilligan, *Milton's Spenser*, 196.

    5. A. C. Hamilton's brief discussion combines the marriage of the rivers with the Garden of Adonis as reflections of the "creative power of love which sustains and restores all life" (*Structure of Allegory*, 168–69). William Nelson discusses the pageant separately from the story as a celebration of the nation through its rivers and as a "symbol of cosmic harmony and plenitude, the work of Venus" (*Poetry of Spenser*, 254–55). Kathleen Williams reads it as symbolic of "the inexhaustible creativeness of the generative world" (*World of Glass*, 144). Roche (*Kindly Flame*, 182) and Berger ("Two Spenserian Retrospects," 15) understand the pageant as also reflecting an evolutionary view of history.

    6. Ebreo, *Philosophy of Love*, 151–52. James Nohrnberg provides a carefully researched discussion of this myth and its relationship to the Venus myth in the Garden of Adonis—but not to the marriage pageant (*Analogy*, 557–67). My purposes lead to a consideration of the way the natural, physical seed functions within characters, not, as do Nohrnberg's, to a consideration of

the cosmic implications of the myth, the birth of Venus as "an allegory for the seminal disposition in which the world was created" (561).

7. Nohrnberg, *Analogy*, 435, 450

8. Huarte, *Examination of Mens Wits*, 279–80.

9. Giamatti, *Play of Double Senses*, 124–30; Renwick, *Edmund Spenser*, 169–74. All of the attempts to understand Proteus, except Giamatti's, are similar to Roche's Neoplatonic interpretation. John Hankins says that Proteus represents "either first matter or the adaptable quality of first matter, the ability to assume all forms" (*Source and Meaning*, 232) and Kathleen Williams says the identification of Proteus as "undifferentiated first matter, or chaos" influenced Spenser's use of Proteus as "a symbol of both change and of constancy in change" (*World of Glass*, 140–41). Nelson sees Proteus as a shape shifter, a symbol of inconstancy (*Poetry of Edmund Spenser*, 247), and Nohrnberg's more detailed discussion (*Analogy*, 581–86) presents Proteus "in sum" as "matter in its infinite receptivity to form, especially generable form" (586).

Chapter 3. Scudamour's Quest for the Love of Amoret

1. Gilde, "The Sweet Lodge of Love and Deare Delight," 63, documents the consensus that Amoret's problem is internal. Roche summarizes and documents the debate with Hieatt in *The Kindly Flame*, n. 129.

2. Hankins, "Hamlet's 'God Kissing Carrion,'" 511–12.

3. Miller, *Poem's Two Bodies*, 250. Miller only touches on the Garden of Adonis as "an allegory of natural reproduction" (274–75); and he does not attempt to find "rot" in this symbolic representation of, among other things, the womb.

4. Hankins, "Hamlet's 'God Kissing Carrion,'" 510.

5. Miller, *Poems Two Bodies*, 250.

6. Jorden, *A Briefe Discourse of a Disease Called the Suffocation of the Mother*, 17–21. I am indebted to Gail Kern Paster, *The Body Embarrassed*, 168, for this reference.

7. Lemmi, "Monster-Spawning Nile-Mud in Spenser," 234–38.

8. Quilligan, *Milton's Spenser*, 82. Miller quotes the first part of Quilligan's passage in *The Poem's Two Bodies*, 249.

9. Lewis, *Allegory of Love*, 342; *Images of Life*, 18–35. Deneef, "Spenser's *Amor Fuggitivo* and the Transfixed Heart," nn. 18–19, points out that Lewis's differentiation of the false and the true Cupid underlies the major studies of Book III by Alpers, Hamilton, Nohrnberg, Roche, and Williams. The most extensive examination of Spenser's Cupid, William V. Nestrick's "Spenser and the Renaissance Mythology of Love," is also heavily dependent on Lewis.

Deneef attempts, through an analysis of the wounds in Book III, to understand Cupid in terms somewhat similar to those I attempt to understand him through psychophysiological analysis of the characters. For Deneef, Cupid is a "principle of love the poet creates in the poem and an ethical action he tries to inculcate in the reader." Cupid represents "the critical transition between the inception of love and subsequent action a character takes on the basis of that love. . ." ("Spenser's *Amor Fuggitivo*, 1). Deneef's focus, however, is not primarily upon the psyches of the characters but on what he perceives to be a pattern in the complex of wounds in Book III, some wounds being "deformative" and some "reformative." Deneef's attempt to understand the actions of the characters without following those actions systematically is typical. All scholars who do so pluck passages out of the quests without regard for the rest of the actions that constitute the whole quest in which the character is engaged, and they inevitably assume complex internal responses on the part of the characters to the situations in which they are involved.

10. By limiting themselves to generalized allegorical interpretation, Lewis and Roche are able to read the meeting of Venus and Diana as a reconciliation. Lewis associates Cupid with courtly love and so Venus's adopting Amoret to take the place of Cupid reflects the shift from courtly love to Christian marriage (*Allegory of Love*, 342–45.) Roche sees the episode as allegorizing the Renaissance revaluation of virginity and marriage as Christian ideals in which Christian marriage becomes the equal of Christian virginity (*Kindly Flame*, 114–16). Kathleen Williams understands the quarrel between Venus and Diana to end, not in reconciliation, but in "armed alliance" (*World of Glass*, 100).

11. Many have touched on the anatomical and/or physiological implications of the Garden: Bennett, "Spenser's Garden of Adonis Revisited," 70; Ellrodt, *Neoplatonism in the Poetry of Spenser*, 88–89; Nelson, *Poetry of Edmund Spenser*, 209; Roche, *Kindly Flame*, 120; Fowler, *Spenser and the Numbers of Time*, 138; Colie, *Paradoxia Epidemica*, 336–37; Cheney, *Spenser's Image of Nature*, 136; and Lewis, *Images of Life*, 51–52. But even those, like Hankins (*Source and Meaning*, 264–72) and Nohrnberg (*Analogy*, 520–33), who do more than touch on the matter, are interested in the physical allegory as a stepping stone to the cosmic. David Lee Miller's examination of cantos 5 and 6 of Book III, under the rubric of "The Wide Womb of the World," is also essentially Neoplatonic (*Poem's Two Bodies*, 215–81). My purposes keep me within the relationship of the Garden to the microcosm. I also use a significantly different, Galenic physiology.

12. According to St. Augustine, "the powers included under the term, *rationes seminales*, may exist in different ways: first, in the Word of God, as ideal reasons; secondly, in the elements of the earth, as universal causes; thirdly, in those things which came forth from the universal causes in the course of time, as in this plant or this animal; fourthly, in the seeds which are produced by these plants and animals" (McKeogh, *The Meaning of the Rationes Seminales in St. Augustine*, 29).

The ideas in the seed are the physiological equivalents of the *rationales seminales*, which Ellrodt used in his attempt to supplant Josephine Bennett's Neoplatonic interpretation of the Garden with a medieval Christian interpretation; Nelson and Hankins used the *rationales seminales* to develop Neoplatonic interpretations of the Garden that were not dependent upon identifying the babes and shapes and forms with Plato's transcendent ideas. My understanding of the ideas in the seed is much closer to the *rationes seminales* as they were perceived in the hexameral tradition and explicated by Ellrodt (*Neoplatonism*, 77–80) than as the *rationes seminales* were perceived by Plotinus and explicated by Nelson (*Poetry of Edmund Spenser*, 211–23). Ellrodt states the difference between the two traditions:

> For the Platonic reflection of the changeless ideal in the ever changing phenomenal world Christian thought had substituted the temporal unfolding of a timeless creation. And though his deeper allegiance may be blurred by the puzzling "transmigration" of the babes, Spenser's thought [in the Garden], as in the Mutabilitie Cantos, is once more in harmony with the Christian point of view. (*Neoplatonism*, 80–81)

13. Ramsay's "The Garden of Adonis and the Garden of Forms" and Cheney's chapter on the Garden of Adonis in *Spenser's Image of Nature* are both helpful but essentially nonphysiological treatments of the sections of, the aspects of, or the myths of the Garden. Ramsay maintained that there were two gardens, a garden of forms (which I call the seminary) where the babes and shapes grow and another place she called the Garden of Adonis (which I call the pleasure garden) where

the lovers live and where Cupid and Psyche rear Amoret. Cheney minimizes the spatial, arguing that "the passage is dialectical rather than descriptive in its structure" (119), that there is a sequence of myths of Adonis, each supplanting the preceding myth or image, which then "fades away" (129). Neoplatonic studies such as those by Josephine Bennett and William Nelson tend not to see the Garden in sections or aspects.

14.   The problem of Time in the Garden has been most vexing, especially to those who have sought to find keys to the Garden in Renaissance Neoplatonism and have consequently attempted to account for a destructive force in an episode in which they find indestructible life forms. Bennett, "Spenser's Garden of Adonis," 68–69, accounts for the presence of Time by shifting the focus from the Garden to the world and back to the Garden again. Nelson slides over the problem by using only a weak word, "troubles," to describe the effect of Time on the creatures in the Garden (*Poetry of Edmund Spenser*, 212–13). Hankins reads the destructiveness of Time as referring only to the destruction of the seminal reasons after a twelve to thirty-nine thousand-year cycle, or, curiously, to the death of embryos (*Source and Meaning*, 276–77). Alpers says that "literally" it is a mistake to put Time, "a principle of sudden and final death" in the Garden; but that "poetically" his presence is valid: "In order to make us aware of earthly mutability, Spenser is willing to neglect both his fable and its philosophical coherence" (*Poetry of The Faerie Queene,* 5–6).

15.   Du Bartas, *Devine Weekes and Works*, trans. Sylvester, 41.

16.   Lewis, *Images of Life*, 50.

17.   Lewis, review of Robert Ellrodt's *Neoplatonism in the Poetry of Spenser*, 112.

18.   For a more traditional examination than Laqueur's of the Renaissance understanding of male and female and masculine and feminine as physiologically determined dualities, see Maclean's chapter, "Medicine, Anatomy, Physiology," in *The Renaissance Notion of Woman*, 28–46.

19.   Hamilton, *Structure of Allegory*, 154; Nelson, *Poetry of Edmund Spenser*, 248; and Berger, "Two Spenserian Retrospects," 12. Williams understands both Scudamour and Amoret to be defective, Amoret with a frightened mind and Scudamour with a confused mind (*World of Glass*, 126).

20.   Hieatt, *Chaucer Spenser Milton*, 145.

21.   Gardner, "Some Reflections on the House of Busyrane," 405.

22.   Hieatt, *Chaucer Spenser Milton*, 103–13.

23.   Hieatt, "Scudamour's Practice of *Maistrye* upon Amoret," 509–10. An expanded treatment of mastery appears in Hieatt's *Chaucer Spenser Milton*, especially pp. 103–33. Apparently, only Reed Way Dasenbrook, "Escaping the Squires' Double Bind," has bought into Hieatt's notions about mastery in the middle books of *The Faerie Queene.*

24.   Galen, *On Semen*, 137.

25.   Lewis, *Allegory of Love*, 340–44.

26.   Gilde, "The Sweet Lodge of Love and Deare Delight," 63.

27.   Roche, *Kindly Flame*, 83–87.

28.   Lewis, *Images of Life*, 23.

29.   Vitruvius, *The Ten Books of Architecture*, trans. Morgan, 211.

30.   Harington, *Orlando Furioso*, 5; Puttenham, *The Arte of English Poesie*, 188 (quoted by Roche, *Kindly Flame*, 16).

31.   Roche, *Kindly Flame*, 80; Nelson, *Poetry of Edmund Spenser*, 230; Alpers, *Poetry of The Faerie Queene,* 18; Hankins, *Source and Meaning*, 163; Gilde, "The Sweet Lodge of Love and Deare Delight," 68; and Hieatt, *Chaucer Spenser Milton*, 124, 129.

32.   Gardner, "Some Reflections on the House of Busyrane," 408.

33. Roche, *Kindly Flame*, 77.
34. Coeffeteau, *A Table of Humane Passions*, 236.
35. Bamborough, *The Little World of Man*, 127.
36. Lewis, *Images of Life*, 33.
37. Cheney, "Spenser's Hermaphrodite and the 1590 *Faerie Queene*," 192–200.
38. MS. Fr. 137, fol. 49. (*Bibliotheque Nationale*, Paris). Found in Jacquart and Thomasset, *Sexuality and Medicine in the Middle Ages*, trans. Adamson, 142.
39. Lewis, *Allegory of Love*, 341.

Chapter 4. Timias's Quest for the Love of Belphoebe

1. Kantorowicz, *The King's Two Bodies*, 270. The only substantial treatment of this concept, which was crucial to the Elizabethan's understanding of their own society, is Miller's postmodern, Lacanian rendition of Books I, II, and III. Montrose refers Belphoebe briefly to Elizabeth in her Body natural ("'Shaping Fantasies,'" 47). References to the two bodies in the earlier studies are brief and unhelpful. Roche comments briefly on Belphoebe's representation of Elizabeth as a private person through the allusion to Dido, who was both woman and queen, and on the possibility of seeing Timias's service to Belphoebe as a "minor analogy" to Arthur's quest for Gloriana (*Kindly Flame*, 100, 148). Nelson comments that Mercilla represents Elizabeth in her Body natural, as well as in her Body politic, because Mercilla exhibits passions (*Poetry of Edmund Spenser*, 125).
2. William Camden, *Annalls*, Book I, 28–29. Quoted by Montrose, "Elizabethan Subject and the Spenserian Text," 309.
3. Lewis, *Images of Life*, 59.
4. For Thomas Roche the allusion to Venus is significant primarily through the allegorical interpretations of Virgil's Venus as "contemplation" and "divinely revealed truth," which relates Belphoebe to the Heavenly Venus of the Neoplatonists, a "conceptual status" that Roche understands to clarify her "ambiguous adventures." Because, for Roche, Belphoebe's central allegorical significance is her representation of Christian virginity (Amoret is Christian marriage), Belphoebe's physical beauty is meaningful only insofar as it is emblematic of her spiritual beauty and virtue (*Kindly Flame*, 100–103).
5. Ibid., 140.
6. Miller, *Poem's Two Bodies*, 226–30.
7. So, apparently do many others. Allan Gilbert comments that the ruby that Belphoebe gave to Timias appears to be a love token and is partly responsible for the common opinion that Belphoebe experiences both love and jealousy ("Belphoebe's Misdeeming of Timias," 631–32).
8. Bennett, *Evolution of The Faerie Queene*, 39–46.

Chapter 5. Social Concord in Miniature

1. John Aylmer, *An Harborowe for Faithful and Trew Servants*, 1559, Sig. H2ᵛ–H3ʳ.
2. From Roche: "We have already seen that Spenser allegorizes the *discordia concors* of the world in the story of Cambell and Triamond, and we shall see that all the good loves of Books III and IV emerge from an initial conflict of man with woman, woman with man. With the love that

moves the sun and stars as example Spenser cannot view chaste love in any other way" and "Out of the distraught passions of Britomart and Artegall, out of the discord prompted by Ate comes the concord of love" (*Kindly Flame*, 55–56, 95). But when we examine the details of the story we find that although Britomart and Artegall fight, Britomart had fallen in love with Artegall long before the fight, and it is not the conflict itself but the accidental revelation of Britomart's beauty that provides the initial stage of Artegall's falling in love. And it is when Britomart saw Artegall's "louely face . . . Tempred with sternesse and stout maiestie" that her "wrathfull courage gan appall, / And haughtie spirits meekely to adaw" (4.6.21,26). Concord between Britomart and Artegall comes after discord, but concord does not "emerge from" discord in the sense of evolving out of it. Nor does, as we shall see, concord arise from the discord caused by Ate and Duessa.

3. Hieatt also examines the tetrad in *Chaucer Spenser Milton*, 75–94, where he is more interested in the characters as fictional personages than as arithmetical and geometrical counters, but his notions of mastery distance his discussions from mine in a radical way. See also Fowler, *Spenser and the Numbers of Time*, 24–33; Nohrnberg, *Analogy*, 621–25; and Heninger, *Touches of Sweet Harmony*, 160–77, who does a most helpful examination of the tetrad generally.

4. Elyot, *The Boke Named The Gouernour*, 2:122, 128.

5. Bennett, *Evolution of The Faerie Queene.*

6. Roche, *Kindly Flame*, 196.

Chapter 6. Toward Mercilla's Castle

1. In one way or another, the classic readings justify Book V by separating a "true" justice, in which clemency and equity are essential ingredients, from justice as embodied in the actions of Artegall. And underlying all of these readings is the assumption that iconography either determines the significance of the fictional situation or is significant apart from the fictional situation. Lewis, *Allegory of Love*, 349; Hamilton, *Structure of Allegory*, 177–80; Nelson, *Poetry of Spenser*, 257–75, esp. 268–71; Williams, *World of Glass*, 166–69; and Aptekar, *Icons of Justice*. I will refer to specifics in Aptekar's study later. Sheila Cavanagh's more recent variation on this theme is that the prince, Arthur, "divinely ordained and supernaturally assisted in battle, represents the poetic ideal of justice," while the justicer, Artegall, as the "representative of the historically based reality of justice," contends with "countless problems, many of which remain insuperable" ("Ideal and Practical Justice: Artegall and Arthur in *Faerie Queene Five*," 20).

It may seem that my understanding of Book V would be closer to T. K. Dunseath's *Spenser's Allegory of Justice* than, say, to Aptekar's. Dunseath also approaches Spenser's characters as fictional personages and focuses on the dramatic action rather than on icons. However, his insistence on seeing character development and on understanding justice apart from Spenser's contemporary concerns radically distances Dunseath's understanding of justice from mine.

2. Starkey, "A Dialogue Between Cardinal Pole and Thomas Lupset," 54–55, 67.

3. Wiltenburg, *Ben Jonson and Self-love*, 108n.

4. Axton, *Queen's Two Bodies*, 69, 105. Spenser uses all of the symbols that Axton found in "The Phoenix and the Turtle" except the phoenix. He has a complete genealogy that, in three separate parts, stretches from Troy to Elizabeth. And Merlin begins his recitation of the history from Britomart and Artegall to Elizabeth with a reference to the tree of succession: "For so must all things excellent begin, / And eke enrooted deepe must be that Tree, / Whose big embodied braunches shall not lin, / Till they to heauens hight forth stretched bee" (3.3.22). Axton points

out that the crown image appears in *The Faerie Queene* in the form of the golden wall that encircles Cleopolis (2.10.72).

5. Greenblatt, *Renaissance Self-fashioning*, 174, 179.

6. See, however, Berger, "Two Spenserian Retrospects" and Fletcher, *Prophetic Moment*, for readings of *The Faerie Queene* in which evolution is found or assumed.

7. *A vewe of the present state of Irelande* (*Variorum*.10.148, 46, 54, 55, and 54).

8. Crowley, "The Beggars Lesson," in *Select Works*, 57 and *The way to Wealth*, 130–45.

9. Bennett, *Evolution of The Faerie Queene*, 1, 163.

10. Aptekar, *Icons of Justice*, 87, 96.

11. Lewis, *Allegory of Love*, 339.

12. Aptekar, *Icons of Justice*, 82–83.

13. Bennett, *Evolution of The Faerie Queene,* 188–89.

14. Tillyard, *Elizabethan World Picture*, 67.

15. Aptekar, *Icons of Justice*, 66–67.

16. Ibid., 46.

Works Cited

Abrams, M. H. *Doing Things with Texts: Essays in Criticism and Critical Theory.* Edited by Michael Fischer. New York: W. W. Norton, 1989.

Adelmann, Howard. *Marcello Malpighi and the Evolution of Embryology.* Ithaca: Cornell University Press, 1966.

Alpers, Paul. *The Poetry of The Faerie Queene.* Princeton: Princeton University Press, 1967.

————. "Review Article: How to Read *The Faerie Queene*. *Essays in Criticism* 18 (1968): 429–43.

Aylmer, John. *An Harborowe for Faithful and Trew Servants*, 1559.

Aptekar, Jane. *Icons of Justice: Iconography & Thematic Imagery in Book V of The Faerie Queene.* New York: Columbia University Press, 1969.

Ariosto, Ludovico. *Orlando Furioso.* Translated by Sir John Harington. 1591. Edited by Robert McNulty. Oxford: Clarendon Press, 1972.

Axton, Marie. *The Queen's Two Bodies: Drama and the Elizabethan Succession.* London: Royal Historical Society, 1977.

Baker, Herschel. *The Image of Man.* New York: Harper, 1961. Originally published in 1947 as *The Dignity of Man.*

Bamborough, J. B. *The Little World of Man.* London: Longman, 1951.

Bennett, Josephine. *The Evolution of The Faerie Queene.* Chicago: University of Chicago Press, 1942.

————. "Spenser's Garden of Adonis." *PMLA* 47 (1936): 46–80.

————. "Spenser's Garden of Adonis Revisited." *Journal of English and Germanic Philology* 41 (1942): 53–78.

Berger, Harry, Jr. "Archaism, Immortality, and the Muse in Spenser's Poetry." *Yale Review* 58 (1968): 214–31.

————. "Narrative as Rhetoric in *The Faerie Queene*." *English Literary Renaissance* 21 (1991): 1–48.

————. "The Spenserian Dynamics." *Studies in English Literature* 8 (1968).

————. "Spenser's Garden of Adonis: Force and Form in the Renaissance Imagination." *University of Toronto Quarterly* 30 (1961): 128–49.

————. "The Structure of Merlin's Chronicle in *The Faerie Queene*, III (iii)." *Studies in English Literature* 9 (1969): 39–51.

————. "Two Spenserian Retrospects: The Antique Temple of Venus and the Primitive Marriage of Rivers." *Texas Studies in Language and Literature* 10 (1968): 5–25.

Bradner, Leicester. *Edmund Spenser and The Faerie Queene*. Chicago: University of Chicago Press, 1948.

Burton, Robert. *The Anatomy of Melancholy*. 3 vols. London: J. M. Dent & Sons, 1932.

Camden, William. *The History and Annalls of Elizabeth, Queen of England*. Translated by Richard Norton. 1630.

Cavanagh, Sheila T. "Ideal and Practical Justice: Artegall and Arthur in *Faerie Queene* Five." In *Renaissance Papers 1984*, edited by Dale B. J. Randall and Joseph A. Porter. Durham, N.C.: The Southeastern Renaissance Conference, 1985.

Cheney, Donald. "Spenser's Hermaphrodite and the 1590 *Faerie Queene*." *PMLA* 87 (1972): 192–200.

———. *Spenser's Image of Nature: Wild Man and Shepherd in The Faerie Queene*. New Haven: Yale University Press, 1966.

Cicero, Marcus Tullius. *The Booke of Freendship*. Translated by John Harington of Stepney. In *John Harington of Stepney: Tudor Gentleman: His Life and Works*, by Ruth Hughey. Columbus: Ohio State University Press, 1971.

Coeffeteau, Nicholas. *A Table of Humane Passions*, 1621.

Colie, Rosalie. *Paradoxia Epidemica: The Renaissance Tradition of Paradox*. Princeton: Princeton University Press, 1966.

Crooke, Helkiah. Μικροκοσμογραφια. *A Description of the Body of Man. Together With The Controversies Thereto Belonging. Collected and Translated out of all the Best Authors of Anatomy, Especially out of Gasper Bauhinus and Andreas Laurentius*. 2d ed. 1631.

Crowley, Robert. *The Select Works of Robert Crowley*. Edited by J. M. Cowper. Early English Text Society, extra series, no. 13. 1871.

Dasenbrook, Reed Way. "Escaping the Squires' Double Bind in Books III and IV of *The Faerie Queene*." *Studies in English Literature* 26 (1986): 25–45.

Deneef, A. Leigh. "Spenser's *Amor Fuggitivo* and the Transfixed Heart." *ELH* 46 (1979): 1–20.

Du Bartas, Guillaume de Salluste. *Bartas: His Devine Weekes and Works*. Translated by Joshua Sylvester. 1605. Introduced by Francis C. Haber. Gainesville, Fla.: Scholars' Facsimiles & Reprints, 1965.

Ebreo, Leone. *The Philosophy of Love* [Dialoghi d'Amore]. Translated by F. Friedeberg-Seeley and Jean H. Barnes. London: Socino Press, 1937.

Ellrodt, Robert. *Neoplatonism in the Poetry of Spenser*. Geneva: Librairie E. Droz, 1960.

Elyot, Sir Thomas. *The Boke Named The Gouernour*. Edited by Henry Herbert Stephen Croft. New York: Burt Franklin, 1967.

Ferguson, Arthur B. *Clio Unbound: Perception of the Social and Cultural Past in Renaissance England*. Duke Monographs in Medieval and Renaissance Studies, number 2. Durham, N.C.: Duke University Press, 1979.

Fletcher, Angus. *The Prophetic Moment: An Essay on Spenser*. Chicago: University of Chicago Press, 1971.

Forest, Elizabeth C. Turner. "A Caveat for Critics Against Invoking Elizabethan Psychology." *PMLA* 61 (1946): 651–72.

Fowler, Alastair. *Spenser and the Numbers of Time*. New York: Barnes and Noble, 1964.

Frye, Northrop. "The Structure of Imagery in *The Faerie Queene*." In *Essential Articles for the Study of Edmund Spenser*, edited by A. C. Hamilton. Hamden, Conn.: Archon Books, 1972.

Galen. *On Semen*. Edited and translated, with a commentary, by Phillip De Lacy. Berlin: Akademie Verlag, 1992.

Gardner, Helen. "Some Reflections on the House of Busyrane." *Review of English Studies* 34 (1983): 403–13.

Geertz, Clifford. *The Interpretation of Cultures: Selected Essays*. New York: Basic Books, 1973.

Giamatti, A. Bartlett. *Play of Double Senses: Spenser's Faerie Queene*. Englewood Cliffs, N.J.: Prentice-Hall, 1975.

Gilbert, Allen H. "Belphoebe's Misdeeming of Timias." *PMLA* 62 (1947): 622–43.

Gilde, Helen Cheney. "'The Sweet Lodge of Love and Deare Delight': The Problem of Amoret." *Philological Quarterly* 50 (1971): 63–74.

Greenblatt, Stephen. *Renaissance Self-Fashioning from More to Shakespeare*. Chicago: University of Chicago Press, 1980.

———. *Shakespearean Negotiations: The Circulation of Social Energy in Renaissance England*. Berkeley: University of California Press, 1988.

Greenlaw, Edwin. "Spenser and British Imperialism." *Modern Philology* 9 (1912): 347–70.

Hamilton, A. C. *The Structure of Allegory in The Faerie Queene* Oxford: Oxford University Press, 1961.

Hankins, John E. "Hamlet's 'God Kissing Carrion': A Theory of the Generation of Life." *PMLA* (54) 1949: 507–16.

———. *Source and Meaning in Spenser's Allegory: A Study of The Faerie Queene*. Oxford: Clarendon Press, 1971.

Heninger, S. K., Jr. *Sidney and Spenser: The Poet as Maker*. University Park: Pennsylvania State University Press, 1989.

———. *Touches of Sweet Harmony: Pythagorean Cosmology and Renaissance Poetics*. San Marino, Calif.: The Huntington Library, 1974.

Hieatt, A. Kent. *Chaucer Spenser Milton: Mythopoeic Continuities and Transformations*. Montreal: McGill-Queen's University Press, 1975.

———. "Scudamour's Practice of *Maistrye* upon Amoret." *PMLA* 77 (1962): 509–10.

Holland, Philemon, trans. *The Philosophie, commonly called The Morals Written by the learned Philosopher Plutarch of Chaeronea*. 1603.

Huarte, John. *Examen de Ingenios. The Examination of Mens Wits*. Translated by R. C. 1594.

Hughes, Felicity. "Psychological Allegory in *The Faerie Queene* III.xi–xii." *Review of English Studies* 29 (1978): 129–46.

Jacquart, Danielle, and Claude Thomasset. *Sexuality and Medicine in the Middle Ages*. Translated by Matthew Adamson. Princeton: Princeton University Press, 1988.

Jorden, Edward. *A Briefe Discourse of a Disease Called the Suffocation of the Mother*. 1603.

Kantorowicz, Ernst H. *The King's Two Bodies: A Study in Mediaeval Political Thought*. Princeton: Princeton University Press, 1957.

Laqueur, Thomas. *Making Sex: Body and Gender from the Greeks to Freud*. Cambridge: Harvard University Press, 1990.

Lewis, C. S. *The Allegory of Love: A Study in Medieval Tradition*. 1936. New York: Oxford University Press, 1958.

————. Review of *Neoplatonism in the Poetry of Spenser*, by Robert Ellrodt. *Etudes Anglaises* 2 (1961): 107–16.

————. *Spenser's Images of Life*. Edited by Alastair Fowler. Cambridge: Cambridge University Press, 1967.

Lockerd, Benjamin. *The Sacred Marriage: Psychic Integration in The Faerie Queene*. Lewisburg, Pa.: Bucknell University Press, 1987.

Maclean, Ian. *The Renaissance Notion of Woman: A Study in the Fortunes of Scholasticism and Medical Science in European Intellectual Life*. Cambridge: Cambridge University Press, 1980.

McKeogh, Rev. Michael J. *The Meaning of the Rationes Seminales in St. Augustine*. Diss., Catholic University of America, 1929.

Miller, David Lee. *The Poem's Two Bodies: The Poetics of the 1590 Faerie Queene*. Princeton: Princeton University Press, 1988.

Montrose, Louis Adrian. "The Elizabethan Subject and the Spenserian Text." In *Literary Theory / Renaissance Texts*, edited by Patricia Parker and David Quint. Baltimore: Johns Hopkins University Press, 1986.

————. Introduction to *Revisionary Play: Studies in the Spenserian Dynamics*, by Harry Berger Jr. Berkeley: University of California Press, 1988.

————. "'Shaping Fantasies': Figuration of Gender and Power in Elizabethan Culture." In *Representing the English Renaissance*, edited by Stephen Greenblatt. Berkeley: University of California Press, 1988.

Nelson, William. *The Poetry of Edmund Spenser: A Study*. New York: Columbia University Press, 1963.

Nestrick, William V. "Spenser and the Renaissance Mythology of Love." In *Literary Monographs*, vol 6, edited by Eric Rothstein and Joseph A. Wittreich Jr., 36–70. Madison: University of Wisconsin Press, 1975.

Nohrnberg, James. *The Analogy of The Faerie Queene*. Princeton: Princeton University Press, 1976.

Notcutt, H. Clement. "The *Faerie Queene* and its Critics." *Essays and Studies by Members of the English Association* 12 (1926): 63–86.

O'Malley, C. D. "Helkiah Crooke, M. D., F. R. C. P., 1576–1648." *Bulletin of the History of Medicine* 42 (1968): 1–18.

Padelford, Frederick M. "The Allegory of Chastity in *The Faerie Queene*." *Studies in Philology* 21 (1924): 367–81.

Paster, Gail Kern. *The Body Embarrassed: Drama and the Disciplines of Shame in Early Modern England*. Ithaca: Cornell University Press, 1993.

Plutarch. *Morals*. See Holland, Philemon.

Preus, Anthony. "Galen's Criticism of Aristotle's Conception Theory." *Journal of the History of Biology* 10 (1977): 65–85.

Primaudaye, Pierre de La. *The Second Part of the French Academie*. Translated by Thomas Bowes, 1594.

Quilligan, Maureen. *Milton's Spenser: The Politics of Reading*. Ithaca: Cornell University Press, 1983.

————. "Words and Sex: The Language of Allegory in the *De planctu naturae*, the *Roman de la Rose*, and Book III of *The Faerie Queene*." *Allegorica* 2 (1977): 195–216.

Ramsay, Judith. "The Garden of Adonis and the Garden of Forms." *University of Toronto Quarterly* 35 (1965–66): 188–206.

Reid, Robert L. "Spenserian Psychology and the Structure of Allegory in Books 1 and 2 of *The Faerie Queene*." *Modern Philology* 79 (1982): 359–75.

Renwick, W. L. *Edmund Spenser: An Essay on Renaissance Poetry*. London: Edward Arnold & Co., 1925.

Roche, Thomas P., Jr. "Britomart at Busyrane's Again; or, Brideshead Revisited." In *Spenser at Kalamazoo 1983*, edited by Francis G. Greco, 121–41. Proceedings of Special Sessions at the Eighteenth International Congress on Medieval Studies. Kalamazoo, Mich., 5–8 May 1983. Clarion, Pa: Clarion University Press, 1983.

————. *The Kindly Flame: A Study of the Third and Fourth Books of Spenser's Faerie Queene*. Princeton: Princeton University Press, 1964.

Siraisi, Nancy G. *Medieval & Early Renaissance Medicine: An Introduction to Knowledge and Practice*. Chicago: University of Chicago Press, 1990.

Spens, Janet. *Spenser's Faerie Queene: An Introduction*. New York: Russell & Russell, 1967. Originally published in London in 1934 by Edward Arnold & Co.

Spenser, Edmund. *The Works of Edmund Spenser: A Variorum Edition*. 10 vols. Edited by Edwin Greenlaw et al. Baltimore: Johns Hopkins University Press, 1932–49.

Starkey, Thomas. "A Dialogue Between Cardinal Pole and Thomas Lupset, Lecturer in Rhetoric at Oxford." In *England in the Reign of Henry the Eighth*, edited by J. M. Cowper, 1–215. Early English Text Society, extra series, no. 12. London, 1871.

Strong, Roy. *The Cult of Elizabeth: Elizabethan Portraiture and Pageantry*. Berkeley: University of California Press, 1977.

Thomasset, Claude. See Jacquart, Danielle.

Tillyard, E. M. W. *The Elizabethan World Picture*. New York: Vintage, n.d.

Vicary, Thomas. *A profitable Treatise of the Anatomie of mans body*. 1577.

Vitruvius, Pollius Marcus. *The Ten Books of Architecture*. Translated by Morris Hicky Morgan. Cambridge: Harvard University Press, 1914.

Williams, Kathleen. *Spenser's World of Glass: A Reading of The Faerie Queene*. Berkeley: University of California Press, 1966.

Wiltenburg, Robert. *Ben Jonson and Self-love: The Subtlest Maze of All*. Columbia: University of Missouri Press, 1990.

Wright, Thomas. *The Passions of the Minde*. 1621.

Index